RICHARD II

THONY S

Princip   qe of
                           ardif

RICHARD II

RICHARD II

BY

ANTHONY STEEL

*Principal of the University College of
South Wales and Monmouthshire
Cardiff*

WITH A FOREWORD BY

G. M. TREVELYAN, O.M.

Formerly Master of Trinity College, Cambridge

CAMBRIDGE
AT THE UNIVERSITY PRESS
1962

PUBLISHED BY

THE SYNDICS OF THE CAMBRIDGE UNIVERSITY PRESS

Bentley House, 200 Euston Road, London, N.W. 1
American Branch: 32 East 57th Street, New York 22, N.Y.
West African Office: P.O. Box 33, Ibadan, Nigeria

First edition 1941
Reprinted 1962

First Printed in Great Britain at the University Press, Cambridge
Reprinted by offset-litho by Bradford & Dickens, London, W.C. 1

CONTENTS

Note on the plate opposite

The following particulars are taken from Dr A. H. Lloyd's *Early History of Christ's College* (Cambridge, 1934), p. 10.

No. 17 in Dr M. R. James's catalogue of the manuscripts in the possession of Trinity Hall, Cambridge, is entitled *Rogeri Dymok, Liber contra duodecim errores et hereses Lollardorum*, and is attributed by Dr James to the late fourteenth century. Dr Lloyd adds:

On the first page the initial has a portrait of King Richard II throned, and the royal arms (France ancient and England quarterly) are blazoned in colours on the right-hand margin, while on the bottom margin is his badge, *stags sejeant guardant gorged crowned and chained or....* Dr James regards it as a copy made for presentation to the King.

After having two intervening owners it passed into the hands of William Byngham (c. 1390–1451), first founder of Christ's College, from whom in turn, after having at least two more known owners, it passed *via* Robert Hare (d. 1611) to Trinity Hall.

FOREWORD

THE REIGN OF RICHARD II has interested people more, perhaps, than any other equally brief period of English medieval history, because of its social and religious happenings. Whether or not it is the period that best represents "the break up of the medieval system", is a question of definition. For "the Middle Ages" began to "break up" in England in the twelfth century as regards the first inroads on the manorial organisation of servile labour; and medieval institutions will not have disappeared from our land unless and until some authoritarian system succeeds in abolishing our Parliament, our Universities, our Churches and our Common Law. In short, the Middle Ages began to come to an end before the fourteenth century and have not finished coming to an end yet. But, in this long-drawn-out process, the reign of Richard II holds a peculiarly important place. For in it the Peasants' Rising of 1381 dramatically illustrated the evolution of the manorial economy into a more modern system, and the rise of Lollardry brought into being the first great heretical movement of English origin, with many distinctively "protestant" features.

And therefore Wyclif and the Peasants' Rising — and Chaucer and Langland to boot—have attracted much attention to the period covered by the life of Richard II. But the biography and psychology of that unfortunate prince, and the purely political struggle between him and his enemies, which to Shakespeare represented the whole content of his reign, these things also are not without interest, whether we regard them as "constitutional developments" or as a mere political struggle for power between selfish factions.

These political events, and the biography of Richard II, have of recent years been subjected to much learned analysis, and Mr Steel has in this volume done a real service to historians and to the reading public in composing a critical and coherent narrative by a collation of the works of these specialists.

Mr Steel's scholarly equipment for the task is undoubted, and the reader may have the satisfaction of feeling that he is being told as much of the truth about these intricate and ill-reported happenings as can now be gleaned.

Possibly the chief impression left by a perusal of the book will be an increased sense of the little wisdom and less honesty with which the world used to be governed in ages gone by. The feudal governing class of that day, in its management of high politics foreign and domestic, here appears as even more un-educated and ill-fitted to rule England than the various ruling classes which have succeeded it—the country gentlemen, the bourgeois, the trade unionists. Yet even these selfish warrior nobles and Caesarian clergy did not permanently ruin England or prevent the evolution in the long run of higher types of society.

G. M. TREVELYAN

PREFACE

THIS book is an attempt to make one coherent whole out of the minutiae, and in certain instances the larger monographs, of recent scholars. The picture of Richard II which emerges, limited though it is to Richard in his political function, seems to me worth the presentation in that I believe it to be largely different from the political pictures of Richard which we have been given in the past. This in itself is understandable, for only one full-length portrait has ever been attempted hitherto (H. Wallon, *Richard II*, 2 vols. Paris, 1864), and although Wallon's work has great and obvious merits much has been discovered since his day.[1]

Forty years ago Professor Trevelyan's *England in the Age of Wycliffe* reached a public which had never heard of Wallon and inspired more students than its author modestly allows, while in the present century the great work of Tout has exposed administrative foundations hitherto unknown; M. Perroy has rewritten the foreign policy of Richard and his governments; and the trenchant studies of the late Miss M. V. Clarke, aided in one important instance by Professor Galbraith, have thrown completely new light on the major crises of the reign. Professor Tait, Mr G. T. Lapsley, Mr J. G. Edwards, Mr H. G. Richardson, and very many others whose names will be found in my footnotes and my bibliography, have laboured fruitfully in the field; if I have sometimes misunderstood their often intricate and always learned arguments I hereby offer my apologies; it is rarely indeed that I have ventured to differ from them.

I am particularly indebted not only to Professor Trevelyan for his Foreword but also to Dr Helen M. Cam, who has been good enough to read the whole book at an early stage in typescript and to make a number of suggestions, nearly all of

---

[1] Notably Adam of Usk's and the Dieulacres chronicles, together with the true relationship of Creton and the *Traïson et Mort de Richard II*.

which I have adopted. I also have to acknowledge with thanks the courtesy of the Master and Fellows of Trinity Hall, Cambridge, in permitting me to reproduce a hitherto unknown portrait of Richard II from an illuminated manuscript in the possession of the college. That this manuscript was once the property of William Byngham, the first founder of Christ's College, Cambridge, has naturally given it an added interest in my own eyes, but it has been more than a mere act of piety on my part to choose it for my frontispiece; for in depicting Richard as a sick man and prematurely old at thirty the unknown artist seems to me to have expressed precisely the interpretation of his later years which I had reached myself some time before the late Dr A. H. Lloyd drew my attention to his work. It is an odd coincidence that the treatise which he decorated should have been Roger Dymok's *Liber contra duodecim errores et hereses Lollardorum*, seeing that I have as far as possible omitted any mention of Wyclif and the Lollards from this book, but few people will dispute the thesis that Lollardry and the story of its founder constitute a separable problem of great difficulty and intricacy which has little to do with the development of Richard's character or the general course of political events during his reign. I have touched on both where absolutely necessary, but it was impossible to cover all the ground—indeed there are many other omissions of which I am just as conscious— and I hope that as the book stands it has a certain unity. Meanwhile, for the general background of the reign the reader may refer to Professor Trevelyan's classic work, already mentioned, to Dr G. G. Coulton's *Chaucer and his England*, or to the many other well-known studies mentioned in my bibliography.

I should have liked to dedicate this book to the memory of Miss M. V. Clarke, but in the first place, to my lasting regret, I had not the honour of her personal acquaintance, and in the second place it falls too far short of what she herself would have written on the theme but for her tragically early death.

ANTHONY STEEL

Cambridge 1940

INTRODUCTION

THE REIGN OF RICHARD II marks in many respects the culminating point in English medieval history. If Henry VII was, as has been claimed for him,[1] the last of the medieval kings of England, Richard II was the last of the old order, the last king ruling by hereditary right, direct and undisputed, from the Conqueror. He is also the last king of England to assert, though vainly, the fullness of the medieval kingly ideal—the ideal of that "almost uninterrupted succession of champions of personal power, passionate and lustful men, who loved domination, strife, war, and the chase".[2] After his violent deposition in 1399 nothing could ever be quite the same again; it was the end of an epoch. Medieval divine right lay dead, smothered in Pontefract castle, and the kings of the next hundred and ten years, medieval as they were in many respects and desperately as they tried to drag together the shredded rags of legitimacy, were essentially kings *de facto*, not *de jure*, successful usurpers recognised after the event, upon conditions, by their fellow-magnates or by parliament. Even Henry V, perhaps the strongest and the most medieval of the series, depended for five-sixths of his revenue on the goodwill of his subjects and could never quite live down the dubiety of his father's title and the precedent of unfortunate concessions exacted from his father's weakness.

It is true that the effective precedent afforded by the events of 1399 was for at least a century or two no more than a precedent of usurpation and that the Lancastrian parliamentary title was in the main imposed on those reluctant sovereigns after the event.[3]

---

[1] C. H. Williams, *The Making of the Tudor Despotism* (1935), p. 9.

[2] Ch. Petit-Dutaillis, *Studies Supplementary to Stubbs's Constitutional History*, English edition, iii, 310.

[3] G. T. Lapsley, "The Parliamentary Title of Henry IV", *English Historical Review*, xlix, 423 ff., 577 ff.

Even Henry IV (and how much more Edward IV and Henry VII) owed the throne not to the sovereign will of the English people, expressing itself through a representative assembly, but effectively to conquest, to some dim pretence of hereditary right and above all to the support of a few wealthy and powerful individuals and the vague fears of the propertied classes in general. All were saviours of society, in the limited medieval sense, against a threatened spoliation or, worse, disintegration. But with the gradual perfecting of the bureaucratic and remorseless Tudor machine of government, with the middle classes' growing sense of wealth, potential power and baffled individualism, old dreams of popular control over a despotic prince revived, and the desperate attempts of jealous fifteenth-century magnates and uneasy fifteenth-century lawyers and knights of the shire to drape and even strangle constitutional indelicacies were resurrected in a new form by a would-be squirearchy grown fat and kicking upon the spoils of the monasteries. In the fifteenth century theory had followed faintly after and had feebly endeavoured to distort fact; in the sixteenth and seventeenth centuries men began with the theory. And so from the last years of Elizabeth's reign onwards there flows a stream of publications whose naked titles tell their own story.

Oddly enough the main fount of this stream is perhaps Shakespeare's *Richard II*; the first quarto appeared in 1597. It is of this play that Elizabeth is said to have exclaimed: "I am Richard II; know ye not that?" and there is little doubt that the subject of Richard II's deposition was a sore point with her and already an encouragement to her enemies: thus on the eve of Essex's rebellion in 1601 the leaders arranged to play *Richard II* (whether actually Shakespeare's play or another is doubtful) in order to encourage the conspirators. From that time to this Shakespeare has often been paradoxically cited as the best historian of Richard II's reign and, curiously, as the only historian to do full justice to Richard's point of view, yet, as Elizabeth and Essex knew, his general tone is really hostile, and though there are touches, drawn direct through Holinshed, of the friendly French chroniclers Creton and the author of the

Traïson et Mort, the groundwork is provided by that unfriendly Tudor, Edward Hall. Thus only the last three years of the reign, the most difficult to defend of all, figure in the play, and Richard is depicted as a weak-kneed tyrant, alternately unmanned by misfortune and drunk with success; his unpleasantness in the early stages is not atoned for by the pathos of the later scenes.[1] The real Richard was perhaps too fond of dramatising himself, but naturally not along these lines, and one feels that he might have protested with justice, though on different grounds, against Shakespeare and "Gordon Daviot" alike.

Shakespeare's *Richard II* was followed within a year or two by the appearance of a book (?1599) entitled *The First Part of the Life and Raigne of King Henrie the IIII*; the author was a certain Sir John Hayward (1564–1627). Hayward's book strongly approves the deposition and was, moreover, dedicated in the usual extravagant terms to Essex. Hence Elizabeth ordered Bacon to read it with a view to discovering whether it concealed treason. Bacon reported in a famous phrase that he found in it no treason but many felonies, since the author had stolen much from Cornelius Tacitus. In spite of this, however, directions were given to remove the dedication and, eventually, to suppress the book, Hayward being brought before the Star Chamber and both he and the printer sentenced to imprisonment. Hayward was not released until after Essex's execution, but the attempt to suppress his history was none the less a failure, for several contemporary copies exist, all containing the offending dedication, and moreover they are all of such variety that it looks as if several presses had been used to keep pace with the demand.[2]

Seventeenth-century politics proved fertile ground for the legend, which began to flourish exceedingly. Its first-fruits are found in *An Historicall Narration of the Manner and Form of that Memorable Parliament which Wrought Wonders, begun at Westminster 1386 in the tenth yeare of the reign of King Richard the*

[1] H. Wallon, *Richard II*, i, 398–9.
[2] H. R. Plomer, *The Library*, iii (N.S.), 13–23.

second.—Related and published by Thomas Fannant, Clerke. Printed (significantly) *in the yeare* 1641. It was thought until quite recently that this tract was, as it pretends to be, a contemporary composition, but the researches of Miss May McKisack[1] have shown that it is actually a rough and incomplete translation of a pretentiously, not to say barbarously, written Latin version composed in 1388–9 by one Thomas Favent or Fovent, probably a clerk in the diocese of Salisbury and certainly a strong supporter of the appellants. It is also worth noting that in fact Favent deals principally with what is usually called the "merciless" parliament of 1388, to which, and not to that of 1386, his epithet "wonderful" should properly be assigned. The mistake, which has been incorporated in nearly all later histories, is of course due to the anonymous translator of the seventeenth century.

It was not long, however, before that century returned to Hayward's practice of rewriting fourteenth-century history instead of plagiarising fourteenth-century pamphleteers. In the year 1681 we have *The Life and Reign of King Richard the Second, By a Person of Quality*. This is wholly a réchauffé of the contemporary chroniclers Walsingham and Knighton, with special emphasis on their anti-curialist tendencies; it is, however, interesting for its reference to Richard's friends as a "cabal". The moral here is clearly that Charles II is as bad as Richard II, just as the translation of Favent was intended to suggest a comparison between the parliaments of 1388 and 1641. Finally, the revolution of 1688–9 produces, among its many *pièces justificatives*, a whole crop of such political histories, one anonymous, another by the Marquis of Halifax (both belonging to 1689), and yet another (1690) by Sir Robert Howard. All three of them are principally, and naturally, concerned for the first time with actual deposition; all three deal with Edward II as well as with Richard II; and their general object is to show that the events alike of 1327 and 1399 afforded precedents

---

[1] *Camden Miscellany*, vol. xiv (1926). Miss McKisack prints the newly discovered complete Latin text with critical notes and introduction.

for the parliamentary removal of princes obnoxious to the people.

This cumulative appeal to history from the time of Elizabeth to that of James II seems to justify Wallon[1] in referring to Richard II's reign as "l'époque où commence...la longue histoire de la Révolution en Angleterre". It culminates in the fine flower of the Whig revolution of 1688–9; the Glorious Revolution, "glorious" because it succeeded,[2] after which the English people may be said to have "constituted" itself, requiring no more political revolutions, though much evolution, ever since. Gradually the long years of silence between 1399 and 1599 came to be forgotten, as the seventeenth-century pamphleteers intended that they should be; Edward II and Richard II take their places at the beginning of one magnificent continuum, and the tradition is complete.

This tradition has been generally followed by most English historians up to the present century; by Hume and Hallam, by Green and Stubbs and Ramsay, a long and honourable procession. Thomas Carte in the eighteenth century and Lingard in the nineteenth mildly questioned it, while more recently Tout,[3] though hostile to Richard personally, doubts the historical value of the constitutional theory involved in the tradition but at the last turns back decisively to administrative history and refuses to answer the constitutional question. Among French historians Wallon, the author of the only full-length history of the reign, after showing much sympathy for Richard, is unable, in the absence of evidence which has since come to light, to modify substantially the orthodox English attitude towards the events of his last three years, while M. Perroy,[4] invaluable as his work is for foreign policy and relations with the papacy, is content, like the *Cambridge Medieval History*, to do little more than follow Tout for domestic affairs. Yet the tendency of most modern specialised research is away from the tradition, and

---

[1] *Op. cit.* i, p. iv.
[2] If we are to accept H. Butterfield, *The Whig Interpretation of History*.
[3] *Chapters in Mediaeval Administrative History*, esp. iv, 64–5.
[4] *L'Angleterre et le grand schisme d'Occident*.

it certainly requires a re-examination of a different kind from the blind, sentimental vindication and romantic modernisation of Richard to be found in the works of certain historical novelists[1] and in that successful play, *Richard of Bordeaux*.

Such a re-examination must be predominantly political and constitutional, because it is in those fields that the real drama of the reign and the main historical perversions of it seem to lie, but that is not to say that in other and equally important respects the close of the fourteenth century does not mark an epoch in English history, or that these other considerations do not, many of them, affect directly the interpretation of Richard's character, politics and the constitution. There is, for example, the linked, but separate, drama of the Peasants' Revolt, that first great uprising of the submerged classes in England, that first attempt of "John Nameless and John the Miller and John the Carter... John Trueman and all his fellows" not only to think, but to act for themselves, fumblingly but spontaneously and on a wide scale. There is again the portentous appearance of Wyclif and his followers. True, Wyclif is essentially a schoolman who looks backwards rather than forwards, and we are told we must no longer regard him as in any sense a morning-star; yet the first appearance of heresy on a large scale in England is an event of inescapable importance, while Wyclif's own subtle dialectic, medieval as it was, is accompanied by his sponsoring of the first vernacular Bible. Moreover, Lollardry apart, the persistent anti-papal legislation of the period, taken in conjunction with the Great Schism in the Church, suggests, to say the least of it, some impending change in medievalism.

In literature the period is marked by the first great burst of vernacular excellence in English history; Chaucer and Langland immeasurably outstrip all English predecessors. They are also the earliest poets whom a modern Englishman, uninstructed in Anglo-Saxon or Middle English, can hope to understand. Yet of the two it is only Langland, the rougher, sadder poet of the

---

[1] E.g. Gillian Olivier, *The Broomscod Collar* (1930); cf. Sir Henry Newbolt's *The New June*. F. Converse, *Long Will*, deals principally with the Peasants' Revolt.

popular awakening, who, however unintentionally,[1] could produce a revolutionary effect, for Chaucer was no more political than mystical and far from primitive; though writing in English, he was the polished, *fin de siècle* poet of a cosmopolitan society unified in a kind of bastard chivalry, and his work is far more complex and sophisticated than is commonly allowed. There are also minor poets, anonymous political lampoonists, the tedious Gower and that worthy but insufferable civil servant, Thomas Hoccleve.

Finally, in art and architecture Richard's reign represents the last great effort of the English Middle Ages. It sees the perfection of the Perpendicular Style, the building of Westminster Hall and New College chapel, and the final triumph, of technique at least, in the draughtsmanship of monumental brasses and in the carving of effigies in the round.[2] Everywhere in the wool-growing districts the great wool-merchants' churches, adorned with stained glass at its loveliest, were beginning to arise; college was added to college in Oxford and Cambridge. Painting, carried to its limits in the art of book-illumination, spread to panels and church walls; more, the two greatest pictures ever known to have been painted in medieval England are, one certainly, and another probably, portraits of the young king. Richard II, like Henry III, was undoubtedly himself a connoisseur of building, sculpture, painting, books and music, as well as of plate, jewellery and dress; there is on record plentiful, if scattered, evidence of these tastes which has never been put together. If for no other reason he should go down to history as the inventor of the handkerchief,[3] the *chef d'œuvre* of a dilettante of genius. Yet the dilettante,

[1] It is the accepted view of scholars such as R. W. Chambers that Langland, if he preached anything, preached resignation. None the less his mysticism is politically dynamic in a sense that Chaucer's work never was.

[2] Cf. Arthur Gardner, *English Medieval Sculpture*. The work of the thirteenth century is spiritually greater, but its mastery over material is less complete, and alabaster as a medium was first introduced in this age.

[3] *parvis peciis factis ad liberandum domino regi ad portandum in manu sua pro naso suo tergendo et mundando*: M. V. Clarke, *Fourteenth Century Studies*, p. 117.

almost connoisseur, is only one aspect, if the most neglected, of the complex personality developed by the sheltered boy who so unexpectedly faced the Peasants' Revolt. There is the distracted son of a professional soldier and an almost equally professional beauty, torn between a desire upon the one hand to emulate, more successfully than his fellows, the impossible standards of knightly prowess bequeathed to a too slight physical frame, and on the other an almost morbid consciousness of the kingly dignity and the necessity of not betraying it. There is the passionate and loyal friend and husband of early manhood, corrupted into bitterness and cynicism by personal insult and the judicial murder of his companions. There is the defender of the church, orthodox and sincerely religious to the last, yet strangely averse from the newfangled idea of burning his subjects when they happened to be heretics.[1] There is the unbalanced widower, half-hearted autocrat and pitiful neurotic of the later years. All these, and many others, are aspects of the more than usually intricate character of the last truly medieval king of England. Any one of them, given the tortuous politics in the background, the uneasy stirring of new forces, unorientated as yet and seeking a direction, towards the close of the Middle Ages, affords an excuse for studying him; taken together, they constitute a problem whose difficulty is only equalled by its fascination. But before beginning the attempt to unravel it, to reinterpret Richard as the essentially medieval product of a medieval generation, something must be said of this background, of the state of politics at home and abroad, but especially at home, since it was these which first affected him, at his accession in June 1377.

[1] Cf. H. G. Richardson, "Heresy and the Lay Power under Richard II", *E.H.R.* li, 1–28.

CHAPTER I

The State of Politics at the Accession of Richard II

IT has been well said that "no accession ever marked less of an epoch than did that of Richard II".[1] There is in fact so little of a break in 1377 that it is necessary to go back as far as 1369 in order to understand the complexities of the position and to trace the emergence of the leading personalities. For in 1369 there is a decisive break, for France as well as England, in the course of fourteenth-century history; it is the year in which France begins to reap the fruits of her new king's policy, while England, after the glories of the first part of the Hundred Years' War, suddenly enters upon a period of "military disaster and economic exhaustion".[2] The Peace of Bretigny (1360) had in fact been the high-water mark both of Edward III's policy and his personal prestige, but before 1369 nobody realised it.

Elsewhere in Europe the year was not particularly eventful. In Bohemia Charles IV, the greatest and most realistic of late medieval emperors, was quietly building up the fortunes of the house of Luxemburg—a policy of little concern to anyone except perhaps to the Electors, to the Wittelsbachs, the Hapsburgs and any other rival dynasty in Germany. In spite of his two visits to Italy he had practically renounced the most fruitful principle of discord, imperial interest in that country, and he was beginning to grow old. It was three hundred years since Canossa and he was on excellent, if distant, terms with the sainted pope Urban V. Urban was more troubled; in 1367 his conscience had driven him from the safety and comforts of Avignon back to a dangerous and half desolate Rome; the loud

---

[1] Tout, *Chapters*, iii, 324.
[2] G. Unwin, Introduction to *Finance and Trade under Edward III*, p. xiii.

protests of his cardinals and the genuine insecurity of central Italy were to bring him back to die upon the banks of the Rhône in 1370. But the spell of the Babylonish captivity had been broken and the seeds of the Great Schism had been sown.

The only other powers that directly concerned England at this time were, besides France, Flanders and Castile. In Flanders the main English wool-market was controlled by the Francophil Louis de Maele, who had become count of Flanders at the age of sixteen when his father was killed at Crécy. He was a peculiarly unpleasing specimen of late medieval class arrogance —the type of knight who did not think it necessary to keep his word to "villeins" and classed as villeins the inhabitants of the great cloth-producing cities. Even Louis de Maele, however, had not been able to prevent the artisans of Ghent from recovering their municipal liberties in 1359, a fact which drove him more than ever in the direction of France. Now, ten years later, he was about to auction the hand of his heiress, Margaret, and the English bid would have to be a high one.

France since 1364 had been ruled by the sickly and unattractive, but extremely able, Charles V, the Wise. He had reformed his army and found a captain of the first rank in du Guesclin, the poor knight of Rennes. Within two years he had broken the power of his most dangerous enemy, Charles the Bad of Navarre, and had forced the Montfort duke of Brittany to acknowledge the suzerainty of the French royal house. The next problem was to dispose of the free companies of mercenaries who were ravaging what was left of France. It was decided to get rid of them by intervening in the question of the Castilian crown, then in dispute between Pedro the Cruel, a protégé of Navarre and England, and Henry of Trastamara, the candidate of Peter IV, the Ceremonious, king of Aragon. In April 1366 du Guesclin at the head of his free companies set Henry on the throne of Castile, but he was driven out again in the following year by his rival, who had successfully invoked the Black Prince from Bordeaux. But the campaign of Navarrete, while apparently undoing Charles's work, was actually of the greatest benefit to France; for it was fought with much the same professionally minded mercenaries as had accompanied du Guesclin, and these suffered so heavily from casualties and disease that they ceased to be a menace to society. Moreover the Black Prince himself, France's bitterest and most dangerous enemy, contracted the disease which was to immobilise him from 1371 and kill him in 1376, while in 1369 du Guesclin had no difficulty in disposing finally of Pedro and placing Henry II permanently on the throne.

It remained only to deal with the English, for the Peace of Bretigny under which the English kept Poitou and Aquitaine, henceforth known as the duchy of Guienne, together with certain lands in the Cotentin, Ponthieu, Calais and the strong places in its neighbourhood, obviously could not be allowed to stand. When the peace had been ratified in the Treaty of Calais (1361) Edward III's promised renunciation of his claim to the French throne had not been carried out, and the Gascon lords of Aquitaine for their part had similarly failed to renounce the suzerainty of France. When the Black Prince returned broken in health and judgment from Castile he endeavoured to refill his treasury at the expense of contumacious Gascons, and these promptly appealed to their overlord, Charles V. Late in 1368 Charles decided to entertain the appeal; hostilities began in January 1369; war was declared the following May; and shortly afterwards Edward III of England resumed the style of king of France.

Parliament was at first enthusiastic, but the war went badly; of the king's sons John of Gaunt was unsuccessful in the north and the Black Prince in the south, while Portsmouth was burnt by the French. The Flemish marriage was decided in favour of Philip the Bold, duke of Burgundy and brother of Charles V; from this time on, though there continued to be unrest in the towns, the government of Flanders was closely united with the French government. The death of queen Philippa in August, during a widespread revisitation of the Black Death, marked the beginning of Edward III's personal deterioration and left the way clear for his rapacious mistress, Alice Perrers, who exploited his declining years. In 1370 things went from bad to worse; the gallant *chevauchée* of Sir Robert Knolles, held up only by the walls of Paris, proved futile and expensive, while the Black Prince's career ended in the inglorious and bloody sacking of Limoges.[1] In January 1371 the prince was back in England, his health finally broken and his finances so exhausted that he was unable to pay his men.

The immediate upshot was the parliamentary crisis of February 1371, "the commencement of those political movements and party combinations which continued through the next fifteen years".[2] There were at this stage two main parties, the first of which, enjoying the support of the enfeebled Black Prince and his household and of the conservative and legitimist elements generally, might be called that of church and customary forms of government.[3] It composed the existing government and its main strength lay in the professional civil service, consisting typically of "Caesarian"[4] clergy, such as William of Wykeham, now chancellor, and Thomas Brantingham, bishop of Exeter and treasurer, the two of them representing a now old tradition. They had formerly enjoyed the confidence of the old

---

[1] The sack of Limoges was due in large part to the initial treachery of the bishop and principal citizens: the Black Prince himself, though he made no effort to prevent it, was too enfeebled by dysentery to take part and indeed showed no signs of wishing to do so. What really interested him was, characteristically, a single combat of three a side fought while the sack was going on. None the less he bears the main responsibility for the event, which outraged opinion on both sides, for he had sworn "by the soul of his father" that he would have the place again and would make the inhabitants pay dearly for their behaviour: he ordered that no quarter should be given, and would not listen to appeals for mercy. In the end more than three thousand men, women and children lost their lives and even Froissart, though at that time pro-English in sentiment, condemned it, "for I trow they were martyrs". Coulton, "The Chronicler of European Chivalry", *The Studio,* p. 92.

[2] G. M. Trevelyan, *England in the Age of Wycliffe,* p. 4.

[3] We must not say "constitution". Cf. Lapsley on 1341 in *E.H.R.* xxx, 193-215—the real functions of the constitution are unsuspected and Edward III did not "break" it in that year because there was not one to be broken, only "precedents pointing in different directions".

[4] See p. 22 below for the explanation of this term, which was a favourite adjective of Wyclif's.

king, but Edward was rapidly breaking up and the mismanagement of the war, together with the wiles of Alice Perrers,
induced him to give the opposition something of a free hand.

This opposition was essentially a court party of laymen,
looking for their shadow government to the only other educated class, the common lawyers. It was nominally led by John
Hastings, earl of Pembroke, but he was only twenty-three
years old, was attending parliament for the first time and was
certainly less a politician than a fighting-man, and not very good
at that. He was, in short, a figurehead or man of straw pushed
forward to conceal the nefarious activities of more sinister
interests in the background, interests represented by the get-
rich-quick policy of the king's mistress, of lord Latimer and
the London merchants Richard Lyons, John Pecche and others,
not to mention the mounting ambitions of the exponents of
common law and a residue of genuinely disgruntled patriots.
In any case Pembroke was defeated by a Franco-Spanish fleet
a year later off La Rochelle and taken prisoner, so that his career
as party leader, if he was a real leader, was destined to be a short
one; his place, unfilled for over three years, was ultimately
taken by John of Gaunt, whose wealth and wide connexions
constituted a party in themselves,[1] but that was not before the
end of 1375.

Meanwhile the general question whether churchmen or laymen should control the medieval state is worth consideration,
and in this connexion the career of William of Wykeham
furnishes an admirable example.[2] He was born about 1324 at
Wickham in southern Hampshire, his mother being of slightly
better family than his father, who seems to have been a small
freeholder. In any case the tradition of noble birth on both
sides of his family is false; William of Wykeham or Wickham
was essentially a *novus homo*. He was taken up at an early age by
Sir John Scures, lord of the manor of Wickham and sheriff of

---

[1] See e.g. M. V. Clarke, *Fourteenth Century Studies*, pp. 36–7.
[2] Details mainly from G. H. Moberly, *Life of William of Wykeham*, much
corrected by Tout, *Chapters*, iii, 235–9. For a brief notice of Brantingham,
see Tout, *op. cit.* pp. 261–2.

Hampshire, who sent him to the priory school at Winchester and then took him as a clerk into his own household, where he remained until 1346, apparently specialising in architecture.[1] On William Edington's[2] becoming bishop of Winchester in that year the young architect seems to have attracted his attention and was recommended by him to the king. Edward III sent him to Windsor to work upon the great castle then being demolished and rebuilt; he must have given satisfaction, for in 1356 he appeared as clerk of the works there as well as at Easthampstead and Henley, and in 1359 as chief keeper and surveyor of other royal castles and manors, when his connexion with Windsor secured him his first mention in a contemporary chronicle.[3] During 1360–9 his completion of the royal apartments there and his building of Queenborough castle, so called after queen Philippa, increased his influence with the king, who now began to heap offices and rewards upon him to such an extent that he has been called "the greatest pluralist of his age".[4]

In 1363 he received his first important political appointment when he became keeper of the privy seal. "At this time", says Froissart,[5] "there reigned a priest in England called Sir William de Wican, and this Sir William de Wican was so much in favour with the king of England, that by him everything was done and without him they did nothing." This alone made him enemies, but for some years yet they were unable to check the triumphant course of his advancement. Thus in 1366 he received what was then the normal reward of a successful civil servant by being nominated to the bishopric of Winchester, which he was to hold until his death in 1404, but though elected by the chapter without opposition to the king's instructions Wykeham found Urban V less complaisant; it was the first hitch in his career. The reason probably lay in the considerable part played by Wykeham on the king's side in the anti-papal controversies of these years; moreover, his own benefice-

---

[1] Tout's adjective "illiterate" (*Chapters*, iii, 255) seems rather strong.
[2] Another "Caesarian", Tout, *Chapters*, iii, 202–5.
[3] *Chronicon Anglie*, p. 41, *virum providum et discretum*.
[4] Tout, *Chapters*, iii, 238.   [5] *Chroniques*, ii, 126.

hunting was against him, for he had not hesitated to profit from a system which he had helped the king to attack. Hence it was not till October 1367, a month after he had reached the top rung of the royal ladder as chancellor of England, that he was actually consecrated bishop, having at last been papally provided to the see. Two years later he bought the first part of the site of New College, Oxford, though the charter is as late as 1379 and building did not begin until 1380.

That the wealthiest bishopric in England should crown the career of a successful architect and minister of the crown may seem scandalous, as it did to Wyclif, yet there is much to be said for a clerical official of this kind in the conditions of the age. Such a man had generally his whole career to make, with the result that he was more efficient than he might otherwise have been and more devoted to his master; what Tout has called "the fierce individualism of a greedy bachelor fighting his way through the world" could sometimes be socially valuable. Again, from the king's point of view the clerical official could be cheaply rewarded with livings, prebends and higher dignities,[1] while the extreme old age of less distinguished men could be provided for by a corrody, or royal order, entitling the recipient to a grant of free board and lodging for life in a religious house. Laymen, on the other hand, needed grants of royal domain, the custody of royal wards, the hands of heiresses in royal keeping or even hard cash pensions. The chief disability of clerks, loudly asserted in 1341, 1371 and 1376, namely that they could not be called to account and disciplined as easily as laymen, might be met by translation *in partes infidelium* (the pope would usually oblige) if they were bishops, or in humbler cases by giving them poor and distant livings, e.g. in Ireland—and requiring residence. Even so, the spiritual objections would remain, but it is too easily assumed that all Caesarian bishops habitually neglected their dioceses; Wykeham's registers show that he was no stepfather to the see of Winchester, and it was not always without reluctance, especially in later life, that he

[1] Cf. R. A. R. Hartridge, "Edward I's Exercise of the right of Presentation to Benefices", *Cambridge Historical Journal*, ii, 171–7.

neglected it from time to time at the king's command to appear upon the troubled stage of politics. In any case, whatever be thought of it, the Caesarian principle was in fact so well established in fourteenth-century England that of the two great departments of government the chancery was entirely clerical in 1369, while the exchequer, though it had always sheltered important lay interests, was tending rapidly in the same direction.

It was the chief object of the new court party in 1371 to check this tendency, or rather practice, at least as far as heads of departments were concerned, and to substitute common lawyers for clerks in control of public affairs. There was even talk of disendowment as an extreme measure; two Austin friars from Oxford brought forward detailed articles to that effect[1] when the clergy in convocation refused to make the grants expected of them. To begin with, the attack succeeded. By harping on the mismanagement of the war Pembroke and his friends were able to extract a joint petition from the lords and commons, as a result of which Edward III reluctantly substituted Sir Robert Thorpe, chief justice of the common pleas, for Wykeham as chancellor, while another layman, Richard le Scrope of Bolton, took Brantingham's place as treasurer. What was more, in Nicholas Carew the privy seal found the first lay keeper in its history. This, however, seems to have been as far as the king was prepared to go; "the only victims", says Tout, "were a few highly-placed ministers".

Moreover the experiment, which had already been made in the years 1341-5, was once more not a success, for it led to heavier expense, if not to greater inefficiency. The reason for the increased expense lay in the fact that the lower ranks of the civil service, being unchanged and therefore still predominantly clerks, had to be provided with board and lodging. When the high officials had been bishops this was easy; the office staffs were maintained in a corporate household at the expense of the see. But the new lay officials, being mostly married men with

---

[1] Published by V. H. Galbraith, *E.H.R.* xxxiv, 579-82.

limited incomes, had to have extra allowances for the support of their clerks.

As regards efficiency the point is more open to dispute. True, in 1371 there was the famous miscalculation—40,000 for 8600—of the number of parishes in England, made in connexion with the new parish-tax of that year, but Tout has disposed of the view that this had anything to do with the new lay ministers,[1] and on other counts the receipt roll evidence is in their favour. Thus there is a drop, which is maintained for years to come, from 52 per cent (tallies) in 1370 to only 4 per cent in 1372 in the dangerous practice of assignment or anticipation of the revenue.[2] Again, while there is great confusion in the receipt rolls for the last two terms of Brantingham's reign as treasurer, there is a marked improvement in method, clarity and order, though not in volume of receipts, after his dismissal. There would therefore seem to be very little difference either way in the matter of efficiency; the subordinate staff remained the same all the time and, as Tout says, there were very few persons of either class, clerk or lawyer, fit to hold high office. It is, however, so easy to over-estimate both the ability and the disinterestedness of medieval lawyers that it may be advisable to say something of their general relations at this time with parliament.

Edward III's reign had been marked by the steady growth of that great lay university, the Inns of Court, and by an increased production, as an alternative to the clerk, of the *miles litteratus* or educated layman. This fact, which can no longer be disregarded by 1371, has filled certain historians with enthusiasm. Sir William Holdsworth, for example, claims[3] that it was due to the presence of lawyers in parliament that the medieval ideal of a rule of law came to be embodied in the concrete fact of a

[1] *Chapters*, iii, 280–1.

[2] A. Steel, "Practice of Assignment", *E.H.R.* xliii, 172–80, and "Some Aspects of English Finance in the Fourteenth Century", *History*, xii, 298–309.

[3] "The Influence of the Legal Profession on the Growth of the English Constitution", *Proceedings of the British Academy*, 1924.

fundamental law which could be changed by parliament; and, furthermore, that because in England alone throughout Europe lawyers and parliament thus united together in an attempt to create what Fortescue in the next century was to call a *dominium politicum et regale*, in England alone at the end of the Middle Ages such a polity actually emerged.

But this is reading history backwards and flattering one great profession. Fourteenth-century common lawyers were neither so far-sighted nor so disinterested as Sir William Holdsworth implies and, as the events of 1372 were to prove, the "lay legislator included in his condemnation the man of law equally with the cleric". The full number of lawyers present in the commons as knights of the shire during the century is quite impossible to discover, and only twenty-six have been identified with any certainty by Miss Wood-Legh[1] for the whole reign of Edward III. There must have been many more, however, for there were probably eleven present in the parliament of 1372 alone. The reason why that parliament objected to them, as given in the statute which resulted from the protest of the commons, was their habit of making parliament into a convenience for transacting their clients' business instead of attending to the interests of the commons as a whole; they were more concerned with private petitions than with the common petitions and were fond of persuading the commons to "colour" such petitions as if they were joint ones. The statute then proceeded to enact that lawyers practising in the royal courts at Westminster should be excluded in future from the commons. The whole incident throws a curious light on the relationship idealised by Sir William Holdsworth; nor was it an isolated incident, for although it is true that the lawyers soon crept back again there was another and more determined attempt to expel them as late as 1404.

A special reason for the ill temper of the commons in November 1372 was provided by the continued misconduct of the war, even after the change of ministers. A great council

[1] "Sheriffs, Lawyers and Belted Knights in the Parliaments of Edward III", *E.H.R.* xlvi, 372–88.

held at Winchester in June 1371[1] had done little to assist matters, and Pembroke's quick defeat in 1372 not only put an end to his career but resulted in the English losing control of the Channel for the next fifteen years, that is, until Arundel's victory at Cadzand (off Margate) in 1387. Moreover, an expensive expedition undertaken by the king himself as a diversion was held up by contrary winds and came to nothing, while before long Thomas Percy had been beaten at Soubise and the English were being rapidly expelled from Poitou as well as Brittany. Yet the new lay ministers, in spite of parliamentary grumbling, stayed in office, with the sole result that the war went from bad to worse in 1373, the year of Gaunt's remarkable, but useless, march from Calais to Bordeaux, on which he was harassed all the way without fighting by du Guesclin and lost nearly all his horses and most of his men.

The parliament of November 1373, called to raise funds, fortunately before Gaunt's failure was definitely known, exhibited much less recalcitrance than might have been expected. Thus the commons meekly accepted the instruction that they must give supply priority over petitions, and although they created an important precedent in not only demanding a joint committee of enquiry with the lords into the conduct of the war but in insisting on their own choice of personnel, this appears to have been done more in perplexity than anger and the committee, when appointed, contained merely William of Wykeham and a collection of respectable nonentities. The presence of Wykeham might suggest a turn in the political tide, but the party grouping was in fact too fluid at this date; Wykeham himself still had "curialist"[2] traces, and he was not heart and soul with the more respectable magnates until 1376.

Meanwhile the war continued to be disastrous; by 1374 only Calais, Brest, Bordeaux and Bayonne were left, and in view of the lethargy which had overtaken the king and prince of Wales

---

[1] *Interim Report of Committee on House of Commons Personnel*, p. 108.

[2] Since Tout's great work on this period "curialist" has become a generally accepted term of art not so much for "courtiers" in the old sense as for persons, groups and interests politically dependent on the royal court.

alike John of Gaunt for the first time began to take a serious interest in politics. For two years he himself was still to be abroad, first fighting then negotiating, but it seems probable that during this time his agents were already effecting contacts which considerably strengthened the camarilla of the new court party by throwing the whole weight of Lancastrian influence into the scale. It was at this time that Latimer, Lyons and the rest, encouraged by Gaunt's advances, began to commit the actual frauds which were afterwards brought to light in the Good Parliament. Gaunt himself can hardly be held responsible for their misdemeanours, of which he may have been completely ignorant; his personal intervention dates only from the winter of 1375–6 after his conclusion of the truce of Bruges in June—a truce for one year only in the first place, though afterwards prolonged into a second year, but for all that an invaluable breathing-space for the English in the desperate straits to which they had been reduced. It was extorted from the triumphant French by papal diplomacy, always anxious to reunite the two great western monarchies for the purpose of a crusade, quite as much as by Gaunt's own bargaining abilities, but he may fairly have the credit of being the first important Englishman of his generation ready to admit that the days of Crécy and Poitiers were over.

Born in March 1340, John of Gaunt was, since the death of Lionel of Clarence in 1368, the second surviving son of Edward III. His first marriage, to Blanche heiress of Lancaster who had died in 1369, had brought him both the wide Lancaster estates and a claim to the hereditary stewardship of England; his second (1371) to Costanza of Castile had made him a candidate for the Castilian throne, and in England titular king of that country. His wealth was colossal; thus, if his manors did not cover, as they were popularly said to do, one-third of England,[1] he could at least maintain at his own expense during the whole period 1372–82 a retinue of 125 knights and 132 esquires, while from 1376 he had for some years a bishop as his chancellor.

[1] Cf. Armitage-Smith's *John of Gaunt, passim,* esp. the map opp. p. 218.

Though naturally anxious to dominate English politics on the failure of his father's and elder brother's health, the contemporary charge that he was aiming at the English throne[1] is groundless; thus he was appointed executor to the Black Prince just before the latter's death at the height of the constitutional crisis of 1376, although for at least six months—probably much longer—he may have been politically opposed to him. Moreover he seems to have made no attempt whatsoever to prevent the succession of his nephew—on the contrary, he tried to secure his position as heir-presumptive against any rival by a proposal to bar succession through females—and although he was sometimes on strained terms with Richard, for example in 1384, he was definitely an influence for peace at home and abroad from 1389 until his death, at the relatively early age of fifty-eight, on the 3rd of February ten years later. In other words the view is probably correct which sees in Gaunt an, on the whole, amiable nonentity of no special attainments—a man neither good nor bad within the conventions of his age, yet always forced to fill a rôle too big for him.[2] He has, however, been alternately blackened and whitewashed to a ludicrous extent, first by contemporaries, to whom a man in his position was bound to bulk large, whatever his true character, and (less excusably) by most modern historians.

In 1376 Gaunt definitely joined, and having joined naturally led, the new curialists, not so much against his invalid elder brother as against the western marcher lords, a majority of the bishops and the clerical civil service. His coalition contained some unattractive elements, such as Alice Perrers, considered useful in controlling the king, who was now a helpless dotard, and also the whole gang of corrupt household servants, courtiers and officials, "of whom Latimer (the chamberlain) was the chief and Lyons was the financial agent".[3] Its most respectable members, outside the powerful northern lords and half a dozen magnates and bishops from the south, were probably the common lawyers, together with a sprinkling of sincere anti-

[1] *Chronicon Anglie*, pp. 92–3.
[2] *Cambridge Medieval History*, vii, 458.   [3] Tout, *Chapters*, iii, 297.

clericals, to whom by September 1376[1] may be added the great name of Wyclif. The reasons for this at first sight rather astonishing addition need examination.

The foundations of the alliance between the very worldly Gaunt and his friends and the unworldly Wyclif undoubtedly lay in the latter's theories of civil and divine dominion, for which he was already famous at Oxford and beyond. As Dr Workman has shown, the fact that these theories in their final form were not yet in writing is of small importance, for in the Middle Ages actual publication in the modern sense marked the end, not the beginning, of long discussions previously held in the Schools. According to these theories all bishops such as Wykeham and Brantingham were simply Caesarian clergy who had left the way of Christ. Wyclif's suggestion that the *gentz de sainte église* should hold no worldly office and furthermore revert to apostolical poverty, an idea partly borrowed from the Spiritual Franciscans, would have brought the whole clerical civil service of tradition to the ground. As such it would be welcomed by Gaunt and the curialists as an effective party cry; they would, however, certainly consider it impossible, and perhaps undesirable, to carry it into practice. But in the improbable event of a wholesale confiscation of church property taking place on Wyclifite lines—something like this was actually proposed by the commons in 1404—they would not be averse from getting their share.

The wealth of the church, though much exaggerated at the time, was proverbial. To the subsidy of 1371 it contributed £50,000 by a levy of two and a half tenths; its assessable total income was therefore in the region of £200,000. Wykeham's income, in the rather exceptionally rich see of Winchester, was about £3000 in 1374,[2] and this figure does not include the feudal incidents, such as fines, reliefs, wardships and marriages, or the fruits of any vacant benefices payable to the bishop in that diocese.[3] The alliance between Gaunt and Wyclif against the

---

[1] I.e. *after* the Good Parliament, *not* at Bruges in 1375: H. B. Workman, *John Wyclif*, i, 275–6.

[2] *Wykeham's Register*, ed. T. F. Kirby, ii, p. ix.   [3] Ramsay, *Genesis*, ii, 60 n.

church party is therefore comprehensible, yet it was political only, and if Wyclif flattered himself that he had converted his patron to his own peculiar religious views he was badly deceived. For Gaunt, like most men of his stamp, managed to combine extreme political latitudinarianism with extreme religious orthodoxy;[1] thus in later years he earnestly requested Wyclif not to disseminate his peculiar views on transsubstantiation. Moreover, his own chancellor at the actual moment of alliance was the Caesarian Ralph Erghum, bishop of Salisbury, while other Caesarian clerks staffed his household on the exact model of the king's.

The effects of the alliance were largely bad for both parties. Wyclif, it is true, may have owed to it his peaceful old age at Lutterworth, yet his adherence to the unpopular Gaunt cost him much support among the common people and among the Londoners, who loathed Gaunt, while the alliance brought neither party any further allies and consolidated the ranks of their enemies. The innocent and academic Wyclif may perhaps be held to have entered on it in optimistic ignorance of the real uses to which it would be put, but it is difficult at first sight to see why Gaunt made so obvious a blunder. The answer is probably to be found in general in the strictly limited nature of his political intelligence and in particular in the quite unsuspected revelation of the strength of the forces marshalled against him in the early summer of 1376 in the best known of all medieval parliaments.

The Good Parliament, which met in April and sat till July of that year, represents in fact the temporary triumph over Gaunt and his faction of a rival coalition consisting of the church party, the magnates jealous of Gaunt and, especially, the two households nearest to the throne. These were those of the dying Black Prince and the earl of March, whose son by Philippa, daughter of Lionel of Clarence, must have been widely held to be next heir after Richard of Bordeaux. Yet this coalition could hardly have effected much without the sudden, violent and

[1] Armitage-Smith, *op. cit.* pp. 176–80.

unexpected encouragement of the commons, which seems to
have gone far beyond their wildest dreams when their members
arranged, as they must have done, that the earl of March's
steward, Peter de la Mare, should act as *prolocutor, commune-
parlour* or *vant-parlour*, a vague office of some few years'
standing which his ability, energy and courage were destined to
convert for all time into that of Speaker, in something distantly
approaching the modern sense. Two chronicles[1] attest Peter's
virtues, one in considerable detail, while the other adds significantly that, even outside parliament, many songs were made
in his praise, an honour hitherto reserved for magnates like
Simon de Montfort or Thomas of Lancaster. Yet even de la
Mare could have done little without willing and numerous
supporters, and it is now[2] clear that, though the lead was taken
by the seventy-four knights representing the thirty-seven
medieval shires, an exceptionally large number of burgesses was
also present; it was not only a very long, a very vigorous and
an extremely independent but also a remarkably well-attended
parliament.

The day after the formal opening on the 29th of April, when
the usual chancellor's speech asking for grants was made, the
lords retired to their usual place of meeting[3] in the White
Chamber, while the commons betook themselves to theirs in
the chapter-house of Westminster Abbey, where after an oath
of mutual loyalty they began deliberation. First, a knight *del
south pais* said the king should live of his own, then another
called attention to the removal of the staple[4] from Calais for the
benefit of Latimer and Lyons, as all men knew, and suggested
that it should be restored. Finally, a third suggested asking for a

[1] *Anonimalle Chronicle*, p. 83 and *Chronicon Anglie*, pp. 72, 392—the
latter for the songs.

[2] From the newly discovered *Anonimalle Chronicle of S. Mary's, York*,
ed. V. H. Galbraith, from pp. 74–94 of which the detail following is taken.
See also Pollard in *E.H.R.* liii, 577–605.

[3] A. F. Pollard, *Evolution of Parliament*, p. 72, for the lords. *Anon. Chron.
loc. cit.* for the chapter-house as "the ancient place of meeting" of the
commons.

[4] The official wool-market.

joint committee with the lords, to be chosen by the commons themselves as in 1373, and this was agreed. De la Mare first came to the fore in summing up after these speakers; an adjournment followed. On the 3rd of May the commons reassembled and until the 9th of May proceeded to work out in detail all their grievances, the raw material of petitions. It was at this second stage that de la Mare so distinguished himself that he was unanimously called on to act as *commune-parlour* before the lords. Consequently, on the 9th he and a few knights appeared before Gaunt, who was representing the king, in the Painted Chamber, where lords and commoners now habitually came together for joint meetings, but on this occasion de la Mare refused to speak until all the commons were present and, with remarkable sang-froid, kept the lords waiting for two or three hours until as many as possible of the commons had been found. The joint committee, containing four bishops, four earls and four barons,[1] was then appointed and the commons went away. It is worth remarking that the committee, though excluding William of Wykeham, was heavily weighted, as we should expect, with the more conservative magnates or their relatives. It included de la Mare's master, the earl of March, in person, together with two young bishops of the magnate as against the self-made class, both of them destined to be prominent in the early years of the next reign. These were William Courtenay of London, grandson of the first earl of Devon, and Henry Despenser of Norwich, grandson of Edward II's favourite, the younger Despenser. Among the barons may be noticed Henry Percy, future earl of Northumberland, the stormy petrel of the late fourteenth century and a far more sinister figure than John of Gaunt. It was not long before Percy found it in his personal interest to change sides, but he remained true all his life to the principles of extreme baronial independence, a danger to all government.

On Monday the 12th of May the joint committee met in the chapter-house and then returned to report in parliament. This

[1] Representing three "estates" of the nobility. Cf. M. V. Clarke, *Medieval Representation and Consent*, p. 321.

was the occasion of de la Mare's great speech. It contained a devastating indictment of the curialists, notably Latimer and Lyons. The old charge concerning the Calais staple was repeated, but more interesting for the light they throw on government finance are the accusations of "chevisaunce" made against these two in that they had in the first place lent the king 20,000 marks, but secured repayment in pounds, and this though William Walworth and another London citizen would have lent free of interest entirely, and secondly that they had bought up exchequer tallies from all and sundry at a 50 per cent discount to their own great profit and without the knowledge of the king.[1] Alice Perrers was accused of drawing a revenue of £2000 to £3000 a year from the king—a sum roughly equal to the income of the see of Winchester—while protests were freely made in the speech against the dissipation on unworthy recipients of the crown's lands and feudal incidents in general.

The next day all these charges were reported to Edward, who agreed to add Brantingham and Scrope to the joint committee for the sake of their evidence as treasurers. Gaunt, however, apparently suppressed all mention of the king's concession and it was not yet known when on Monday the 19th of May the lords met once more in the White Chamber and the commons and the joint committee in the chapter-house. In the parliament which followed Gaunt endeavoured to obtain a grant from the commons without paying further attention to their grievances. His bluff was called by de la Mare, whereupon Gaunt at last gave way, and revealed the king's consent to the afforcement of the joint committee by the expert witnesses. Richard le Scrope at once confirmed the truth of the main charges, adding that a new figure, one John Pyel, was concerned; Pyel, however, promptly turned king's evidence and seems to have got off scot-free. Latimer and Lyons did not escape so easily, the now infuriated commons demanding their arrest and trial by

[1] Cf. A. Steel, "Some Aspects of English Finance in the Fourteenth Century", *History*, xii, 298–309, for technical explanations. The "mark", which was purely money of account, was valued at 13s. 4d., i.e. two-thirds of a pound.

the lords, that is, their impeachment.[1] Shortly afterwards
Lyons was in fact sentenced to forfeiture and imprisonment,
while the magnates Latimer and John Neville of Raby were
deprived of their household offices and Latimer placed temporarily under arrest; minor victims included another London
merchant, John Pecche, and a fraudulent collector of customs,
apparently Lyons's agent, at Yarmouth. All this was the
result of renewed deliberation by the lords and commons
separately from the 20th of May onwards, concluded by
another joint meeting and another great speech by de la Mare
on Saturday the 24th. Incidentally, in this speech de la Mare
renewed the attack on Alice Perrers and had the satisfaction of
seeing her formally dismissed the court a few days later, the
king professing cynical surprise to learn that she had in fact
been married all the time to Sir William de Windsor, his
extremely vigorous and unscrupulous "governor and guardian"
of Ireland.[2]

The commons, and their friends among the magnates, were
not however merely content to remove and punish enemies;
there is an interesting attempt, recalling those of 1258 and 1311,
to bind the king in future and prevent a repetition of these
offences. De la Mare's demands upon the 24th included a
request not only that the treasurer and chancellor should be
put on oath but also that a "continual council" should be
appointed, to consist of three bishops, three earls and three
barons, without whose consent no grants of feudal revenue
were to be made or any important business carried on. The
lords agreed to it, and on Monday, May the 26th, this decision
was carried to the king, who promptly appointed the council
they advised, omitting Gaunt but including William of
Wykeham. Unfortunately the appointment was robbed of
much value by the provision that the five principal ministers

[1] The word is first used in the technical modern sense on this occasion.
See M. V. Clarke, "The Origin of Impeachment", in *Fourteenth Century
Studies*, pp. 242–71.

[2] For Windsor's career see M. V. Clarke, *Medieval Representation and
Consent*, pp. 50 ff., and *Fourteenth Century Studies*, pp. 146–271.

should be allowed to *faire et esploiter les busoignes qe touchent lour offices sanz la presence des ditz conseille(r)s*;[1] parliament had not as yet the full courage of its convictions. Moreover, Edward's skilful acquiescence in accepting for the moment the personnel suggested to him left it open to the crown to choose future councillors at will, a fact of which Gaunt was not slow to avail himself. None the less, the idea of a " continual " council took root and, modified by strictly parliamentary appointment, was to flourish fitfully during the reign of Richard II.

There followed the melancholy interlude of the Black Prince's final illness at Kennington and his death on the 8th of June. This made his eldest surviving son, Richard of Bordeaux, next heir to the throne, but had little other practical effect; to all intents and purposes the prince had died five years before. The Good Parliament was scarcely interrupted; meeting again in full shortly after his death, it heard the king's consent to its wishes, had the new council presented to it and was admonished for the last time by Peter de la Mare. It ended in the second week of July[2] with *une tres-graunt et excellent fest* given by the knights to the lords, the celebration of a party victory which was not to be overclouded by the accident of a royal funeral.

It is not easy to assess the importance of the Good Parliament. Stubbs, for example, was inclined to disparage it because most of its acts were promptly reversed, and of its many petitions not one became a statute. He would not even allow much importance to the freedom of its language—"these debates, if debates they can be called".[3] It is certainly true that it displayed much essential weakness for all its bold front; the knights alone were vocal, for we hear nothing of the burgesses, and even the knights depended upon an alliance with a solid and determined majority among the lords, while their leader was the steward of the lords' leader. Irresistible while sitting, the parliament was helpless after it had broken up, especially when the magnates who had supported it began to split into factions, as

---

[1] *Rot. Parl.* ii, 322.   [2] *Anon. Chron.* p. 94.
[3] *The Constitutional History of England* (1875), ii, 429. Stubbs, however, did not have access to the *Anonimalle Chronicle*.

they were always prone to do in the hour of victory; Henry
Percy, for example, joining Gaunt's party, together with Sir
Richard Stafford, both of whom had sat on the original joint
committee, while Percy at least was a member of the continual
council. It is, again, possible to question the extent to which
this parliament was genuinely representative of the politically
conscious classes; was there no minority feeling? was it all as
unanimous as it sounds? The general impression is that public
was asserted against private interest and yet there is a taint of
party feeling and a sense of narrower loyalties; an air of
conscious virtue, accompanied by much loud speaking from a
few leaders and the stampeding of the rank and file, sits ill
on even fourteenth-century politicians. We may agree that
March and de la Mare led the less disreputable of two parties,
but for all that it did not cease to be a party which they led.

If we do not know what effect public opinion had on the
Good Parliament, what is quite clear is the effect of that parliament on public opinion.[1] This is evident not only from the
chronicles, especially the *Anonimalle Chronicle* of York, but
from popular sermons and popular literature. Skeat, for
example, dates the new recension of the B Text in his edition of
Piers Plowman to the early months of 1377, and although Dr
Workman somewhat exaggerates in calling this recension "full
of new political utterances",[2] much has certainly been added to
the original poem and the new matter does contain a good deal
of politics. In particular there is the well-known fable of the
rats (the lords), who agreed to try and bell the cat (the court)
but were dissuaded by a wise mouse (commoner), who said
that even a cat has his uses, since without him mice would eat
men's malt and rats prevent them from sleeping at night. The
moral is clearly not that of the Good Parliament, but it may
well be applied to the "reactionary" parliament of January
1377 and in any case the point is that *some* parliament is clearly
intended. Moreover, a recent theory suggests that the now
parliament-conscious Langland is here reflecting a widely held

[1] Cf. Tout in *Mélanges...à...Pirenne* (1926), pp. 545–62.
[2] *John Wyclif*, i, 271.

point of view associated with popular sermons (the widest form of fourteenth-century publicity) and with one well-known preacher in particular.[1]

When this passage was composed Langland was a poor clerk living "in a little house in Cornhill not far from St Paul's", and regularly attending, as he himself says,[2] the sermons at St Paul's Cross. The most famous preacher there at that time was Thomas Brunton, bishop of Rochester from about 1373 to 1389. A former Benedictine monk at Norwich, Brunton became a royal confessor and sat as an anti-Wyclifite on the Blackfriars council in 1382. Walsingham[3] says he delivered the sermon at St Paul's Cross *in processione* on the day of Richard's coronation, and later records his death in 1389 as a national misfortune, while, in the *Chronicon Anglie*[4] he adds that he was one of the four bishops singled out to give counsel in 1376 to the knights of the shires. One manuscript copy of his Latin sermons survives and among these Gasquet has identified no. 69, from its references to Alice Perrers, Lord Latimer and others, as belonging to April of that year.

Comparison makes it clear that in the B Text of the Prologue Langland drew *verbatim* on this and other sermons of Brunton's; thus the fable of the rat parliament occurs in both. The "Angel" of the Prologue is perhaps Brunton himself—an angel is a common medieval figure for a preacher—and the "Goliardeys, a glotoun of wordes", who next appears in the poem, may be none other than Peter de la Mare. Again, both poet and preacher advance well beyond the stock feudal conception of Priest, Knight and Labourer as the components of society, into a more complex and national system. Thus Brunton tells the other bishops to follow his own example and preach faithfully not only in their own dioceses but also in London, because of its national importance; further, he con-

---

[1] G. R. Owst, *Literature and Pulpit in Medieval England*, pp. 576 ff., for this and what follows.
[2] Skeat's B Text, Passus XIII, ll. 65–6.   [3] *Historia Anglicana*, i, 338–9.
[4] p. 69. Cf. generally R. L. Poole's short notice on "Brinton" (*sic*) in the *Dictionary of National Biography*.

centrates on specifically English knights, English magnates and English shortcomings, and here too Langland follows him. This growth of national sentiment as a form in which a conscious public opinion can express itself is also reflected in the Good Parliament, which produced no less than thirteen petitions aimed at the pope and foreign clergy, not so much as clergy but as foreigners.[1] As a result the government—soon in Gaunt's hands again, but Gaunt had no objection to this particular line of policy—was able to bring pressure to bear on Gregory XI by forbidding the reception of bulls, and in September 1376 Gaunt himself was not afraid, as we have seen, to ally himself openly with Wyclif. It may be then·that Stubbs under-estimates the indirect influence of this parliament when he says that it "asserted some sound principles without being the starting-point of new history",[2] and perhaps tradition is right in hearing in its debates the striking of a new note which is to dominate the rest of the century. Whether this be so or not, the immediate result was otherwise; there was, in fact, a considerable reaction from the Good Parliament, the measure, so Perroy thinks,[3] of its own violence.

In the first place the sole effective action taken in deference to its requests was the restoration of the staple to Calais (24th July 1376). It is true that this raised a principle of some importance,[4] since the complaint was that it had been removed without parliamentary consent and contrary to statute, but the victory on this point only represented a small fraction of the parliamentary demands. Even its cherished victims had been mostly released on bail by the end of August to appear before a great council, finally held from October to December, at Westminster. Moreover, in this council Gaunt won over a majority of the inconstant lords to dissolve the continual council and declare all the acts of the Good Parliament invalid; it

[1] E. Perroy, *L'Angleterre et le grand schisme d'Occident*, pp. 41–3, for an analysis of these petitions.

[2] *Constitutional History*, ii, 428.   [3] *Schisme*, p. 43.

[4] Cf. G. Sayles and H. G. Richardson, "The Parliaments of Edward III (concluded)", *Bull. Inst. Hist. Research*, ix, 1–18.

should, on the other hand, be noted in his favour that he made no attempt to oppose Richard's creation as prince of Wales on November 20th. He and Latimer, who was now at liberty again, then proceeded to assault the persons prominent in the Good Parliament. Of these, William of Wykeham, though important only in its later stages, had ultimately joined in pressing the attack on Latimer before the lords, while from the mere extent of his possessions he was obviously vulnerable. He was therefore forbidden the court and deprived of his temporalities, probably by a special commission appointed in this council—the charges against him being an ingenious reflection of those he had urged against the newer curialists. The earl of March, on the other hand, was not directly attacked, but he was frightened into resigning the marshalship of England, which was promptly used as a bribe to secure the renegade Percy, while March's steward, the unfortunate de la Mare, was flung into Nottingham castle, it is uncertain by what authority or upon what charge. Finally, a new parliament was called in legal form for January 1377.

There has been a good deal of debate about the composition of the commons in this last parliament of Edward III. Tout,[1] for example, repeats the tradition that Gaunt, having learnt his lesson in the previous summer, was now careful to secure the return of his own friends; if so, this is of interest as the first occasion on which it was thought worth while to pack the commons, but the tradition has recently been challenged.[2] It apparently goes back to the very hostile *Chronicon Anglie*, reinforced in modern times by Armitage-Smith's suggestion[3] that the duke may well have used some of his 125 knights and 132 esquires[4] for the purpose. Yet actually only thirty of these knights, and not more than nineteen esquires, sat in all twelve parliaments taken together of the period 1372–82, and there were never more than seven Lancastrians sitting at any one

[1] *Chapters*, iii, 312.
[2] By Col. J. Wedgwood, in "John of Gaunt and the Packing of Parliament", *E.H.R.* xlv, 623–5.
[3] *Op. cit.* p. 441.   [4] Above, p. 20.

time in any one parliament. In the Good Parliament itself there were in fact four Lancastrian knights and one esquire—the nucleus, no doubt, of an overborne minority—and there were only four such knights and two esquires in that of January 1377. That is, in both parliaments Gaunt's personal following had just about its fair share of seats, and no more.

However, it might be argued that even if Gaunt did not put his own retinue into the commons he may have used his influence with the sheriffs appointed in the autumn of 1376 to keep known opponents out. The sheriff of Cambridgeshire and Huntingdonshire for 1376–7, Sir John Dengayne, was for example one of Gaunt's men and, though nothing has as yet been proved for other shires, it is certainly remarkable that only eight knights and five burgesses out of all those attending the Good Parliament were re-elected in January 1377, whereas the average re-election figures are sixteen and ten respectively.[1] Moreover, out of the eight knights re-elected three sat for Lancashire and Leicestershire, both counties almost wholly under the influence of Gaunt, while as soon as Gaunt lost power again on Edward's death twenty-two of the knights of the Good Parliament were re-elected to that of October 1377. These figures seem to tell at first sight in favour of what might be called an *un*-packing theory, but it is doubtful if they are really very conclusive. What is remarkable is that this supposedly submissive parliament of January, whose speaker was Sir Thomas Hungerford, steward of Gaunt's lands in Wales and the south and a member of his council, did in fact raise some effective protests against Gaunt's policy and party, while at least four of its petitions virtually repealed those of its predecessor.

The parliament certainly began by respecting Gaunt's wishes; thus, when the lords under protest[2] once more agreed to

[1] N. B. Lewis, "Re-Election to Parliament in the Reign of Richard II", *E.H.R.* xlviii, 364–94, for this passage.

[2] They complained that "such manner was never before seen in any Parliament, save in the three Parliaments last past", D. Hughes, *Illustrations of Chaucer's England*, p. 224.

the appointment of a joint committee with the commons, the committee appointed contained a clear predominance of Lancastrians, notably the bishop of Salisbury, still Gaunt's chancellor and ally. It was complaisant too in approving the conversion of Lancashire into a county palatine with the rights of Chester, that is, with full regalian rights and a separate chancery,[1] a grant made in the first place for life and confirmed as such in November 1378 but extended to the heirs male of Gaunt in February 1390. Moreover it exempted Wykeham from the general amnesty now proclaimed for all late offenders in connexion with the king's jubilee, but it did this reluctantly—there were petitions in favour of Wykeham and the lords refused to associate themselves with the exception, while condoning it— and it is doubtful whether the remaining activities of this parliament were specially congenial to Gaunt.

Of these activities the most significant was the invention of the "tallage of groats". This was a poll-tax, the first of a notorious series, to be paid by all persons over the age of fourteen other than genuine beggars, at a flat rate of fourpence per head. It was an entirely new form of taxation—an experiment comparable to the unfortunate parish-tax of 1371—and it was deliberately adopted in preference to a double subsidy and other more unpractical suggestions, apparently with the idea of spreading the burden of taxation as widely as possible. In this respect it throws a peculiarly unpleasant light on the substantial knights and burgesses who were increasingly ready to criticise the government while endeavouring to make others pay for it, for the tax was obviously unjust to the poorer classes who were not represented in parliament. As such, it may have laid the foundations of Gaunt's remarkable unpopularity in the country during the following years, since most of the actions of this parliament would, rightly or wrongly, be popularly attributed to him, though there is no evidence that he was in fact responsible for this particular experiment.

[1] There are important details in Armitage-Smith, *op. cit.* pp. 203–10. The extension to heirs male in 1390 may well help to explain Richard's arbitrary confiscation on Gaunt's death in 1399.

Another commons' innovation in this parliament with which Gaunt can hardly be associated was a demand for four special treasurers to administer the proceeds of the new tax; this was reluctantly withdrawn in answer to the plea of expense, on condition that the entire yield should be specially earmarked for the war, which was on the point of being renewed as the truce of Bruges ran out—but though withdrawn on this occasion we shall hear much of this and similar demands again. Altogether, this touchiness on the subject of taxation, together with the appearance among its petitions of pleas not only for Wykeham but also for de la Mare, certainly suggests that the real extent of Gaunt's influence in this parliament can easily be exaggerated. However this may be, in convocation, which was sitting at the same time, Gaunt clearly had no influence at all.

Here Courtenay, bishop of London, was vigorously fighting for Wykeham and the church by carrying a proposal that all grants should be refused until Wykeham, who was still forbidden the court, should appear. Gaunt's retort was to give Wyclif, whom he had been keeping for just such an occasion, an opportunity to expound his views upon civil and divine dominion, on grace and, above all, on ecclesiastical poverty. This resulted in Wyclif's first citation before the bishops—even Sudbury, the mild archbishop of Canterbury, being "roused as from deep sleep"—which in turn produced a riot in St Paul's. In the course of this riot the Londoners took up the demand for justice to Wykeham and de la Mare, and Gaunt was temporarily discomfited. The incident has importance in decisively revealing, as it did, the permanent danger of London to all fourteenth-century governments with their unprotected headquarters at Westminster, only a mile or two outside the walls, and the consequent importance to every government of making friends with one party in London and of keeping that party in power.[1] It was a lesson which the young Richard was soon to learn—the events of his childhood, from this time on, may well have impressed it on him—and he was to

[1] Tout, "Beginnings of a Modern Capital", *Collected Papers*, iii, 249–75. Cf. G. Unwin, *Gilds and Companies of London*, ch. x.

discover that it extended beyond politics and brawling to the question of loans and high finance.

Meanwhile in the spring of 1377 a compromise was reached. Wykeham bought back his temporalities by a promise to make fine in £2000, later excused him, with the king, and also, according to tradition, by abasing himself before Alice Perrers, now triumphantly installed at court again—but that was probably malicious gossip. Convocation in return followed parliament in making a grant, and Wyclif was outwardly left in peace, though secretly denounced, by no means for the first time, to the pope. Finally, the household servants and advisers of the new prince of Wales and of his mother, Joan of Kent, came effectively on the scene by arranging, first, a reconciliation between Gaunt and London and, secondly, a concordat of their own with the duke, which ensured a peaceful succession and lasted well into the next reign. In virtue of it de la Mare was at last released with compensation from Nottingham castle; this occurred on the 30th of June 1377, eight days after the death of Edward III. The new reign had begun.

It might seem unnecessary to recite at such length the history of the unfortunate years 1369–77, but apart from the fact that it is perhaps the only way of making clear the complex political situation which existed in England in June 1377 this period is really of a piece with the four or five years which follow. The uncertainties of the international situation, the ever-growing futilities of the French war, the muddled anti-clericalism, directed partly against the Caesarian clergy, partly against a papacy itself about to be divided by the Great Schism, the mounting political ambitions of the common lawyers, the intrigues of the magnates and the curialists, the involved finance and the unhappy experiments in that connexion, the irresponsibility of the commons, the failure of "continual councils", the rising temper of the people, all these are the very stuff of Richard's reign. We shall see these and other forces continuing to act and interact remorselessly, warping the sensitive adolescent unwillingly involved in them and, almost incidentally, producing that abrupt explosion which we call the Peasants' Revolt.

CHAPTER II

The Minority

EDWARD III was succeeded without interregnum by Richard of Bordeaux; the hereditary, as opposed to the elective, view of the succession was gaining ground and at the coronation archbishop Sudbury administered the oath before turning to the people to ask whether they would have Richard as their king.[1]

Richard was born in the abbey of St Andrew, Bordeaux, on the 6th of January 1367 and was baptised in the cathedral three days later. James, titular king of Majorca, was his chief sponsor and this, together with the possible presence of Peter the Cruel and the fact of Richard's birth on Twelfth Day, no doubt gave rise to the Messianic story of the three kings who offered him gifts. At the end of his life hostile legend added that he was born "without a skin and nourished in the skins of goats" and was no true son of the Black Prince but of a certain French canon in the household.[2] His nurse, Mundina Danos, "of Aquitaine", received a pension in 1378 and subsequently married the king's tailor.[3] Richard himself was taken to England by his parents in January 1371, at the age of four, shortly after the death of his seven-year old elder brother, Edward of Angoulême—an event which is said to have deeply disturbed the Black Prince and no doubt reinforced the medical advice

---

[1] Ramsay, *Genesis*, ii, 104, 108. The contrary suggestion in the B Text of *Piers Plowman* (Prologue, ll. 112-13) is misleading. The lines—

> "Thanne came there a kyng: knyghthod hym ladde,
> Migt of the comunes: made hym to regne..."

probably refer to the commons' successful demand for the production of Richard before parliament on the 25th of June 1376, after the death of his father, "that they might see and honour him as very heir apparent". They do not enshrine any political theory.

[2] *D.N.B.* "Richard II".   [3] *Cal. Pat. Rolls*, 1377–81, p. 609.

which led to his retirement to Berkhamsted, where from this date Richard was brought up.

It is a matter of some importance but great difficulty to reconstruct the influences which were brought to bear on Richard as a child. Clearly we should place his mother first among them; she still had charge of him when he opened the parliament of January 1377 for his grandfather. Joan, princess of Wales,[1] was born in 1328; she was a younger child of Edmund of Woodstock, earl of Kent and sixth son of Edward I. Her father having been beheaded in March 1330 she was brought up by queen Philippa according to Froissart, who describes her as *en son temps la plus belle de tout la roiaulme d'Engleterre et la plus amoureuse*; hence no doubt her later nickname, the Fair Maid of Kent. William de Montacute, second earl of Salisbury, and the steward of his household, Sir Thomas Holland, both wished to marry her, but it was Holland whom she preferred. They seem to have lived together under a pre-contract of matrimony, but Holland was called away to the French wars, whereupon Salisbury took advantage of his absence to enter into a marriage contract himself with Joan, presumably against her wishes. Holland, however, petitioned Clement VI on his return to England to restore his rights and obtained judgment in November 1349. Three years later, on the death of her brothers, Joan became countess of Kent in her own right, her husband assuming the title of earl by the courtesy of England. Within a very few months of his death in December 1360 Joan, now nearly thirty-three and the mother of two surviving sons, entered into a clandestine love affair with the Black Prince. As the parties were related in the third degree and there was, in the eyes of the church, a spiritual relationship since the Black Prince had been godfather to Joan's elder son, Thomas Holland, it was doubtful whether they could marry and in any case a papal dispensation would be necessary.[2] However, according to Froissart,[3] so great was the love between them that the old king was taken into their confidence, a papal

---

[1] *D.N.B.* for this paragraph in general.
[2] *D.N.B.* "Black Prince".   [3] *Œuvres*, vi, 366–7.

dispensation obtained and the marriage solemnised by archbishop Simon Islip at Lambeth in October 1361 in the presence
of the whole royal family. In 1361–2 and again from 1371 the
couple lived at Berkhamsted, but the intervening years were
spent by Joan, mainly with her husband, at various places in
Aquitaine. One son, as we have seen, was born at Angoulême
and a second, Richard, at Bordeaux. There were no other
children.

What are we to make of all this? The facts suggest beauty
and desirability in Richard's mother rather than strength of
character; the Salisbury episode in particular is odd. Moreover
there were two vulnerable points in her career: if either the papal
decision of 1349 or the dispensation of 1361 were reversed—
and such things were not unknown—her children might be
declared illegitimate; Richard in particular had a double chance
of illegitimacy.[1] The fact that no steps were taken at any time to
procure the reversal of either or both of these decisions goes a
long way to clear the character of Gaunt, the person most
immediately interested, and incidentally suggests that the
princess of Wales, sheltered no doubt even after his death by the
great name of her second husband, made no abiding enemies.
She had the reputation of a peace-maker in later life in spite of
the advancing years and corpulence which might easily have
embittered her; thus she was affectionately greeted by the
rebels who intercepted her on the road from Canterbury to
London in 1381.[2] Richard was consistently devoted to her to
the day of her death at Wallingford in August 1385, but it
seems to have been a gentle, obvious affection and anything
abnormal in his relationship with his parents was connected
with his father.

There is no evidence that Richard ever felt differently from
his contemporaries towards the much-admired Black Prince;
on the contrary, it is probable that like the rest of his world he
admired him far too much. The prince was in fact universally
agreed to be the perfect type of the debased and complicated

[1] H. Wallon, *Richard II*, i, 4, stresses the first chance only.
[2] Kissed, according to Froissart, *Œuvres*, ix, 391.

chivalry of the later Middle Ages;[1] great in tournaments, great in war, and master of a social code remarkable alike for senselessness, extravagance and complete indifference to the interest of classes other than its own. He was famous not only for Crécy, Poitiers and Najera, but for the ostentatious entertainment in England of his royal captive, John II of France, and of another great knight errant, Peter I of Cyprus, at Angoulême in 1363, when however he was careful to excuse both his lords and himself from taking the cross. He played a great part, it is true, in negotiating the impracticable Peace of Bretigny and it is said that the English clergy trusted him; but there is really nothing to suggest the statesman in him or that when he died before his father England lost the chance of having another great king. A good, but not a brilliant soldier—he could never cope with the reformed tactics of the French captain du Guesclin—he began a military career prematurely at fifteen, ruined his health in the pursuit of it and died at forty-six. His Castilian wild-goose chase and his misgovernment of Gascony had helped to undo his own diplomatic work by producing a renewal of the French war—of this danger, it is true, he had had the insight to warn Edward, though in vain—and on his deathbed, having roused a storm he could never have controlled, he turned aside to insist above everything on the confirmation of his personal gifts, the payment of his personal debts and the protection of his son's succession. His last interview with Richard hinged once more on the extraction of an oath from this child of nine that his father's gifts would be respected, and he seems to have died without ever having learnt to distinguish the interests of the country from those of the royal family. Romance apart, the record is not an impressive one.[2]

Richard cannot in fact have seen very much of his father; the

[1] Cf. J. Huizinga, *Waning of the Middle Ages* (London, 1924), *passim*, for a brilliant analysis of western European "chivalry" at a slightly later date.

[2] Facts mainly from the *D.N.B.*, but I am responsible for the unfavourable interpretation. Cf. P. Shaw, "The Black Prince", *History*, xxiv, 1–15, for a slightly kinder view. He notes that the traditional sobriquet dates only from Grafton's *Chronicle*, 1569.

prince left Bordeaux for Dax shortly after he was born, and during the next few years was mainly engaged in campaigning, while from 1371 he was in broken health with the exception of a few weeks of temporary improvement during the summer of 1372, when he was at sea with Edward III on an abortive expedition. Moreover, his distress at the death of his elder son suggests that it was not unnaturally Edward of Angoulême, rather than Richard of Bordeaux, who up to 1371 claimed most of his scanty attention. None the less, from that year at least Richard had no rival and, however much or little he saw of his father, he could not help being brought up under the shadow of a name not only great, but great in certain specific respects. The prince's choice of tutors for him was significant; they were two old companions in arms, Guichard d'Angle, created earl of Huntingdon at Richard's coronation, who died without issue a few years later, and Simon Burley, executed by the appellants in 1388. Here as elsewhere the Black Prince displayed a complete lack of insight, sympathy and imagination; the son was to be formed in the image of his father, despite the physical incapacity suggested by the surviving portraits, which seem to indicate a build too slight for the requirements of knight errantry, and despite the nervous temperament which he can hardly have failed to observe. Richard was not a physical coward, but he was very probably a physical weakling, and the imposition from an early age of his father's standards of physical prowess as the sole avenue to distinction must have weighed heavily upon him. When we add to this the insistence on the kingly dignity and regality which was more and more stressed by his tutors the nearer he approached to the throne, the position must have become intolerable. Richard was apparently being told that to be a great king he must be a great knight, like his father; he was physically incapable of becoming a great knight; how then could he become a great king? Yet a great king he was determined to be. The solution to be reached through rejecting the standards proffered to him was too difficult; Richard possessed a sensitive, and far from unintelligent, but at the same time a lazy and profoundly conventional mind, and it would not have occurred to him at any time to reject what all his circle not only admitted but insisted on. So the conflict of two ideals incompatible in his case remained to torture him all his days; it was to be resolved for one short moment only in the presence of Wat Tyler, probably the supreme moment of his life, but it returned to haunt him almost at once, not unassisted by the jealous intrigues of his enemies, and may help to explain such curious actions of his later days as the sudden termination of the duel between the dukes of Hereford and Norfolk at Coventry in 1398.

Apart from their too orthodox scale of values the two tutors seem to have been reasonable and kindly men. We hear little of Guichard d'Angle in this particular connexion, but Richard never seems to have felt any ill-will towards him, while to Burley, who was to play a great part in what is sometimes known as his first "tyranny", he became warmly attached. It may well have been Burley who instilled into him an exaggerated idea of kingship—in itself a questionable service, but certainly not one which Richard was disposed to resent. It is possible that the secret of his affection—an affection which later made him let his queen kneel to the earl of Arundel for Burley's life, while he himself for three weeks risked his throne—lay in some persuasion of the ultimate compatibility of kingship with a certain lack of chivalric distinction which Burley, himself an old soldier of merit, and only Burley, was occasionally able to effect. But this is guesswork; what is certain is that Richard's education was carried on along the most strictly orthodox fourteenth-century lines, orthodox, that is, among noble families; in other words, in most important respects, it was neglected.

We do not know very much about the other companions of Richard's childhood; there is in fact a certain solitariness about him during most of the early and some of the middle years of his life—another handicap, for his was not a nature which gained from solitude. It is commonly said that he was brought up with his two Holland half-brothers, and their allegedly violent, selfish and avaricious characters are then adduced as unfortunate influences on him in palliation of his later life. But apart from the question whether his later life needs or gains much from this excuse, and passing over the rather arbitrary characterisation of the Hollands, who were certainly violent but perhaps not remarkably selfish or avaricious for the age in which they lived, the facts of chronology make the whole theory absurd.[1] Thomas Holland, second earl of Kent, was born in 1350, seventeen years before Richard, and was in fact knighted by the Black Prince, while fighting in Castile, in the year of Richard's birth. His younger brother, John Holland, later earl of Huntingdon and duke of Exeter, is generally supposed to have been only about two years younger than Thomas, and though we hear nothing of him before 1381 it is highly un-likely that a boy fifteen years older than Richard, and so famous in later life for knightly prowess that he must have begun his military exercises early, could ever have been "brought up" with him in any sense of the words. What is true is that John's skill in tournaments and Thomas's military distinction must have been continually held up to Richard as further instances of the ideal at which he was to aim and may well have obscured his eyes to their less admirable characteristics. While increasing his sense of inferiority and forcing it still more strongly to look for compensation in the regality, their careers do not seem to have inspired him with jealousy; on the contrary, Richard was clearly on good terms with Thomas until his death in 1397, although owing to ill-health in later life he was never an effective ally, and on even better terms with his young son (born in 1374) of the same name, while John was certainly one of the intimates and stalwarts of his later years. But it is time to turn from the early character of Richard and the influences which affected it to the practical arrangements for government which were made at the beginning of his reign.

Passing over the frequently described pageantry of the corona-tion, elaborate accounts of which survive in more than one chronicle, we come to the changes produced in the political situation by the death of the old king. These as a matter of fact were slight, but it is important to note that from this time on

[1] See *D.N.B.* "Thomas and John Holland".

the term "court party" is naturally applied to the household, dependents and allies of the princess of Wales and her son; the old court party dissolves into an opposition rabble, more or less discredited. The king himself was, of course, too young to affect politics directly for at least four years to come, but there was no regency; Joan of Kent acted as his informal guardian and the centre of his court, while Richard himself had his own great seal, privy seal and signet from the beginning. The actual government was carried on by a "continual council" of twelve persons, appointed in a great council held in July 1377;[1] it excluded not only Gaunt but also his younger brothers, Edmund of Langley (1342–1402), earl of Cambridge and future duke of York, and Thomas of Woodstock (1355–97), earl of Buckingham and future duke of Gloucester. Apart from these notable exclusions some attempt seems to have been made to represent all parties on this first continual council—thus creatures of Gaunt, if not Gaunt himself, appear on it—yet the Lancastrian coalition which had been powerful at the beginning of the year was held to have suffered a setback sufficient for the duke to retire moodily to his castle of Kenilworth and for Percy to be compelled to resign the marshalship of England to Sir John Arundel.

This balancing of rival factions among the magnates, reasonable and moderate as it may seem, had in fact disastrous results. For the next four years the failure of any one clique to triumph over the rest produced a lack of leadership and a steady shelving of responsibility which found expression first in a series of restless experiments with parliaments, great councils and small councils "continual" only in name, and finally in a complete breakdown of government. The period is therefore dreary in the extreme; it is marked by an unimaginative persistence in the war with France, accompanied by the crudest military, financial and administrative incompetence. The ruling classes could neither

[1] J. F. Baldwin, *The King's Council*, ch. vi, misdates the first two continual councils of the reign, and makes other mistakes corrected by N. B. Lewis, "The 'Continual Council' in the early years of Richard II, 1377–80", *E.H.R.* xli, 246–51.

bring themselves to make peace, because that involved concessions to the French, nor yet endure to find the money for a
decisive campaign. At the same time it is essential to sketch,
however roughly, the class selfishness and futilities of the
minority, as an introduction both to the Peasants' Revolt and
to later, rather half-hearted, attempts at administrative reform,
coupled with a more realistic foreign policy.

The first parliament of Richard II, which met in October 1377,
clearly reverted to the policy of the Good Parliament. The
reason is to be found in the French raids on the south coast
of England, made repeatedly since the expiry of the extended
truce of Bruges the previous June. De la Mare was once more
speaker, and although it is true that the commons invited Gaunt
to sit on a joint committee with the lords and consulted his ally
Wyclif about papal exactions,[1] the rest of their behaviour can
hardly have been congenial to the Lancastrians or their allies.
Thus the continual council was remodelled by the committee
in such a way[2] as to exclude Latimer and greatly reduce
Lancastrian representation; a more serious mistake was the
insertion of a self-denying provision, by which its members
were to hold office for one year only and then be ineligible for
the next two years, thus effectively destroying administrative
experience and continuity. The commons further insisted that
during the king's minority not only the continual council
but the five principal ministers, the chief justices and other
important officials ought to be chosen by parliament.

This last demand, though described by an historian so hostile
to autocracy as Oman as an "enormous encroachment"[3] on the
ancient rights of the crown, was none the less substantially
conceded,[4] whereupon the commons reached the limits of their
audacity in expressing a wish that the actual household staff of
the king should also be appointed and dismissed in parliament.

---

[1] This provoked the nineteen Conclusions, embodying Wyclif's theory
of dominion. See *Historia Anglicana*, i, 353–5.
[2] By reducing the total number from twelve to eight.
[3] *The Political History of England*, 1377–1485, p. 8.
[4] Details in Tout, *Chapters*, iii, 335–6.

Finally, when the lords, greedy for power as they were, felt
that this was going too far and rejected the petition, the
commons delivered a Parthian shot in the shape of a request,
which was allowed them, that future measures agreed in parliament should not be altered or repealed without their consent.[1]
In return for these concessions, however, they made the first
generous money grant for some years in the shape of a double
subsidy and the renewal for three years of the existing customs
on wool and hides.[2] Yet in doing so they revived, and this time
carried into effect, the demand made but dropped in January
1377, for the appointment of special receivers of the proceeds of
these grants, such receivers to be named by the government.
Two prominent citizens of London, William Walworth
and John Philipot, were appointed[3] and their joint account
is still extant at the end of the ordinary receipt roll. Altogether, the degree of continuity between this parliament
and its two predecessors is remarkable enough to illustrate still further the slightness of the changes in the general
situation brought about by the accession of the new king. The
records are not complete, but it is known that at least twenty-
two knights and nine burgesses of the Good Parliament reappeared in October 1377, and many of its petitions are repeated, while a more surprising continuity with the supposedly
reactionary parliament of January 1377 is shown not only by
the appointment of treasurers of war but by the almost identical
form of the petitions concerning aliens. It is clear, moreover,
that this continuity is not merely one of parliamentary personnel,
which changed considerably, at least in the January parliament,
but of what may now perhaps be called "public" opinion, that is,
the opinion of those classes returning members to parliament.[4]
It is not therefore lords and commons only; it is the upper

[1] This may be regarded as an attack on Gaunt's virtual nullification of
the measures taken in the Good Parliament.
[2] Ramsay, *Revenues*, ii, 300.
[3] Adams and Stephens, *Select Documents of English Constitutional History*,
p. 137.
[4] N. B. Lewis, *E.H.R.* xlviii, 364–94.

and upper middle classes of the country generally which must
bear the responsibility for the rising tide of mismanagement
which continued through the next few years.

For mismanagement there was in all departments, military,
naval and financial, and the percentage of cash entries on the
receipt rolls as against entries recording anticipated revenue
drops from 76 per cent in the Easter term of 1379 to 33 per cent
in the Michaelmas term of 1381–2, following the Peasants'
Revolt.[1] Much money was wasted in the late summer of 1378
on Gaunt's abortive siege of St Malo, and the government was
further shaken in his absence by the scandal arising out of a
murderous violation of sanctuary at Westminster, caused by a
dispute over the ransom of the count of Denia, who had been
for years a prisoner in England.[2] It was not a good time to
summon parliament again, but fresh supplies were imperative,
and accordingly writs were issued for a meeting at Gloucester
in October 1378. It was the first time for thirty-nine years that
parliament had met elsewhere than at Westminster, but men's
feelings, those of the Londoners in particular, had been too
much roused by the recent violation of sanctuary there to make
Westminster any longer a safe place for assembly, and moreover it was hoped that the comforts and conveniences of the
great abbey of St Peter might do something to soothe the
unpleasant temper in which the commons were undoubtedly
going to meet a tottering government.

Besides the Westminster scandal and the expensive fiasco at
St Malo there were other pressing questions, notably in the
field of foreign policy, which had suddenly extended its
difficulties far beyond the familiar limits of the dragging war
with France. It was already clear that the year 1378 would
mark the beginning of a new age in European, if not in
English, history; the great Emperor Charles IV, if not yet dead,[3]

[1] A. Steel, "Practice of Assignment", *E.H.R.* xliii, 172–80.
[2] This is the famous Hawley-Shakell episode, for which see Walsingham,
Hist. Anglic. i, 375–9, 411–12. The act of sacrilege was committed by
members of Gaunt's following and he, though absent, was held largely
responsible for it.   [3] He died on the 29th of November.

was dying and his son and successor Wenzel was scarcely
eighteen; the French king himself, it is true, like du Guesclin,
the greatest of his servants, had still two years to live, but he was
growing old and feeble and wavering in judgment; he had just
alienated the Bretons, in spite of the opportunity with which the
weakness of the English had presented him; his principal ally,
Flanders, was on the verge of an anti-French popular revolution,
which in fact broke out the next year; the dauphin was a boy of
ten, possessing three ambitious uncles. In Castile, 1379 would see
the death of Henry II of Trastamara and the active renewal in
the Peninsula of Gaunt's ambitions, coupled at first with those
of his brother Edmund, earl of Cambridge, this time at the
instigation of the Portuguese; it was a world of shifting land-
marks, of uneasy popular mutterings, from which all the elder
statesmen, one after another, were quietly slipping away. As
such, it was a world of great opportunities which the leaderless
English government, with its eyes fixed firmly on its feudal
past, was quite unable to perceive, much less utilise; moreover,
it was obsessed by the one great change which had already
actually occurred by October 1378, and was not merely
threatening; for in March Pope Gregory XI, who had finally
returned to Rome in the autumn of 1376, had died there, and
towards the end of September the Great Schism had begun.
Europe was being rapidly divided into two camps, armed
camps if the more ardent supporters of each pope could have
their way, and it was necessary for the English, as for other
people, to make their choice.

It was no ordinary schism. The first of the two rival popes,
Urban VI, had been elected early in April amid the uproar of a
Roman mob. It is not disputed that all the proper forms were
observed and it was not for some weeks that certain of the
participating cardinals, not unreasonably disappointed in the
man they had chosen, declared that they had been unduly
influenced by fear of the Roman people. Their statement, at
first sight plausible, was in fact a dubious one, not only through
the long interval which elapsed before it was made, but because
they themselves had imagined at the time that in choosing the

archbishop of Bari they were choosing a man uncongenial to the Romans, who wanted one of themselves, and also because immediately after the election they went out of their way to make an extraordinary declaration to the cardinals remaining at Avignon that the vote had been free. None the less by August they had repudiated the authority of Urban and in September thirteen of them, all Frenchmen, proceeded, with three Italian abstentions, to elect as pope cardinal Robert of Geneva, who took the title of Clement VII.

The real reasons for this remarkable conduct are to be found, first and foremost, in the desire of a predominantly French conclave to return to Avignon, and secondly in the unfortunate personality of Urban VI. Urban had been expected to return to Avignon; he not only failed to do so but adopted an overbearing tone towards the sacred college, seized the property of some cardinals and even attacked their persons. Clement's line of action was not in doubt; he naturally made an attempt, which failed, to drive his rival out of Rome and Italy, but he was expected to betake himself ultimately to Avignon as his headquarters and there in due course he went, though not until 1379; nor did he maltreat his cardinals. The special nature of the schism is seen in the fact that two rival popes had never before been elected by the same body of cardinals, observing all the main rules of election and possessing anything like as much excuse, feeble as it may seem, for the second election as they had on this occasion. To a modern in possession of what facts there are it may seem easy to make up one's mind, but the Roman church has never actually pronounced on the validity of either election and to contemporaries, relatively ill-informed and subject to all the passions and propaganda of the day, the two claims seemed so evenly balanced that their settlement was simply made a matter of political convenience. France naturally supported Clement; the Empire mostly Urban; Scotland held by France; Flanders, now rapidly drifting out of the French orbit, by the Empire; Italy and the Spanish states were more evenly divided, but Castile in 1381 and Aragon in 1387 eventually became Clementist, and Portugal Urbanist by 1385, all from the same type of political consideration. Perroy indeed has shown in convincing detail how the exigencies of the Schism dominated European affairs for a whole generation; it is the main theme of his book,[1] but it is treated from the stand-point of English policy. For England too had to decide, and though the obvious decision was lightly taken it is none the less perhaps the main title to remembrance of the parliament of Gloucester.

English recognition of Urban was fortified by the prospect of confiscating all the benefices of Clementist cardinals held in England, but it earned the immediate gratitude of the Roman pope, for it came so promptly that for some time the English monarchy was his sole prominent supporter. In return Urban did his best, not without success, to reverse the pro-French policy of his imperial friends, for early in 1378 Charles IV had actually visited Paris and had conferred on the dauphin the vicariate of the extinct kingdom of Arles. But after Charles's death in November Urban's diplomacy, which aimed at the encirclement of France, began to take effect and its ultimate fruit was to be the marriage of Richard little over three years later to Wenzel's sister, Anne of Bohemia. Chance had halved the resources of the "sinful city of Avenon" and had given England a new diplomatic ally in the French war, together with an opportunity for attack, which was to be disgracefully abused in 1383, in Flanders; more, Urban and his successors were too hard pressed to haggle much over the terms of the alliance, a fact which was to influence powerfully the relations between church and state in England.

Yet clear as it may seem to-day that the most important business of the parliament of Gloucester was to declare England's part in the Great Schism, it is doubtful if that was the contemporary view. The parliament began, as was expected, with an immediate explosion about the sacrilege at West-minster, in reply to which Gaunt, now returned from Brittany, very unwisely and quite ineffectively introduced Wyclif into politics, for the last time as it happened, in order to argue

[1] *L'Angleterre et le grand schisme d'Occident*, esp. pp. 54–62.

against rights of sanctuary in general.[1] The sole effect of this move was to re-form the clerical and conservative coalition which had confronted Gaunt in 1376, and although it is true that, perhaps as a result of this discussion, the following parliament of April 1379 declared against the abuse of sanctuary by debtors, it was sufficiently clear that church and commons acting together had defeated that section of the magnates led by the Lancastrians. Thus the continual council was remodelled in parliament for the second time so as to eliminate the Lancastrian influence entirely, some of the changes to take effect immediately and others later at the ministers' discretion.[2] The only possible concession made to Gaunt lay in the choice of his friend, the moderate Richard le Scrope of Bolton, who was popular with the commons, as chancellor. As regards the necessary money grant even Scrope was able to extract no more than a reluctant and strictly temporary prolongation of the wool duties at a slightly higher rate,[3] and only this by conceding an account of the way in which the last subsidy had been spent, "on this agreement, that this shall not in future be considered a precedent".[4] This demand may be attributed to an erroneous belief that Gaunt had been corrupting the special treasurers of war; in making it the commons once more found themselves in advance of the lords, who retorted by refusing to sit on the usual joint committee.

It was the lords again—for with all their faults they showed much more conception of public responsibility than the commons—who came to the rescue of the government in the desperate matter of finance. They attended a great council in February 1379 in which they agreed to force the commons' hands by raising not altogether voluntary loans on a large scale

[1] His arguments are predominantly medieval: see H. B. Workman, *John Wyclif*, i, 323-4. E.g. that a foreign army invading England might take sanctuary, if attacked, and so prepare unharmed for further depredations!

[2] This is the last of the three continual councils of the minority, for which see Tout, *Chapters*, iii, 344, revising J. F. Baldwin, *The King's Council*, ch. vi.

[3] Ramsay, *Revenues*, ii, 303.   [4] Adams and Stephens, *op. cit.* pp. 137-8.

from many magnates, monasteries and towns and then calling a
parliament at Easter in order to raise money to repay them. The
incident is of some importance, not merely as a political
manœuvre but because it is an early example of the forced or
semi-forced loan being employed upon a large scale—we hear
much of the iniquity of Richard's action when he employed the
same machinery at the beginning of his *coup d'état* of 1397, but
little enough about it when it was used by the amorphous
government of the minority and still less when it became the
engine, as it habitually did, of the "constitutional" Henry IV
and the both popular and "constitutional" Henry V.[1]

In 1379 the measure was of course a desperate one; the money
might be raised, but the method of raising it left the government
helpless before an outraged commons who did at least flatter
themselves that since the beginning of the century they had
secured undisputed control over finance. This explains the weakness shown by the ministers in actually offering an account, instead
of conceding one under protest, in this parliament, and in acquiesc-
ing without a struggle in the commons' further demand for
the appointment of a lords' committee to enquire generally into
expenditure and revenue.[2] The fact was, however, that the
spirit of compromise was not all on one side; the commons
themselves had been alarmed by the hostility of the lords and
by spy scares and stories of an imminent French invasion;[3]
the committee they asked for was now an exclusively lords'
committee and they were content to give up the device of
special treasurers of war as not having accomplished what was
expected of it. They showed themselves more reasonable too in
the most important of all ways by making a substantial grant,
and if this was only at first sight a renewal of the vicious tallage
of groats of 1377, at least the most objectionable feature of a
poll-tax was removed by the introduction of a system of
graduation according to the means of the payers which was
intended to lessen the gross social injustices of the earlier

---

[1] A. Steel, "English Government Finance, 1377–1413", *E.H.R.* li, 44–8.
[2] Adams and Stephens, *op. cit.* p. 138.   [3] Perroy, *Schisme*, p. 79.

experiment.[1] It is perhaps worth noting that in this graduated system lawyers were assessed at an exceptionally high rate, in some cases as high as barons, a fact which may perhaps be connected with the petitions against default of justice and arbitrary decisions by the household courts made in this parliament. In spite of this the proceeds were inadequate, owing to corrupt administration; Ramsay[2] thinks the yield was not more than £27,000, and though that was £5000 higher than the supposed yield of the tallage of groats it was not enough, and the second form of poll-tax was in its turn discredited.

But the cup was not yet full; for some months yet the dreary attempts to raise money for what had almost ceased to be a war were to be matched by the even drearier incompetence of the commanders who had the spending of it. December 1379 saw the great storm which engulfed Sir John Arundel's Breton expedition, to the ill-concealed delight of Walsingham,[3] who disapproved of Arundel as a blasphemer and ravisher of nuns. This led inevitably to fresh demands by the chancellor which could only be expressed in yet another parliament, held at Westminster in January 1380. Scrope's speech was pathetic; he had to confess that what money there was had all been spent without result, and the king was not even able to repay the loans made by the magnates, monasteries and towns as the result of the great council of February 1379.[4] This produced a violent and unsympathetic reaction in the commons.

In the first place it was recognised that the continual councils of the past three or four years had failed, and the whole system was swept away in favour of directly appointing or at least approving the five chief ministers in parliament and then giving them a free hand. There was also to be another committee of enquiry into the raising and spending of the revenue

---

[1] Adams and Stephens, *op. cit.* pp. 141-2, for the scale. The mayor of London paid as an earl and the aldermen as barons. Walsingham (*Hist. Anglic.* i, 392-3) complains bitterly that abbots had to pay twice over, once for themselves and once for each of their monks, but Walsingham, as a monk himself, was an interested party.

[2] *Genesis*, ii, 132.   [3] *Hist. Anglic.* i, 418-25.   [4] *Rot. Parl.* iii, 72-3.

on the analogy of that of April 1379. But whereas the former
committee had consisted of magnates and had apparently never
reported, the new one contained many commoners,[1] and was
definitely instructed to report, though it never seems to have
done so. As regards the ministers the commons contented
themselves with implementing their new principle in the case
of the chancellorship only, archbishop Sudbury being substituted for Scrope and thereby sent to his death in the next year.
Finally a generous grant was made in the shape of one and a half
subsidies of the old type and a prolongation of the existing
customs dues,[2] but only on condition that no new parliament
should be called before Michaelmas 1381. This, however,
proved impossible, for the summer of 1380 witnessed yet
another English fiasco in Brittany, namely an expedition in
being from July to October, led this time by the king's youngest
uncle, Thomas earl of Buckingham. The money had all been
spent on old debts and the new failure remained to be paid for.
Hence with some trepidation the ministers broke their promise
and summoned a new parliament, not to Westminster but
to Northampton, for November 1380. It was this parliament
which provoked the Peasants' Revolt.

Walsingham says[3] that the reason why the expedient of 1378
was repeated and Westminster avoided as a place of assembly is
to be found in the proposed condemnation of John de Kirkby,
a Londoner, for the murder of a Genoese merchant, the
object being to avoid interruption by the London mob. The
Kirkby trial in short played the part which the Westminster
sacrilege had played two years earlier, but it is also probable
that in 1380 as in 1378 it was felt that the commons themselves
might prove more amenable away from Westminster. This in
fact they did, but for rather different reasons, for whereas at
Gloucester it had been the comforts of St Peter's which, it was
hoped, would mollify them, at Northampton the scarcity of
food and lodging was such that they were anxious to make

---

[1] About one-third.   [2] Ramsay, *Revenues*, ii, 308.
[3] *Hist. Anglic.* i, 449. For the motive of the murder and the reason for
bad feeling between the Londoners and Genoese generally at this time, see
ibid. i, 407–9, 450; ii, 83–4.

their grant and get away from the place; they could not, moreover, altogether escape the increased responsibility for the government which they had assumed earlier in the year. Hence, in spite of much grumbling at the inconveniences they were suffering and at the state of affairs in general, the commons did not in fact take advantage of the absence of most magnates, either with Buckingham in Brittany or with Gaunt on the Scottish marches, but duly endeavoured to produce funds. Moreover, their petitions even seem to show a curious confidence in the government; they request for example that the present ministers shall not be changed until the next parliament. In spite of this the chamberlain was changed at the end of the year and, which was more important, another future victim of the rebels, Sir John Hales, prior of St John of Jerusalem in England, took the place of the elderly Brantingham as treasurer in February 1381. Possibly this last change may be connected with another petition of the commons, namely that the slumbering committee of enquiry into the revenue should wake up and get to work, and again the prospect of this enquiry may help to explain the extremely hasty and ill-considered nature of the grant which was actually made. For the commons, while recognising the real need for money, were not prepared for the moment to tax themselves, the prosperous classes, any further; they were determined to spread the burden as widely as possible, so they not only reverted to the worse of the two poll-taxes, that of 1377, thus abandoning the principle of graduation, but insisted that this time the flat rate should be made to yield results.

Apparently the problem was merely one of simple arithmetic. The government had demanded the colossal sum of £160,000; this of course was ridiculous, but parliament agreed that £100,000 might be necessary, of which they were prepared to find two-thirds, or approximately £66,000,[1] provided that the clergy found the rest. Now the tallage of groats had yielded rather over £22,000, so the problem was easy; the same tax must be levied at three times the rate and the slight excess which that would produce could make possible the generous

---

[1] Not the whole £100,000, as Tout, *Chapters*, iii, 355 implies. See Ramsay, *Revenues*, ii, 311.

concession of raising the age of exemption from fourteen to fifteen. It was added as an afterthought that the rich should help the poor, but no machinery was devised to compel them to do so,[1] nor in fact could they do it very generously if they had wished, since there was an additional clause to the effect that no man and wife together were to pay more than 20s.—contrast this with the £6. 13s. 4d. payable by a solitary duke in 1379—or less than 4d. The effect of this on the very poor may be gauged by the fact that 1s. was at this time approximately the monthly wage of what might be a married man with a family; thus the wages of carters, ploughmen and shepherds averaged only 13s. 4d. a year.

There were in fact two fatal objections to the whole scheme, either of which alone would have been enough to settle its fate. In the first place by abandoning the principle of graduation introduced in 1379 it exposed the new tax to three times the unpopularity (for it was three times as severe) of the already sufficiently unpopular tax of 1377; it was of course well known on both occasions that these poll-taxes were merely substitutes for the old subsidies or taxes on movables, standardised since 1334, which, however far-reaching in their incidence, were taxes on property and not on human beings. In other words the poll-tax was, and was known to be, a deliberate piece of class legislation, an attempt to push a larger share of the burden of taxation on to the shoulders of the very poor. Moreover, besides being unjust between rich and poor individuals it was, like modern rating, unjust between rich and poor districts. Secondly, and quite apart from these considerations, the schedule of the new tax made no attempt whatsoever to provide against the defects of collection and administration which had wrecked the graduated tax of 1379, but blandly left such points to be settled between the government and the tax-payers. Even upper-class contemporaries were not wholly blind to these defects, so obvious were they; thus the *Anonimalle Chronicle* records[2] that "divers lords and commons think the tax unfairly

---

[1] The fact that vills and boroughs were assessed at so many heads and then left to repartition their gross contribution as they pleased had of course a limited permissive effect.   [2] Ed. V. H. Galbraith, p. 134.

levied from the poor and not from the rich, and that in any case the collectors have retained most of the yield".

In view of all this it is not surprising that there were from the first embittered and wholesale attempts at resistance; these in turn were followed by desperate and increasingly complicated efforts on the part of the bankrupt government at enforcement and collection, and such efforts[1] were the immediate occasion of the Peasants' Revolt. The causes of the revolt lay deeper, but it is not difficult to understand how the blundering incompetence and selfishness, prolonged over so many years, of an upper class which could not even fulfil its own ends of existence yet continued to believe that the world was made to gratify its own pleasure and ambition, proved the last straw to a people now rapidly becoming conscious that they too had a destiny. Rich clerks, lawyers, burgesses, knights and nobles might perhaps expect to get their work of government and even war paid for by others, however well they could afford to pay for it themselves, if it was gloriously or even decently done, but when these same classes chose a moment at the end of twelve years' deepening failure and disgrace to send the bill to their inferiors the time had come at last to raise the basic question of inferiority for good and all. Nor was the revolt when it came barren of all practical result, as it is frequently said to have been, for one lesson at least was drawn from it by the governing classes when they had heaved themselves back into the saddle; there were no more poll-taxes, no more attempts to make the poor man pay, for the rest of the English Middle Ages; in future the standard customs and subsidies, the orthodox fifteenths and tenths drawn from those who could afford to pay them, were to be varied only, and that very occasionally, by fresh experimental taxes on land and other forms of property, but not on lives.

[1] For these efforts, which throw much light on the revolt, see the very important passage in Tout, *Chapters*, iii, 359–65, drawn principally from the *Calendars of the Fine* and *of the Patent Rolls*, in which many of the actual commissions of enforcement and collection may be found.

CHAPTER III

The Peasants' Revolt

IT would be difficult to exaggerate the air of helpless be-
wilderment with which the governing classes greeted the
events of June 1381; the foundations of society as they knew
it had suddenly disappeared and their world was in chaos, they
were at a loss to know why. For days, even weeks, they were
stunned into hopeless inaction; probably no social revolution in
history achieved a greater element of surprise. To the more pious
among them, such as the monk Walsingham,[1] the revolt was the
judgment of God upon an evil and adulterous generation; only
the more cynical could connect it with the poll-tax, and there is
no trace of any contemporary consciousness of deeper causes.
Yet historians are agreed, even if they continue to quarrel about
their nature, that causes far more complex and deep-rooted
than the poll-tax did exist and need to be taken into account.
Two features of the revolt make it particularly difficult to
arrive at them: the spontaneous, unconnected yet simultaneous
character of the rising in different localities, and its comparatively limited field, for the only serious trouble occurred in the
south and east of England, apart from certain isolated exceptions, such as Scarborough, Beverley and the Wirral, Bridgwater, Winchester and a few manors in Northamptonshire.

Its spontaneous character suggests at first careful preparation
and organisation over the whole disturbed area, but this is not
borne out by the facts, and contemporary attempts to link it
with the already widespread dissemination of Lollard doctrines
break down as hopelessly as the Lollard counter-charges against
the friars. There seems actually to have been little or no
connexion between the different centres of the revolt until it
had broken out, and not very much then; it was, however, in

[1] *Historia Anglicana*, ii, 11-13.

the interest of the governing classes to exaggerate the degree of organisation and intention after the event, partly in order to excuse the punishment which they proceeded to inflict and partly to conceal the real fact that the grievances produced by the existing system had actually been strong enough to produce a widespread and unrelated revolt. But we are still left asking what these grievances were and why they were so largely limited to not much more than half a dozen counties, and these are difficult questions.

There is first of all the general disturbance of social relationships on the land produced by the slow decay of the manorial organisation. This in turn had been accelerated by the severe famines of Edward II's reign[1] and later by repeated visits of the Black Death. From it had sprung the savage and reactionary labour legislation of 1350–1, reinforced ten years later by a statute which prescribed branding for all those who left their native town or district to look for higher wages, while every year from 1377 to 1380 the commons in parliament had been steadily demanding that this whole code should be rigidly enforced. Yet while this attempt to restrict wages and the mobility of labour was undoubtedly one cause of the rising it does not explain the popular hostility to the magnates and great landowners, including the monasteries, because in England, as in France, it was not so much the rich men as the smaller country gentry who were driven to demand its enforcement. There is in fact a marked contrast between conditions in western Europe and in Prussia or Italy, where similar wage tariffs are found but are the work of great capitalists, whereas in England it is the knights of the shire rather than the nobles, the commons rather than the lords, who insist.[2]

But apart from the question of responsibility for the labour code it is clear that from the rebels' point of view restriction of wages and the accompanying attempt to prevent the spread of

[1] Notably 1308–22 (practically continuous). See C. Petit-Dutaillis, "The Peasants' Revolt", in *Studies Supplementary to Stubbs*, vol. i, for much of the opening part of this chapter.

[2] Eileen Power in *Cambridge Medieval History*, vii, 720, 734.

commutation of bond-services are only two irritating factors among many; there had, for example, been little commutation at any time during the fourteenth century on the great monastic estates, such as those of St Albans, where none the less the risings were fiercest. What was wanted was freedom—freedom from merchet, leyr-wite and heriot[1] as well as from bond-services; it was the contradiction between legal condition and material progress which, as far as the villeins, themselves only one element among the rebels, were concerned, was at the back of the rising.[2]

As regards legal condition it was still true in theory at any rate during the fourteenth century, as an abbot of Burton had once remarked, that the villein owned *nihil praeter ventrem*, but this was very far from being the fact. Moreover, what he possessed was subject not only to the fines already mentioned but also to the mortuary. When a male villein died the lord took the best beast, the best suit of clothes and if there were no son even the best tools; when a female died, he took the best dress and also the best bed, if there were no surviving un-married daughter. This was bad enough, but on top of that the church took the second-best of all these things, as well as taking tithe from villeins in their lifetime. When, finally, the lord's rights and the church's rights were combined in one hand, as was often the case with monasteries, it is easy to understand popular hostility to religious houses.

All this was the more irritating because by 1381 most villeins had in fact, as the mortuary lists suggest, considerable property to lose. The decline in the purchasing power of money which had marked the fourteenth century had greatly benefited those peasants who had early obtained commutation of their services at fixed rates, and the gradual breakdown of the manorial system in general was steadily diverting profits from the lord into the pockets of those tenants who had been able to keep any hold on the land. On the other hand, those who had lost their

---

[1] Fines exacted from the villein for the marriage or pregnancy of his daughter and for entering on his inheritance.

[2] Petit-Dutaillis, *loc. cit.*

hold were passing more and more easily into the position of free and relatively highly paid,[1] if landless, labourers, for in the existing labour conditions it was becoming very difficult for lords to maintain personal villeinage without attachment to the land. All this helps to explain why in fact it was largely the question of free labour, its wages and conditions of employment, rather than merely one, as Thorold Rogers used to think, of bond-services and commutation—itself a concession which might still leave a man a villein—which was the real problem of the later Middle Ages.

Froissart is therefore broadly right,[2] in spite of his class prejudice, in attributing the revolt of 1381 to "the ease and riches that the common people were of". Precisely the same is true of the free and well-to-do peasants of western Flanders, who fought from 1322 to 1328, successfully in the end in spite of their great defeat at Cassel, to prevent serfdom being forced upon them.[3]

There is, however, still another important feature of the decaying manorial system which has recently been brought to light.[4] This is of special value in explaining the hostility felt towards the great; it is to be found in the collapse of the manorial court before the onslaughts of the baronial council. The powerful part played by the early manorial court and the custom of the manor in protecting tenants, bond and free, against their lord is not always recognised. Once that is done, however—and the fact is not consciously disputed—and once it is realised that in the fourteenth century many of these courts were already falling into decay, an additional source of discontent appears. This decay was due in part to the intervention,

[1] It was in practice very difficult for competing employers in a general scarcity of labour to observe the wage regulations of the labour code.

[2] Quoted in *Camb. Med. Hist.* vii, 738.

[3] Cf. W. J. Ashley, *James and Philip van Artevelde*, pp. 65-9.

[4] By the late Miss Levett, *Studies in Manorial History*, pp. 21-40. The whole of what follows is taken from this suggestive paper. Mr N. Denholm Young's strictures (*Seigneurial Administration*, pp. 26-7) seem to be unnecessarily severe.

first of justices of labourers, then of justices of the peace, between lord and man and to the regulation of wages by parliament, but it was also due to the much earlier breakdown of the old system of bond-services which lessened the need for frequent meetings of the manorial court, for by the fourteenth century services were sometimes twenty years in arrears. Nor must the growing practice of leasing the lord's demesne, with or without the control of the court, be neglected as a powerful solvent of the manor; yet when all these contributory causes have been taken into account the fact remains that the greatest damage of all was probably done by the new-fangled baronial council.

In the fourteenth century[1] all great laymen, many bishops and some monasteries, such as St Albans, possessed councils: thus the statutes of livery in the fifteenth century seem to regard one as a normal part of any baronial household. They consisted in the first place of a core of expert professionals, both clerks and laymen, usually described as being "learned in the one law or the other", that is in canon or civil (Roman) law. Then there would be officials such as the steward, or the coroner of a liberty—in the case of an abbey an abbot might be supported by his prior—together with important tenants, or even fellow-magnates: thus one of the de la Pole family (Edmund) was a member of Gaunt's council. The final touch would be supplied in some instances by the presence of an official of the king himself, a serjeant-at-law or even a judge. These councils were clearly itinerant in practice and their functions varied, but among other things they undoubtedly entertained difficult cases pending in the manorial courts among the customary tenants, and in settling them by the scientific principles of canon or civil law they helped to bring about the decay of the time-honoured custom of the manor. The great abbot of St Albans, Thomas de la Mare, was particularly proud of his learned councillors, skilled in both laws, who first annoyed the townspeople by refusing to give a written answer to their

[1] And of course very much earlier. See F. M. Stenton, *English Feudalism*, 1066–1166, *passim*, for widespread baronial mimicry of all royal institutions.

demands and then, in 1381, fled with the prior as far as Tyne-
mouth at the first onset of the revolt. It is clear that this St
Albans' council had forced Roman law upon the tenants,[1] who
would have none of it, and in fact the more "expert" such
councillors became the more likely they were to lose patience
with local rules and customs. This certainly helps to account for
villein rage against legal records, for their famous determination
nec jura civilia nec canonica de cetero frequentare and, finally,
explains better than the labour code the reason for their hatred
of great landowners as well as small ones. If to all these causes
we add the general protests against the lords' hunting and
fishing rights—this again was a special grievance at St Albans—
and the widespread resentment at the way in which enclosure
for sheep-farming was already affecting rights of public pasture,[1]
we shall have gone a long way towards explaining the revolt as
far as peasants were concerned.

But the revolt, although it bears their name, was not limited
to the peasants; there was almost everywhere a strong artisan
element in the rising. Its motive is to be found partly no doubt
in the labour legislation, but also in the notable expansion of
the English cloth industry, which was producing a class of
wage-earners with no future, excluded from the gild system.
In this, as in other respects, there is a marked parallel between
the English revolt and the French Jacquerie of 1357, which was
reluctantly supported by the bourgeois leader Étienne Marcel as
well as by a number of more enthusiastic artisans. In England
these workers were beginning to form their own illicit journey-
men's gilds,[2] and though these are hard to trace quite as early as
1381 there is at least much evidence for quarrels about wages
and invocations of the labour codes as far back as 1350.[3] Their
unrest was accompanied by a special hatred of foreigners,
notably Flemings, which took its origin not, as some have

[1] Petit-Dutaillis, *loc. cit.*

[2] E.g. in 1383 (undeterred by the failure of the revolt) the yeoman saddlers
of London. In 1396 they put forward a religious excuse for their association
which failed to satisfy the masters.

[3] Petit-Dutaillis, *loc. cit.* and *C.P.R. passim.*

thought, from an un-medieval objection to the employment of foreign sweated labour but from a natural hostility to a close organisation which kept secret, instead of sharing, the details of its superior technique and thereby drove native products off the market. Many of these malcontents, artisan and peasant as well, might be ex-soldiers, and almost all would have experience of service in watch and ward, in hue and cry, in the rudimentary police activities of the day, and this no doubt explains their speed of mobilisation, their comparatively good discipline and perhaps their readiness for collective bargaining.[1] But in this last respect they must also have owed much to the educated men, the poor clerks, who were so often to be found among their leaders.

This complicity of the lower clergy—John Ball, John Wrawe and William Grindecobbe at once spring to the mind—was no doubt due in part to the pressure of papal taxation. The government in 1381 was on excellent terms with Urban VI, and besides confirming his frequent collations and provisions to benefices was actively supporting his tax-collectors, one of the most famous of whom, cardinal Pileo di Prata, was touring England just before the revolt.[2] Hence the papacy and the foreign clergy at large were special objects of attack, but so too were most of the higher native clergy, and for that a different reason must be found. It lies in the aristocratic or Caesarian nature of most of them and the consequent difficulty of promotion except through the king's service or through that of some other great man in an entirely non-spiritual capacity. At the same time the total number of poor clerks actually induced by these considerations to take part in the revolt must not be

[1] G. G. Coulton, "The Peasants' Revolt", in *Great Events in History*, ed. G. R. Stirling-Taylor (Cassell, 1934), pp. 197-274, esp. p. 256.

[2] E. Perroy (*L'Angleterre et le grand schisme d'Occident*, p. 150) remarks that the object of this visit was really diplomatic—it was concerned with Richard's marriage—but admits that the cardinal took the opportunity to drive a roaring trade in indulgences, letters of confession, titles of chaplain and papal notary, licences for portable altars, dispensations from Lent and absolutions. He did not, however, take the title of legate, which he left to the archbishop of Canterbury (*ibid*. p. 151 n.).

exaggerated; they were probably never very numerous and were mostly half-mad independents of the type of John Ball, for only those of doubtful orthodoxy (both Ball and Grindecobbe had been excommunicated) would succumb to the temptation. It is for this reason that the Lollards, or rather Wyclif's Poor Preachers, were so freely accused of having fomented the rising, and though there was in fact little or nothing in the accusation it is at first sight a specious one and needs examining.

The case really rests on what is known as the Oxford letter of the four mendicant Orders addressed to Gaunt on the 22nd of February 1382[1] and on the statute of May 1382. Of these, the letter taxes Wyclif in person with having first caused the rising and having then tried to blame it on the friars. This charge may be dismissed at once; the statute does not mention Wyclif and in any case it is clear that whatever the ultimate implications of his doctrine he did in fact hold the most conservative views on the possession of property by laymen and on the duty of obedience to the lay power.[2] It is true that he had attacked the rich at large and not only the rich monks and higher clergy, but he had only done so in terms common to almost every medieval preacher, and he had certainly never incited men to revolution. Even if the puritanical idea that riches are damnable in themselves did find some reflection in the revolt, for example, when the rebels prevented the looting of Gaunt's palace, the Savoy, in favour of its complete destruction, there were as we shall see many possible sources other than the teaching of Wyclif for this idea. Moreover, he certainly deprecated the actual revolt.[3]

Wyclif's Poor Preachers, on the other hand, were in a category slightly different from their master's. The statute of 1382

---

[1] *Fasciculi Zizaniorum*, p. 292.

[2] Cf. H. Wallon, *Richard II*, i, 49: "Wicleff ne se levait avec tant de violence contre le pouvoir spirituel, que pour le mieux assujettir au pouvoir temporel."

[3] In his treatise *On Blasphemy* assigned to 1382. But cf. H. B. Workman, *John Wyclif*, ii, 241–5, for a contrast with Luther: Wyclif's attitude was a mild one.

mentioned heresies and definitely alluded to the Blackfriars council, which had just condemned the doctrines though not the person of Wyclif; it ordered the arrest of all travelling preachers who had no licence from the pope or the ordinary and it is certain that Lollard preachers were particularly intended.[1] But what is true of 1382 and later—for after that date the Poor Preachers were certainly beginning to create disturbances—is not necessarily true of 1381 and earlier. Even if we accept the outraged Walsingham's statement[2] that Wyclif had begun to send them out as early as 1377, on which Lechler has thrown doubt,[3] four years is not a very long time for Wyclif's doctrines to have become widely known and popular in medieval England; moreover, his characteristic doctrines of the priesthood were nowhere found among the rebels, while it is certainly odd that heretical Leicestershire should have been so quiet during the revolt, while orthodox London murdered the archbishop of Canterbury. Hence, although it remains possible that even at this early date some of the more enthusiastic disciples far outran their master and although Wyclif and his followers must bear their share of indirect responsibility for the rising, the verdict on the Poor Preachers as a class can hardly be more decisive than "not proven".[4] We can, however, give a more definite answer to their alleged counter-charges against the friars.

It is true that in July and November 1381 royal mandates

---

[1] Archbishop Courtenay's letter to Oxford (*Fasc. Ziz.* p. 275) clinches the point.   [2] *Hist. Anglic.* i, 324.

[3] *John Wycliffe and his English Precursors*, tr. W. Lorimer, pp. 189 ff.

[4] The lost confession of John Ball (referred to in *Fasc. Ziz.* pp. 273–4), which is said to have directly implicated Wyclif, can be dismissed, though it is characteristically supported by Walsingham, *Hist. Anglic.* ii, 32–4. Apart from the general consideration that confessions extorted on the scaffold have little value it is well known that Ball had been preaching his peculiar doctrines for twenty years or more and had been condemned by several archbishops. He was a half-witted reformer who, according to the *Anonimalle Chronicle*, pp. 137–8, wished to kill all the clergy, regular and secular, in England, except one bishop. On the other hand it is quite likely that he approved of some of the more startling of Wyclif's social doctrines, as confirming some of his own.

were directed against travelling friars and runaway monks,[1] while Walsingham venomously notes the rebel fondness for friars and Langland definitely accuses them of preaching communism. On the other hand the statute of May 1382 was clearly not directed against them, because it mentioned only unlicensed preachers and the friars were licensed; again, Walsingham's accusation may be dismissed as the spleen of a Benedictine, Langland's as that of a poor chantry priest. Moreover, although the friars are frequently attacked in other fourteenth-century sources, it is always for greed, idleness, immorality and luxury, not for communism. Nor can the plausible accusation of Richard Fitzralph, bishop of Armagh, in the preceding generation, be held particularly damaging; he maintained chiefly that they encouraged the withholding of dues from the parish clergy, and this, though probably true enough, is hardly subversive, much less communistic, doctrine. Finally, the mandates of 1381 are matched by large numbers of royal protections and favours to friars in the four years after the revolt;[2] in some of these they are even described as *oratores assidui pro statu nostro et tocius regni*, which would have been inconceivable if they had actually incited the rebels.

Vagabonds, brigands and criminals in general, on the other hand, obviously took their opportunity, and so did a few irresponsible upper-class ne'er-do-wells anxious to pay off old scores against a neighbouring knight or squire.[3] Jusserand[4] would see in these disreputable figures the shock troops and liaison officers of the revolt, though in view of the purely moral indignation which the rebels often expressed, and their not infrequent abstinence from looting, this is perhaps giving the criminal classes too large a share. Jusserand means to include,

---

[1] *C.C.R.* 1381–5, e.g. pp. 9, 22.   [2] *C.P.R.* 1381–5, *passim.*

[3] E.g. in Cambridgeshire John Hanchach, a considerable landowner in Shudy Camps, may have led the attack against Thomas Hasilden's property in the Mordens because Hasilden had forestalled him in marrying Joan de Burgh, the heiress of Borough Green: W. M. Palmer and H. W. Saunders, *Documents Relating to Cambridgeshire Villages*, ii, 20.

[4] *English Wayfaring Life in the Middle Ages*, pp. 271–2.

however, not only professional criminals but fugitive villeins, artisans ruined by the labour code, discharged soldiers, who were clearly a menace from the statute of 34 Edward III directed against them,[1] runaways from the poll-tax and common outlaws. He would add pilgrims, pedlars and merchants travelling to the fairs as a likely means both of spreading news of the revolt once it had begun and perhaps of helping to disseminate some of the revolutionary literature which actually provoked it.

Revolutionary literature, current up and down the land, was indeed clearly a major cause. It includes such cycles as the Robin Hood ballads, mentioned by Langland, of which two original texts survive, viz. the *Litel Geste of Robin Hood* and *Robin Hood and the Potter*, while in Shakespeare and later writers are to be found the echoes of many more such stories. Robin Hood is of course the "good yeoman", the redresser of social injustice, and he is not the only one; there is, for example, the *Tale of Gamelin*, once attributed to Chaucer, but now believed to be older. Gamelin is another righter of wrongs who attacks clerks and regulars and, when cited to court, usurps the places of sheriff, judge and jury with his friends, condemns them all to death and hangs the lot—this is not unlike what was actually done in 1381. Ultimately, however, Gamelin wins the king's approval, makes a good marriage and lives happily ever after; the whole story is obviously a legendary wish-fulfilment of the common people. Langland's great epic, *Piers Plowman*, on the other hand, though perhaps equally inflammatory, is much less direct. In date it goes back in part to 1362 and as a whole is well prior to 1381, while its great popularity is attested by the survival of forty-five contemporary manuscripts and the catchwords taken from it in the actual rising. Yet its author, William Langland, a poor chantry priest of London, was nominally at least a conservative. His poem is in fact only half socialist, while the other half is mystical, in a way often paralleled in the German revolts of the

[1] Cf. C. G. Crump and C. Johnson, "The Powers of Justices of the Peace", *E.H.R.* xxvii, 226–38.

fifteenth and early sixteenth centuries. Thus for Piers the labourer was before all things the "type of holiness, whose sweat quenched hell-fire and washed the soul clean",[1] and he was emphatically not the murderer of an archbishop of Canterbury.

More recently stress has been laid on the wide appeal and revolutionary influence of the medieval pulpit. André Réville in 1896 was perhaps the first to point out the extreme violence of the language commonly used about the rich by even orthodox priests and monks; thus the Austin friar, Dr John de Waldeby, a highly respectable contemporary of Wyclif's, an Oxford man and protégé of abbot Thomas de la Mare, flayed unsparingly the vices of the higher clergy. Other equally orthodox preachers castigated continually the egotism of the upper classes and the greed of lawyers. Such attacks were admittedly common form all over medieval Europe; they occurred especially in France and Germany. But they had a peculiar reality in the England of 1381, and the latest scholar to work on them, Dr Owst,[2] would assign them an overwhelming importance; moreover, while admitting their European character, he boldly asserts that on the continent, as in England, they explain all the democratic movements of the fourteenth century. To him practically every problem of medieval England can be explained by reference to sermons, and sermons underlie all English medieval literature. There is probably much truth in his theories, if not the sole and exclusive truth which he claims, and the evidence on which they are based deserves to be taken into consideration.

In general Dr Owst suggests that practically all the surviving political verse and satire[3] of the English Middle Ages is the work of clerks and, as such, is directly based on pulpit denunciation; that whole generations of the same stuff lie behind Wyclif and Langland, and that even the characters in the *Canterbury Tales* are stock types taken from sermons and homilies rather than

[1] *Camb. Med. Hist.* vii, 739. Cf. Petit-Dutaillis, *loc. cit.*
[2] *Literature and Pulpit in Medieval England* (1933).
[3] Much of it printed by T. Wright in the Rolls Series (14, i and ii) and Camden Society Publications (1839).

individuals observed by Chaucer. This leads him to attack most
recent authorities, such as Trevelyan, W. P. Ker and Workman,
on the ground that they apparently credit only Wyclif and
Langland with seeing both sides of the social question, whereas
in fact both Langland and Wyclif are merely reflecting pulpit
commonplaces, which issue not merely from the lower clergy
but from courtiers like Waldeby and bishop Brunton. Other
preachers he quotes, besides these two, are John Bromyard, an
orthodox Dominican and "distinguished opponent of Wyclif,
one actually summoned to sit in judgment on his heresies, and
a pillar of the Church", and Master William de Rymyngton,
S.T.P., chancellor of Oxford university, sometime prior of the
Cistercian abbey of Sawley, and author of several treatises
confuting the errors of Wyclif,[1] against whom he is said to have
worked "night and day to discover his crafty designs".
Rymyngton specialised on the three vices of lust, pride and
avarice; Master Robert Rypon, sub-prior of Durham, sometime
Benedictine prior of Finchale and another noted anti-Lollard,
concentrated on gluttony; while John Myrc, prior of a house
of Austin canons at Lilleshall, ranged over the whole field
of clerical misdemeanour;[2] so too did Master Thomas
Wimbledon, of whom nothing is known but one famous
sermon delivered by him at St Paul's Cross in 1388.

Dr Owst, however, does not draw the obvious conclusion,
suggested by the date of Wimbledon's sermon from which he
quotes freely and frequently, that if pulpit denunciation goes on
as it does after the revolt in exactly the same strain as it had done
for centuries before it, its effect upon the revolt itself, which he
thinks decisive, may easily be exaggerated. His evidence does,
however, suggest that such historians as Oman are wrong in
saying that the clergy were not attacked as clergy in 1381 but
only as "possessioners", for it makes it clear that avarice was
not the only clerical vice which was commonly denounced,

---

[1] Cf. Workman, *op. cit.* ii, 122–3.
[2] Cf. the chapter-headings of his *Manuale Sacerdotum*, "The Priest who
loves the tavern more than the Church", "The Priest as Gambler", "The
Priest as Fornicator" and "The Priest as Business Man", Owst, *loc. cit.*

just as among the rich it was not only the higher clergy who were singled out for abuse.

For Dr Owst shows that the famous couplet

> When Adam delved and Eve span,
> Who was then the gentleman?

was not the invention of John Ball but was common in early fourteenth-century sermon literature; it is used by Brunton, Bromyard and others, though with no direct revolutionary intent as Ball used it, but merely to humble the pride of the rich laity and to turn them into good Christians. Detailed vices attacked by these preachers included pride of ancestry and office, together with selfishness and inhumanity, the preference of lapdogs, apes and palfreys, falcons and hounds to human beings. First there were the nobles, lions in hall and hares in the field, preferring jousts to the ardours and rigours of a crusade, though "the tournament of the rich is the torment of the poor". Moreover, they vilified God's ministers (which is perhaps not surprising) and had no respect for the church. As for the smaller country gentry, besides being fully as foul-mouthed, they aped all the other vices of their lords and masters. Lawyers too were corrupt, whether judges or advocates, and even jurors could not be relied on; indeed there was no justice for the poor man, what with the law's delays and undue influence, of which Pilate, who let himself be influenced by the Jews, is the type. Finally there was the willingness of the pleader to undertake even cases which he knew to be unjust, and his skill in making the worse cause seem the better one.

Physicians and merchants were also freely attacked in the sermons for equally obvious vices, though it is difficult to agree with Dr Owst here, as against Dr Workman, that this is in itself a sufficient reason why the urban mobs should have attacked foreign merchants, for as a matter of fact Dr Owst quotes no sermon denunciation whatsoever of foreign merchants as foreigners, and Dr Workman is probably right in assigning the assaults upon them to "almost wholly secular forces".

It will be noticed that this list of classes abused by the

preachers does roughly coincide with those classes singled out for attack in the revolt, namely the rich in general, whether bishops, monks, nobles (such as John of Gaunt), profiteer merchants (such as Lyons), lawyers or all kinds of officials. This might seem to support Dr Owst's theories, but as in fact both lists are fairly exhaustive it would be odd if they did not coincide. Moreover, Dr Owst himself admits that there was one other class which suffered from pulpit invective, to wit the artisans and labourers themselves. The preachers were strictly impartial, though he thinks they were rather more lenient to the poorest classes in England than they were on the continent. Thus no serious anti-social charges were ever made against the poor except, as we might expect, a reluctance to pay the tithe out of which the sermons were financed; it was scamped work, petty meannesses and individual immoralities which were attacked. Even the poor, however, could display pride and avarice in their attempts to rise above their station—the church showed something of the cloven hoof here—whereas they should have remained contented with their lot in this life and trusted to compensation in the next.

Yet what were the poor to think of vivid pictures of the Judgment—often on the church wall before their eyes as well as in the preacher's mouth—and of the tales of torture awaiting the rich in the next world, where "in place of the torment which for a time they inflicted on others they shall have eternal torment"?[1] For although the official church undoubtedly tried to restrain with one hand, by forbidding self-help in this world to the poor and oppressed, the passions which it lashed on with the other, such sermons are, to Dr Owst at any rate, quite enough in themselves to explain the revolt without invoking, as Dr Workman for example does, the Wyclifite theory of dominion or the Spiritual Franciscans' theory of evangelical poverty. Dr Owst goes so far in fact as to claim that there was no distinctively Wyclifite view of the situation; to him "all

[1] Of course this had long been a theological commonplace; cf. Aquinas's doctrine that the bliss of the redeemed in Paradise will be heightened by the sight of the agonies of the damned. Dante, it is true, was wiser.

preachers of rebuke and complaint" were equally guilty, and
not guilty. He is careful to point out that "the great Judgment-
theme of revenge" in the next world took shape as early as the
thirteenth century in the medieval pulpit, and indeed if they
had been nurtured for over a hundred and fifty years on stories
like this it is perhaps surprising that the rebels did not commit
greater atrocities than they did when they at last got their
chance in 1381. And yet for a hundred and fifty years these
stories had not moved them.

To sum up, that the revolt broke out when it did seems to be
due first and foremost to the increased self-consciousness of the
politically depressed classes at the end of the fourteenth century,
caused in part no doubt by the age-old stimulus of these
perpetual sermons, but also by the decay of the manor, the
more recent growth of lay education, discontent with authority,
increased linguistic unity, and a dawning sense of nationality,
due in part to the French wars and to the industrial and commercial competition of Flemings and Italians. Moreover, the
coming of the long bow had caused the English yeoman to
think of himself not only as an Englishman but as a soldier who
both won battles for his feudal masters and furthermore risked
his life for them—a thing which the gradual introduction of
plate armour, the trade in ransoms and the international give
and take of chivalry was making comparatively rare among the
well-to-do. There is furthermore another irritating factor in the
increased amount of visible wealth in the country, due to these
very ransoms, and to loot and piracy as well as to the wool
trade, its obviously unequal distribution, and the oligarchical
tendencies which accompanied it in London and elsewhere.
There was a general sense that the use and wont of a primitive
feudal community were anachronisms in a more complex state of
society, an un-medieval demand for something new, as against
the mere "restoration" of supposedly ancient privileges.

All this was aggravated by the administrative incompetence
and selfishness superadded by the ruling classes to their normal
display of luxury and cruelty, by the unpopularity of a government which did not work in any sense of the word, was

corruptly administered, supported by heavy taxation and inclined to shift the burden of taxation, as far as it dared, from the rich on to the poor.[1] The fact that as a result of the Black Death perhaps two-thirds of the population were left to support a French war[2] which few of them were disposed to terminate was no doubt lost sight of; what struck the eye was the particularly blatant example of administrative stupidity and callousness in the poll tax of 1380, the actual occasion of the revolt. Why it should have broken out, broadly speaking, in the south-east of England only must be explained by the fact that it was only in these comparatively thickly populated and prosperous areas that most of the causes we have been examining (with the exception of the sermons) could be said to operate; serfdom had always been less prevalent in the north and west than in the east and south,[3] and it is principally in the south-east part of England that we find the decay of the manor, the linguistic unity of the East Midland literary dialect, the educational centres of Oxford, Cambridge and London, the contact with the continent demanded by wool and war, and even the home of piracy, for in this age the towns on the North Sea and the Wash, Lynn, Blakeney and the rest, were still more important in that respect with their as yet unsilted harbours than the admittedly rising seaports of Devon and Cornwall. Accordingly, it was in the east and south that the fiercest and most widespread revolts broke out and from the first the government had to face the possibility, in at least the second of these areas, that the rebels would receive help from abroad. It was not perhaps very likely, since the governments of France and Castile preferred other governments, even those with which they were at war, to rebels anywhere, and in fact it did not happen, but it is interesting to find that the first military action the paralysed English government took that summer was to send archers to Southampton and other south coast ports to

[1] Cambridge, for example, was highly restive *before* the revolt. Cf. the "illicit conventicles" mentioned by Cooper, *Annals*, i, 119.

[2] Cf. A. E. Feavearyear, *The Pound Sterling*, ch. l.

[3] *Camb. Med. Hist.* vii, 728.

hold them against the rebels,[1] as well as against the French and
Spanish, and that was after it was clear that the revolt was a
failure. For the rest, the revolt while in being was, as we shall
see, only seriously opposed by a handful of vigorous but
isolated individuals.

The story of it has frequently been told in detail and it will
not be necessary to do more than summarise it here; for the
present purpose the reactions of the young king and of the
governing classes are of more interest than the narrative.
Disturbances which took place in Essex early in May culmi-
nated towards the end of the month in the stoning of one of
the poll-tax commissioners and his men. On the 2nd of June
Robert Bealknap, the chief justice of the common pleas, who
had been sent down to deal with this outbreak, was lucky to
escape with his life and three jurors were actually killed.
Meanwhile, Kent had a rising on its own account; there is,
however, no good authority for the famous story of the clash
between John Legge and Wat Tyler as the occasion of this
revolt. On the contrary, according to the *Anonimalle Chronicle*,
the real cause of the trouble, which began at Gravesend on the
3rd of June, was an escaped serf of Simon Burley's, whom
Legge, himself a royal serjeant-at-arms and inspector of the
poll-tax in Kent, helped to recapture and imprison in Rochester
castle; Tyler does not appear at all until a week later. There is
no reason to reject this explanation, but it is worth noting for
future reference, in view of charges made against him in 1388,
that Burley, who was vice-chamberlain at the time,[2] was not in
England; he had left for Bohemia in the middle of May in
order to hurry on the negotiations for the king's marriage, and
remained abroad until January 1382.

On the 4th of June there was rioting at Dartford and on the
6th there followed the sack of Rochester castle and further
risings in Maidstone and Canterbury. It was in Maidstone and on
the 10th of June that Wat Tyler—actually an Essex man settled
in Kent[3]—made his first appearance; another famous leader,

[1] Perroy, *Schisme*, p. 220.   [2] Tout, *Chapters*, iii, 368.
[3] Ramsay, *Genesis*, ii, 148.

the renegade priest John Ball, seems to have been released from the prison of the archbishop of Canterbury on the following day.[1] The march of the Kentishmen on London under the leadership of these two followed; they had reached Blackheath by the evening of Wednesday the 12th of June. Being unable to cross the river, they looted Southwark and sacked Lambeth palace, archbishop Sudbury, the chancellor, escaping by river and eventually taking refuge with the king in the Tower. On the same evening Richard seems to have insisted on an attempt to negotiate with the rebels at Greenwich from a barge, but was handicapped by the nervousness of his ministers, who broke off the interview almost as soon as it had begun. It was perhaps the first independent action of his life, but it was to be followed before long by others; however, it will be more convenient to deal rather later with his general attitude to the revolt.

Meanwhile, the Essex mob had burnt at least two manor-houses of persons connected with Gaunt or the government, and on Thursday the 13th of June bands of them, reinforced by others from Hertfordshire, and led by a man calling himself Jack Strawe, seized Highbury and Mile End, while on the other side of the city the treachery of the alderman in charge of London Bridge—his name was John Horne[2]—let the Kentishmen into the town. Had the bridge been held another twenty-four hours the attack must have failed for want of food. However, as things were, the southerners broke into London on the 13th, released the prisoners in the Fleet, sacked the New Temple, belonging to the knights of St John, whose prior, Hales, was treasurer of England, and to their lawyer tenants, and also Gaunt's palace of the Savoy, together with the Hospitallers' central house at Clerkenwell, while Strawe and the eastern rebels were sacking their manor at Highbury. They failed, however, on the next day to break into the exchequer at

---

[1] Auth. Knighton, ii, 132, though he puts it *after* the Blackheath interview. The *Anon. Chron.* pp. 137–8 says nothing about imprisonment.

[2] This treachery can only have been due to the ferocious internecine rivalries of the London craft gilds and the possible uses in this rivalry to which Horne may have thought the rebels could be put.

Westminster. During the next forty-eight hours Newgate and the abbot's prison at Westminster were cleared and several people murdered, notably Richard Lyons, the embezzler of 1376, and a large number of Flemings. But the king and his mother, together with the earls of Buckingham,[1] Warwick, Oxford, Kent and Derby, Sir Thomas Percy, then admiral, Sir Robert Knolles (a famous *condottiere*), archbishop Sudbury, treasurer Hales, John Legge and others, were all safe in the Tower, which was certainly well garrisoned and is supposed to have been adequately supplied.

On Friday the 14th of June[2] Richard again asserted himself by insisting on another personal interview, this time by the much more dangerous method of proceeding on land to Mile End, where he is said to have freely promised charters of manumission and pardons to the men of Essex and to have persuaded most of them to go home. It is said that his half-brothers, Sir John Holland and Thomas earl of Kent, began by accompanying him, but lost their nerve and deserted him on the way to the meeting-place.[3] Meanwhile an almost inexplicable event occurred in London when during the king's absence the rebels somehow succeeded in bursting into the Tower—it is not clear for one thing why the drawbridge was not up—whence they dragged out for execution Sudbury, Hales, Legge and others, while the young earl of Derby, the future Henry IV, was only saved from the same fate by one John Ferrour of Southwark.[4] His offence lay entirely in being the son and heir of the much-hated John of Gaunt who, fortunately for himself, was away negotiating with the Scots in the midsummer of 1381. Richard and his friends on their return dared not enter the Tower, which was being plundered, but took refuge in the royal office known as the

---

[1] Wallon, *op. cit.* i, 61, repeats without giving his authority a rumour that Buckingham was in sympathy with the rebels. This seems at first sight incredible in view of his repressive activities at Billericay a fortnight later, but it is possible that like Horne he had the idea of using the rebels for some obscure purpose of his own which was abandoned after their defeat was clear and purged by exceptional severity in suppressing the defeated.

[2] Tout, *Chapters*, iii, 371, erroneously says the 13th.

[3] Cf. Froissart, *Œuvres*, ix, 404.　　　　[4] Ramsay, *Genesis*, ii, 155.

great wardrobe, near Blackfriars. Here Richard, earl of
Arundel, when Sudbury's death was known, took temporary
charge of the great seal.[1]

The next day, Saturday the 15th of June, came the famous
Smithfield interview between the king, Wat Tyler and the
Kentishmen and with it, thanks to Richard's personal gallantry,
the turn of the tide. After the murder of Wat Tyler, the mayor
William Walworth who accomplished it, rode unmolested into
the city with only one servant to fetch help from the better
class of citizen, but the citizens came so quickly that they were
probably already armed and mustered against the continual
looting and disorder when he arrived.[2] He and Sir Robert
Knolles took command of them, rescued the king and dispersed
the Kentishmen; this, the really decisive action, which in effect
put an end to the southern rising, was done so easily that one
wonders why it had not been tried before. The answer is
perhaps to be found in the fact that, after Horne's treachery, the
authorities were not certain of the temper of the citizens,[3]
besides which the rebels were undoubtedly much more formidable while Tyler was still alive.

Before turning to the provincial centres of revolt it is necessary
to mention certain difficulties in this, the accepted account of
events in London, and to make some more accurate assessment
of Richard's share in them. There is in the first place no adequate
explanation of the surrender of the Tower. It is just possible
that it was after all not fully provisioned for a long siege and
that the rebels had successfully intercepted its supplies,[4] but this
does not explain why the drawbridge was not raised during
Richard's temporary absence at Mile End and why the garrison
made no attempt to protect the refugees inside it. The answer
seems to lie in a complete lack of leadership and absence of
instructions to the men-at-arms; the responsible persons in the

[1] *Anon. Chron.* p. 146.
[2] Wallon, *op. cit.* i, 81, says Knolles now wanted to massacre the Kentishmen but Richard restrained him.
[3] Wallon, *op. cit.* i, 69, says the point was discussed in the Tower before
Mile End, but inconclusively.   [4] Cf. *Hist. Anglic.* i, 458.

Tower were evidently one and all paralysed with fright. It may be true that the test was a severe one; as has been said, the suddenness and unexpectedness of this unheard-of rising, aggravated by the suspicion of collusion inside London, must have seemed to the feudal classes for the moment the abrupt and catastrophic end of their world and of society as they had known it, but the fact remains that of all these men for whose comfort and dignity, in return for their supposed powers of governance, the whole of life was organised in 1381, not one could keep his wits about him, with the exception of the fourteen-year old boy whose political education they had studiously neglected and to whom they had been careful not to entrust even the shadow of power. The two things Richard had been taught were first and foremost to be a good knight, a *preux chevalier*, and secondly a king, a sacrosanct person hallowed with the sacred oil, yet hitherto a king who reigned but did not govern. In 1381, acting on his own responsibility, he put his lessons for the first time into practice; the successes of knighthood at least had so far eluded him, but now it was his hour. For this and for his independence of action where they had failed the older genera-tion, with the exception of Gaunt who had not been present to share in the betrayal of his class, was never to forgive him; besides, when they had recovered their poise, the older men were not to give up so easily the power which they had abused during the minority; on the contrary Richard, just because of his behaviour in the revolt, was to be hastily put back into leading-strings. We shall see that during the next few months there was a persistent and successful attempt to humiliate Richard and to convince him of the inexperience and futility of his negotiations with the rebels; only a few more far-sighted men like Burley, who again had not been there during the revolt, were to realise that there was after all something in the weakling which could not be kept under, which on the contrary within a very short time would make necessary the formation of a powerful court party, in which Richard would be something more than a cipher. It might be possible in fact to rule through Richard, but it would not be possible to rule, as hitherto, ignoring him.

There is admittedly another interpretation of Richard's conduct during the revolt. Kriehn[1] notes that the active and prominent part assigned to Richard began, according to the *Anonimalle Chronicle* (incidentally the best single source for the events in London), in the Tower itself, before the party left for Mile End. He argues that in view of Richard's youth and of his unimportance for some time to come this seems improbable; he may have been the figure-head, but it looks as if there was somebody behind him. Kriehn suggests, rather improbably, the princess Joan, but if we are inclined to accept this hypothesis at all, which is not necessary, it is much more likely to have been the old soldier, Robert Knolles. In any case the *a priori* improbability of Richard having led the councils in the Tower at the age of fourteen, however desperate the circumstances, makes Kriehn go on to look for evidence against the well-attested tradition of his courage in the open, a tradition all the more remarkable, it may be noted in passing, in that Richard, because of his later history, has not in general had a good historical press. The evidence he is looking for Kriehn finds in the Monk of Evesham, the author of an undoubtedly contemporary general chronicle covering the years 1377–1402.[2]

The Monk of Evesham's account of the revolt is thought by him to share a common source with Walsingham's (which incidentally is only of first-rate value for the happenings at St Albans), but also to contain certain matter of its own, and it is this additional matter which reflects upon the bravery of Richard. Kriehn takes it very seriously, but does not in effect offer any evidence to show that it is not the work of imagination, which is the more likely since the whole chronicle is strongly Lancastrian in tone. Moreover, the relevant passage is concerned only with what happened at the one interview of Mile End and on the way there.

According to Froissart, who knew London personally, Mile

---

[1] In the *American Historical Review*, vii, 254–85.

[2] Printed in an appendix to *Adami Murimuthensis Chronica* (London, 1846), ed. T. Hog, for the Royal Historical Society. The title *Vita Ricardi Secundi* is a misnomer; it is really a general history. For a fuller edition of the Monk of Evesham (by T. Hearne), see Bibliography, p. 302.

End was then an attractive village in a fine meadow and a well-
known holiday resort for Londoners. Richard was accompanied by a considerable retinue, which included his mother
and three foreign noblemen. But Kriehn points out that his
reputed bravery on his arrival also rests solely on the friendly
authority of Froissart; no other chronicle mentions it, and the
Monk of Evesham on the contrary says that he showed timidity
from the first moment of leaving the Tower, "as one in great
dread of his life". The Monk adds further that Richard did not
venture to leave Mile End without the rebels' permission, and
this, together with the unlikelihood of Richard having dominated
his councillors at so early an age, is quite enough for Kriehn; he
seems to regard the legends of Richard's courage in the revolt as
all but finally disproved.

Yet much of the Monk of Evesham's account is, for the
reason already given, quite as likely to be imaginative rancour
as fact, and in any case we are left wondering where he obtained his exclusive information. It is true that Froissart, who is
guilty of more than one proved inaccuracy in his account of the
revolt, is no good authority for what happened at Mile End,
but nobody has ever impugned the well-attested accounts of
Richard's subsequent conduct at Smithfield, and it is certain
that he was naturally high-spirited and of a dramatic turn of
mind. It is therefore quite legitimate to suppose that while, at
his age, he may not really have been prominent in the councils
in the Tower, he may yet have shown an unexpected courage in
the crises outside it. As for afterwards breaking his promises to
the rebels, of which Kriehn makes much, no argument can be
drawn from that in view of the pressure which was brought to
bear on him and indeed, however high-spirited and honourable
Richard may have been, even his detractor notes that he could
not easily have disposed of landlords' rights and property
without the consent of parliament, much less have annulled
laws which parliament had enacted or executed councillors,
as he had had to promise to do, without trial.

Yet to defend the real merit of Richard's conduct during the
revolt is not to say that he was in any sense democratically

inclined or had any real sympathy with the rebels. Riçhard had been brought up in the prevailing code of chivalry and it must be remembered that in somewhat similar circumstances a fully adult ornament of that code, the count of Flanders, had not thought it incumbent on him to keep his word. Richard can have known little about the peasants and artisans; he may have been touched by the repeated signs of personal loyalty which they gave him, but his real motive was much more probably the desire to make a gesture, to teach his masters their own business, to show for the first time that he really could do effectively what he had been brought up to do and was not after all an unworthy son of his great father, than any real understanding or sympathy with the cause of the oppressed. He certainly showed no such tendencies in the later part of his reign, and it is not necessary to suppose that they were forcibly crushed in him together with the rebels; he may never have had any, indeed he would have been a much more unusual medieval king than he was if he had had principles of that sort. But even if the question of honour did not arise, according to the standards of the day, in the breaking of the promises with which he had cheated the rebels, it must even so have been deeply humiliating for him to be trailed around the countryside in the wake of his own judges, silently witnessing the execution in batches of the only men among his subjects who had hitherto cared to call him king.[1]

But we must return to the movements outside London which account for the wide extension of Richard's bloody assize later in the year. Early on Friday the 14th of June a message arrived from the rebels inviting the co-operation of St Albans,[2] which the abbot Thomas de la Mare was too wise to prevent. The men of St Albans accordingly set out and passed by Highbury,

[1] The Cambridgeshire rebels actually cited royal authority (e.g. at Wood Ditton, Palmer, *op. cit.* p. 36), while the password of the London rebels, as given in the *Anon. Chron.* p. 139, was "Wyth kynge Richarde and wyth the trew communes!"

[2] For the account of events at St Albans Walsingham is naturally the main authority, *Hist. Anglic.* i, 458, 467–84.

where many of them took an oath of loyalty to Richard and the
commons in the presence of Jack Strawe and on the ruins of the
Hospitallers' manor there. A deputation of these people, led by
one William Grindecobbe, an excommunicated priest, made its
way to the king himself and extorted from Richard a signet
letter ordering the abbot to give up to the burgesses the royal
charters which he was thought to have suppressed. This was
brought down next day by the chief tenant of the abbey,
Richard of Wallingford.[1] Meanwhile, on the triumphant return
of Grindecobbe and the rest a certain amount of destruction of
abbey property took place in which the men of Barnet played a
part. After the arrival of the royal signet letter the abbot, under
great pressure, gave up all the bonds, title-deeds and books of
civil and canon law in his possession for destruction, but
steadily denied the existence of an alleged royal charter of Offa
engrossed in uncial letters of purple and gold. Eventually, on
Sunday the 16th of June, a compromise was reached, the terms
of which were as follows.

The abbot in the first place sealed a bond to produce the said
charter, if it could be found, by the 25th of March 1382 under
penalty of £1000. Secondly, he agreed to grant his tenants a
new charter of liberties at their own dictation; fortunately the
news of Wat Tyler's death had reached St Albans by this time
and their demands were therefore not unreasonable. They
included extensive rights of pasturage on the waste, some
liberty of hunting and fishing in the abbey's woods and ponds,
release from the monopoly of the abbey mill (an especially sore
point), and the right of self-government by elected magistrates
instead of remaining under the control of the bailiff appointed
by the monastery. To all this the abbot assented though,
according to Walsingham,[2] with certain private reservations,
upon the advice of the steward of the king's household, Hugh
Segrave, and of the king's knight, Sir Thomas Percy, who had

[1] For what may be his later history see *C.F.R.* x, 18, 218, 266, where
a man of this name is found acting as a collector of tenths and fifteenths in
Hertfordshire in 1383 and 1388.

[2] *Hist. Anglic.* i, 482–3.

been specially sent from London to induce him to give way.[1] It is in short quite clear that the whole St Albans' rising was concerned with local grievances which were skilfully compromised by prudence and moderation on both sides, but as we shall see this did not prevent the town being the scene of particularly savage reprisals at a later date.

Throughout East Anglia in general there was as little principle as at St Albans, and much more violence and bloodshed. In Suffolk the leader was a priest, John Wrawe, formerly vicar of Ringsfield near Beccles, but in touch with Tyler from an early point in the rising. He collected a considerable number of men[2] and, unlike other leaders, began with downright plundering, both on a manor belonging to Richard Lyons and in the village of Cavendish on the Stour, the latter at the expense of John Cavendish, chief justice of the king's bench, who had deposited plate and other valuables in the church for safe keeping; Cavendish was specially hated in East Anglia for his strictness in enforcing the statutes of labourers.[3] Before long the revolt spread to Bury St Edmunds, where the townspeople, as at St Albans, were generally in a state of smouldering resentment against the abbey; and at Bury there was no abbot to control it, for there had been a disputed election[4] and the prior, John of Cambridge, was temporarily in charge. The prior fled at the news of Wrawe's approach and on Friday the 14th of June the rebels sacked his house, together with one belonging to John Cavendish, and sent a party, which incidentally contained a knight and a squire, probably serving under compulsion, to levy blackmail on Thetford, in which they were successful. Meanwhile Cavendish himself had been caught and murdered at Brandon and the prior of St Edmund had experienced the same fate at Mildenhall,[5] while two more murders took place in

[1] Tout, *Chapters*, iii, 373.

[2] 50,000 according to *Hist. Anglic.* ii, 2, 10,000 in *Anon. Chron.* p. 150.

[3] Tout, *Chapters*, iii, 374 n., shows Ramsay is wrong in saying (*Genesis*, ii, 167) that he was chancellor of the university of Cambridge, but there is no doubt of his brutality on circuit long before the revolt.

[4] See *Hist. Anglic.* i, 414–18, 428–30 for the details.

[5] Tout, *Chapters*, iii, 374, says both murders took place "near Lakenheath".

Bury itself, the monastic charters and muniments were destroyed and a general charter of liberties for the townspeople extorted from the terrified monks, as at St Albans. It is worth noting, however, that the actual townspeople of Bury dissociated themselves as far as possible from the more violent proceedings of Wrawe and his country followers; left to itself there, and given a strong abbot, the revolt might have followed much the same course as at St Albans.[1]

In East Suffolk the details are less vivid, but here too there was a holocaust of manorial records and widespread assaults upon anyone connected with the poll-tax, while once again two squires are mentioned among the rioters. In Cambridgeshire two emissaries from London, one of whom, however, may have been Wrawe,[2] helped to cause the outbreak of riots in nearly twenty different places, directed especially against the property of the Hospitallers and of John of Gaunt or his men; thus in the town of Cambridge Corpus Christi alone out of the four or five halls or colleges then in existence suffered serious damage, because "of the patronage of the king's uncle, the duke of Lancaster". Apart from this the records and library of the university were seized and burnt on Market Hill and the plate stolen, while the mayor reluctantly led an attack which did some damage to Barnwell priory.[3] Recent work on the county of Cambridge,[4] however, suggests that Ramsay and Powell both exaggerate, for there were altogether only three days of rioting and during them only one village in three experienced any trouble at all and only one in six any serious trouble. Court rolls were destroyed in this county in only four cases, and it is quite clear that the main objectives were the property and persons of the numerous assessors, collectors, commissioners and surveyors or inspectors of the poll-tax, since this accounts for all the worst disturbances at no less than fourteen villages. The

[1] The most recent account of the events at Bury is contained in M. D. Nobel's *The Borough of Bury St Edmunds*, pp. 150 ff.

[2] *Anon. Chron.* p. 150 says he visited Cambridge.

[3] E. Powell, *The Rising in East Anglia in* 1381, p. 53.

[4] Palmer, *op. cit.* vol. ii.

status of the insurgents in Cambridgeshire was mostly low, with
the exception of Geoffrey Cobbe of Wimpole, who had lands
worth about £20 a year in all in eight different places, and John
Hanchach, whose family had held a manor in Shudy Camps
since at least the middle of the thirteenth century, while John
himself had acquired a fifth share in seven other manors in the
Linton neighbourhood only a year earlier. These two, especially
Hanchach, may have been influenced by personal jealousies—
they were certainly unconstrained leaders—but apart from them
the long list of Cambridgeshire rebels contains nobody with
landed property of any value and only seven others who have
anything substantial in goods. This seems to suggest that while
the revolt as a whole possessed a few common features of importance from shire to shire it is unsafe to generalise too freely,
and very easy to exaggerate.

At Ely a justice of the peace and a lawyer were beheaded, the
bishop's jail was forced and his records at Balsham seized and
burnt. But when, encouraged by these successes, the men of
Ely tried to assault in turn Huntingdon and Ramsey Abbey, the
men of both places combined to scatter them, apparently under
the leadership of one of the very few royal officials active during
the rising,[1] William Wightman, spigurnel of chancery,[2] who was
subsequently rewarded with a share in the chattels of the rebels.[3]

The revolt in Norfolk[4] was probably the best organised and
the most dangerous of all outside London, since one of the two
leaders, Roger Bacon of Baconsthorpe, was an intelligent
knight with real sympathy for the revolt, and the other,
Geoffrey Lytster of Felmingham, though only a poor dyer, was
also a most intelligent and gallant personality. These two raised
a regular army on Mousehold Heath just outside the great town
of Norwich, one of the most important industrial centres in
medieval England, and formed the ingenious plan of kidnapping
all the local gentry and compelling them to act as officers and

[1] One of Gaunt's knights, Sir John Dengayne, a justice of the peace, had
the courage to arrest a rebel redhanded in Cambridgeshire, Palmer, *op. cit.*
[2] *Anon. Chron.* p. 150; Tout, *Chapters,* iii, 374.
[3] *C.C.R.* 1385–9, p. 113.   [4] *Hist. Anglic.* ii, 5–8.

military experts. They did in fact catch five, of whom only one, Sir Robert Sale, preferred death to being seen in their company, and they very nearly caught the earl of Suffolk. The poorer citizens of Norwich then opened the gates of the town to them, but here too they behaved with considerable moderation. Lytster formed a regular headquarters and court-martial for doing summary justice in the castle, while systematic expeditions, mainly for the destruction of manorial muniments, were sent out through the county. Bacon in particular led a special force to the chastisement of Yarmouth for its exclusive market rights and harbour dues—Norwich was then, as it still is, a port—and for its sheltering of foreigners; he killed six Flemings there, presumably for what was regarded as unfair competition with the weavers of Norwich.

However, by the 21st of June news reached Norfolk that Tyler was dead and the king was raising an army; hence Lytster sent two of his captive knights and three rebels to ask for a "Mile End charter" and a special pardon for the county. Near Mildenhall this mission fell in with Henry Despenser, the youthful bishop of Norwich, who almost alone among the governing classes had kept his sense of proportion and his wits about him. He had been staying at his manor of Burleigh by Stamford with a retinue of eight lances and some archers when news of the revolt had reached him. He had at once set out for his diocese,[1] proceeding first to Peterborough where, finding the abbey tenants inclined to emulate those at Bury and St Albans, he had fallen upon them and cut them to pieces.[2] At Ramsey on the 18th of June he had taken prisoner and handed over to the abbot a mounted party of about twenty rioters, who had just arrived and were trying to blackmail the abbey. He had hurried thence to Cambridge, where he had beheaded and imprisoned without mercy for two days, and now near Mildenhall he captured Lytster's embassy, dismissing the knights but executing the other three envoys at Wymondham

---

[1] *Anon. Chron.* p. 151 says he first sent letters to the rebels in Norfolk, ordering them to disperse. If so, he cannot have waited for an answer.

[2] Knighton, ii, 141.

on his way to Norwich, which Lytster had now evacuated. The end of the Norfolk rising came in what is sometimes known as the "battle" of North Walsham, where Lytster had built a crudely fortified camp. Here he was routed, caught and executed by Despenser, who may have deserved a kind of gloomy credit for rediscovering that ill-armed peasants, however desperate, could not in fact stand up to men-at-arms,[1] but had hardly earned the military reputation which he was to cherish so dearly to his own undoing at the hands of a real army in the plains of Flanders two years later.

Shortly after this the Suffolk rising was ended by the reappearance of the earl with five hundred lances from London. Wrawe went into hiding, but was captured some months later and rightly executed while trying to turn king's evidence; he had been one of the least reputable of the leaders. There was no more serious trouble in any of the disturbed areas, except that before the end of June the Essex men mustered once more in defence of the Mile End charters, which were now clearly worthless, at Billericay, only to be ridden down by the earl of Buckingham and Sir Thomas Percy,[2] who like others had now recovered their nerve. There were also isolated disturbances, as has been said already, in more distant parts of the country,[3] but these were mainly due to local causes and none of them ever looked like becoming general or dangerous; in time they were all easily put down.

The punishment of the rebels varied a good deal in intensity from place to place, but taken as a whole it was probably rather lenient according to fourteenth-century standards; for example, it compares favourably with the suppression of the French Jacquerie in 1358, perhaps because the rebels themselves had committed fewer atrocities.[4] The work was entrusted to the

---

[1] Knighton, ii, 141: "they wished to destroy the Church and they perished at its hands".　　　　　　　　　[2] *Hist. Anglic.* ii, 18–19.

[3] For a fiasco at Leicester see Knighton, ii, 142–3.

[4] So the *Camb. Med. Hist.* vii, 738 and Réville (*ap.* Petit-Dutaillis, *op. cit.*). *Hist. Anglic.* ii, 13–14 says that the government was first lenient and then more drastic; *Anon. Chron.* p. 151 exactly reverses this and says there were at first many executions, but later the king issued fresh charters and pardons costing twenty shillings each "pur luy fair riche".

special commissions normal in this period,[1] all of which were to act on the proclamation of the 2nd of July that the king, with the advice of his council, had revoked the letters patent of manumission and pardon "lately issued in haste" to the rebels. In London Sir Robert Knolles, Walworth and two prominent citizens, John Philipot and his brother-in-law, Nicholas Brembre, the last three of whom had just been knighted by the king, got to work as early as the 15th of June; before long Bealknap, the judge whose visit had been the occasion of the Essex rising, was added to their number. This was a good commission; its members behaved with great caution and showed leniency, at least where London citizens were concerned. Only Jack Strawe and a few peasants were arrested and beheaded,[2] though it is true that many Londoners were later excepted from a general amnesty granted in December. But after all, though they had been drawn into it, it had never been a Londoners' revolt.

In Essex and Hertfordshire, on the other hand, the new chief justice of the king's bench, Robert Tresilian, who had succeeded the murdered Cavendish, was exceptionally severe; even Walsingham, who shows little mercy for the rebels, stresses his bloody assize at Colchester, where nineteen rebels might be seen hanging from one beam.[3] At St Albans[4] there was a complete travesty of justice for, when the jurors refused to present, Tresilian produced a black list of persons whom three juries in succession were forced to indict, with the result that fifteen men were drawn and hung and eighty imprisoned, the victims including William Grindecobbe and John Ball, who was supposed to have made a confession on the scaffold implicating Wyclif.[5] All this was going far beyond the abbot's own

[1] Cf. *Hist. Anglic.* ii, 16–17, 20–2. Besides proclamations enjoining resistance to the rebels the calendar of the patent rolls contains at least seven commissions, or sets of commissions, for the rest of 1381 and at least two for 1382 (*C.P.R.* 1381–5).

[2] *Hist. Anglic.* ii, 9–10, 14–15.

[3] *Hist. Anglic.* ii, 19–20: Knighton, ii, 150, *sive juste sive ex odio.*

[4] *Hist. Anglic.* ii, 15–16, 22–31, 35–41.   [5] *Ibid.* ii, 32–4

wishes and in fact it was so abnormal that there must clearly
have been a special reason for it. Wallon[1] is probably right in
finding this reason in the presence of the young king, who was
forced to accompany Tresilian and witness the executions. He
was to be given the clearest possible proof how little his word
was worth, and the people for their part were to be taught not
to rely on it; nothing could have been more humiliating. Oddly
enough Tresilian himself, a pliant if ferocious judge, was to
become a notorious royalist within the next few years and to
suffer himself in 1388 at the hands of the appellants the fate
which he had dealt out to others seven years before.

Most of the other commissions—for instance, that presided
over by the earl of Kent in his own county—followed the
example of London rather than that of Essex. In Cambridgeshire the punishment of the rebels, which began within a
fortnight, was distinctly lenient. There were more than forty
pardons for serious offences and only fourteen clear cases
of beheading or outlawry, though the totals for the latter
should probably be swelled by a fair proportion of some sixty
persons who ran away rather than face the commissions of
enquiry, and it is true that the escheators' rolls show that even in
cases of pardon goods only, and not lands, were returned to
those rare persons who had possessed and forfeited both.[2]
The towns were everywhere separately punished—Canterbury,
Bury, Beverley, Bridgwater, Scarborough and Cambridge[3] all
being severely fined. Towards the end of the year, however,
parliament extended a general pardon, with a very few named
exceptions, to all those who had taken part in the rising, and
to this must be added a considerable number of individual
pardons granted at the nominal request of the new queen,
Anne of Bohemia, during 1382–3.[4]

---

[1] *Op. cit.* i, 101.   [2] Palmer, *op. cit.*

[3] At Cambridge the special local issue of Town and Gown, which had
produced a bonfire of university deeds and books, led to the town charters
being forfeited and the university at last securing the assize of bread and ale,
etc.—a serious setback for town liberties. C. H. Cooper, *Annals*, i, 124–5.

[4] *C.P.R.* 1381–5, *passim.*

There is little to be said of the effects of the revolt. The direct results were not absolutely nothing, as is commonly said, since, as we have seen, the revolt did at least put an end once and for all to the new experiments in taxation designed to transfer the burden from the rich to the poor. The manor continued to decay slowly, and the only effect of the rising in this connexion was to intensify class feeling and make any ameliorative legislation impossible.[1] When the struggle between Richard and his enemies developed, both sides alike adopted a repressive attitude towards the poorer classes, whose interests played no part in the crises of the middle and end of the reign. Administrative incompetence was as great as ever; according to Tout,[2] within a few weeks of the revolt and for some years after it there was no attempt at reform in spite of much complaining in the commons. *Quid juvant statuta?* asks Walsingham bitterly in 1382,[3] though whether the root of the trouble lay, as he goes on to suggest, in sabotage by the king and his "secret" council is more than doubtful; in keeping statutes Richard, though not blameless, was to have a rather better record than his opponents.

All this is true, yet the importance of the indirect results of the revolt can hardly be exaggerated. Three centuries of a new rebelliousness are heralded by this sudden revelation of the deep-rooted anti-clericalism, the growing independence of mind, the tendency towards violence and unrest among the English poor. If, as Wallon has said, the deposition of Richard marks the beginning of the long history of the Whig revolution in England, the Peasants' Revolt marks the beginning of the social revolution. Yet all this lay far ahead; its more immediate importance for our purpose lies rather in the effect it produced on the mind of a king who was too young and too conventionally educated to draw the true lessons from it, but who could at any rate learn this much, that he himself was after all as good a man as another, and that before very long no one would be able to prevent him from personally choosing new advisers.

[1] Ramsay, *Genesis*, ii, 176. [2] *Chapters*, iii, 385.
[3] *Chron. Angl.* p. 333.

CHAPTER IV

The Struggle for Power

IN Edward II's reign the leader of the baronial opposition to
the crown was for many years the king's cousin Thomas,
earl of Lancaster, who was finally put to death for bearing
arms against him. His descendants made their peace with
Edward III, fought manfully in the French wars and left an
heiress, Blanche, to carry the Lancastrian lands and title, now
raised to a dukedom, back into the royal family by marrying
John of Gaunt, the king's son. Such are the bare facts, and they
are simple enough, but there has grown up a legend concerning
them.

The legend is based upon the supposed "constitutionalism"
of the extremely unattractive earl of Edward II's day. He is held
to have died, if not for the principle of parliamentarism, which
is palpably absurd, at least for the policy of imposing regular
restraint upon the crown, and his descendants are believed to
have so cherished and preserved this tradition, though certainly
with greater caution and restraint, that it actually became an
integral part of the inheritance which Blanche brought John of
Gaunt. In this way a "Lancastrian legend" was created and the
term "Lancastrian" was used to denote a set of "constitutional"
principles for which there is little contemporary evidence. The
onus is on the framers of this legend, the greatest of whom was
Stubbs, to prove its truth, but even if it were true of the original
earl Thomas—and most modern research on his career makes
nonsense of the claim[1]—a plea for continuity which overleaps
attainder, reconciliation, the failure of heirs male and a royal
marriage is obviously fantastic.

But if "Lancastrian" in at least the later fourteenth century
can no longer be automatically equated with anti-royal and
"constitutional"—in itself a term of which we have now learnt

[1] See e.g. J. Conway Davies, *The Baronial Opposition to Edward II* (Cambridge, 1918), *passim*.

to fight shy—"Lancastrian" is none the less a convenient adjective for describing a major element in the party groupings of Richard II's reign, and there seems to be no good reason why we should forgo the use of it merely because of its misleading associations. Miss Clarke in particular has revived the term in a new and more limited sense to mean exactly what it says, namely the personal following or faction of the duke of Lancaster.[1] No question of principle is involved in Miss Clarke's usage, but it cannot be over-emphasised that in accepting it, both throughout this chapter and elsewhere in this book, a sense is being attached to the term "Lancastrian" exactly opposite to the sense given to it by Stubbs; it no longer refers to a set of "constitutional" principles, but to the changing, day-to-day opportunism of an individual great man and his faction—no less and no more.

It is perhaps not surprising to find this Lancastrian faction more firmly entrenched in power than ever after the Peasants' Revolt. Unpopularity with the rebels was hardly a handicap to the duke of Lancaster, especially after the rebels had been cheated, broken and dispersed, and as a matter of fact Gaunt, owing to his fortunate mission to the Scots, which had not only proved successful in itself but had effectively kept him out of harm's way, was one of the few members of his class to emerge with credit from the events of 1381.[2] Richard, in spite of his one act of self-assertion, was still too young to count and in any case had been brought under control again, while to make matters surer two guardians, one of them an old and tried Lancastrian, were appointed for him in the November parliament. The only weakness of Gaunt's position lay in the bitter quarrel with his former confederate, the Percy earl of Northumberland, who could not forgive his appointment as king's

[1] Notably in the valuable paper printed on pp. 36–52 of her *Fourteenth Century Studies*, much use of which has been made in this chapter.

[2] He had succeeded in obtaining a form of truce with Scotland to last to the 2nd of February 1383. See Armitage-Smith, *John of Gaunt*, p. 245; Ramsay, *Genesis*, ii, 130, 138; *ibid.* p. 177 wrongly says to 1384. Walsingham (*Historia Anglicana*, i, 446–7) as usual does not do Gaunt justice. Cf. *Anonimalle Chronicle*, pp. 152–4.

lieutenant in the marches; yet even that quarrel appeared to be settled by Northumberland's apology in parliament and "his neutrality, if not his friendship, was bought by a long series of favours"[1] from 1383 to 1390. Both the earl and his famous son, Hotspur, were to play a leading part in placing Gaunt's son, Henry, on the throne, and it was not until the early years of the fifteenth century that the underlying jealousy between the two great families was to reach a fatal conclusion.

There were, of course, other cliques among the magnates, but none of them could rival Lancaster's. The Mortimer interest, though gravely diminished, was not dead; there were the younger uncles and cousins of the king, who were already beginning to carve out policies of their own; there were the Courtenays, the Beauchamps and the Mowbrays; there was the earl of Arundel. Arundel's appointment at this time as one of Richard's guardians seems to suggest that some weight was still being given to non-Lancastrian influences in parliament, for though he was descended through his mother from the third earl of Lancaster and had served under John of Gaunt in France there is little to suggest that this arrogant and tactless nobleman, with his purely military preoccupations and his mixed military record,[2] was ever ready to accept a leader or to promote interests other than his own. A certain generosity towards his favourite religious foundations and a fitful popularity among the commons cannot redeem the less amiable characteristics, which were to make him one of the storm-centres of the reign. Opposition to the crown was in his blood; he could not possibly subscribe to the doctrines of divine right and prerogative defined by Gaunt,[3] and indeed by 1393 Gaunt himself was not

[1] Clarke, *op. cit.* p. 38.

[2] See *D.N.B.* (article by Tout). He had saved Southampton from the French in 1377 and had captured Cherbourg in 1378; on the other hand, he failed at Harfleur, was defeated at sea by the Spanish, ruined Gaunt's expedition against St Malo by his negligence and did nothing to protect his Sussex tenants against the raiding parties of the French.

[3] In the parliaments of 1377 and at Richard's coronation, according to Miss Clarke, *Fourteenth Century Studies*, p. 36.

immune from his attacks. He was in short a jealous, restless, dangerous individual, who spent most of his career positively courting the fate which eventually overtook him in 1397.

There is no evidence that Arundel felt any weight in his duties as Richard's guardian, though he was present on the Scottish expedition, led by Richard in person, in 1385. Two years earlier he had been anxious to serve with the bishop of Norwich in the Flemish crusade—another indication that he was no friend of Gaunt's, since at that time Gaunt was trying to divert the national resources from the "way of Flanders" to the "way of Portugal". If we are to judge by later history Arundel and Richard were particularly uncongenial to each other, and in the years after 1381 the earl seems to have made the mistake of treating the young king with absolute indifference, if not contempt. It was a mistake which the Lancastrian faction did not share; Richard and his eldest uncle may not yet have been upon the friendly terms which they achieved a few years later[1]— indeed they quarrelled violently, though temporarily, in 1384— but on the other hand Gaunt seems to have appreciated the fact that his nephew was rapidly growing up and must soon be given at least the appearance of power and, what is more, he chose one of the most experienced and devoted of his followers to act as Richard's other guardian, namely Michael de la Pole, who became chancellor two years later, in March 1383. Pole set himself to win the young king's confidence, if indeed, as the immediate agent of his marriage, he did not possess it already, to such purpose that his former ward risked deposition for his sake when he was in grave personal danger from his enemies in the winter of 1386–7.

Pole's career up to this point is of considerable interest in view of the violent charges levied against him by his contemporaries[2] and the mistaken belief of Stubbs,[3] which can no longer be maintained, that he was actually a personal enemy, instead

[1] Perhaps as a result of the appellant episode.
[2] E.g. Walsingham, *Hist. Anglic.* ii, 146 *et passim* and the articles of accusation, 1386, for which see N. B. Lewis, *E.H.R.* xlii, 402–7.
[3] *The Constitutional History of England* (1875), ii, 467.

of being, as in fact he was, the personal agent of the duke of
Lancaster. The son of a wealthy Hull merchant, Sir William
de la Pole,[1] he was already a knight when attached to the
retinue of duke Henry of Lancaster as early as 1355. He had
proceeded to serve in France under the Black Prince and Gaunt
in succession, was twice taken prisoner and was at one time
captain of Calais. He was summoned to parliament as a baron
in his own right in January 1366, strongly supported Gaunt in
the Good Parliament and held two commissions as admiral in
1376 and 1377. After serving on the continual councils of the
new reign he had, in March 1379, headed an embassy to Milan
in order to negotiate a marriage between Richard and Catherine
Visconti, which had rather surprisingly ended as a marriage
between Richard and Anne of Bohemia, a daughter of
Charles IV. Even apart from Pole's Lancastrian connexions[2] it
is clearly absurd to treat this seasoned soldier, diplomat and
administrator as a royal "favourite"—the "favourite" moreover of a boy of fifteen—and as a matter of fact no protest was
made at the time of his appointment as Richard's guardian; his
bad name came later. It seems to have been due to his consistent refusal as chancellor to allow either parliamentary or
aristocratic inroads on the royal prerogative, in which, like
Gaunt but unlike Arundel, he seems to have seen the sole hope
of the state.

Pole was, of course, like all his contemporaries, openly on
the make, but he did not really outrage in this respect the
accepted canons of the day, and was easily able to clear himself
of charges of positive corruption in 1384 and again in 1386.
Much of his great wealth was due to his marriage with a
Suffolk heiress and, as Tout[3] says, "his mansions at Hull and

[1] Interesting as one of the first great English financiers to support the
crown. See *D.N.B. sub nom.*

[2] For a brief biography of his equally Lancastrian younger brother, Sir
Edmund de la Pole, see A. Steel, "Sheriffs of Cambridgeshire and
Huntingdonshire in the reign of Richard II", *Proceedings of the Cambridge
Antiquarian Society*, xxxvi, 1–34.

[3] *Chapters*, iii, 403.

London, his castellated manor at Wingfield, and his foundation of the Hull Charterhouse showed his magnificence, his liberality and his piety". As a statesman Pole, with or without Gaunt's guidance, certainly had clear ideas of what was meant by sound bureaucratic government resting on the prerogative. He taught Richard in the ensuing years the rudiments of a consistent foreign policy. He may have persuaded him at any rate to acquiesce in some reform of internal administration.[1] He must have shown him how to play off clique against clique not only among the magnates but among the warring gilds of London, and how to use the royal executive power through the council, the chamber and the signet in the best existing traditions of the English crown. Richard's first lessons in politics in short were learned, if not at Pole's knee, at least from Pole's example; it was unfortunate for Richard that they were not better learned.

Now that the rebel peasants were safely out of the way the most pressing problems confronting the Lancastrian faction were once more those of foreign affairs. Here Richard's sudden and unconscious change of bride had played a central part in a new and grandiose system, the real architect of which was certainly not Pole, perhaps not even Gaunt[2] but, most probably, Urban VI.[3] This was nothing less than a "Grand League of Urbanists" against France, to include not only England but the Empire, the Rhine princes, Portugal and Naples. The next step was to be a continental expedition, led by Richard in person, which was to rally the Germans to Urban's cause. Fortunately the expense of this scheme, which could hardly have been successful, proved prohibitive; even the modest grant of £60,000 demanded by the Lancastrian chancellor, le Scrope of Bolton, was refused by parliament[4] and the proposal had to be abandoned. What revenue there was had mostly been antici-

[1] While Pole was chancellor the *expensa hospicii* were lower than at any other period in the reign: Tout, *Chapters*, iv, 207; Clarke, *op. cit.* p. 39.

[2] Clarke, *op. cit.* p. 42, attributes it to Gaunt.

[3] So E. Perroy, *L'Angleterre et le grand schisme d'Occident*, ch. iv, *passim*.

[4] May 1382.

pated to pay for Richard's marriage and the foreign pensions
which went with it, so that, far from leading military expeditions, Richard was practically bankrupt by the summer of 1382,
while all attempts to make his still more penniless brother-in-
law Wenzel, king of the Romans,[1] play any active part against
the French had broken down completely by the end of the year.

This collapse appears to have done something to discredit
Gaunt and his friends; the English clergy too were alarmed by
the Wyclifite propaganda which had accompanied the Anglo-
imperial alliance and the open revival of doctrines associated
with the reign of Lewis of Bavaria.[2] Already in the October
parliament of the same year an episcopal chancellor[3] had made
his appearance in le Scrope's place and in his opening speech
fresh proposals were placed before the commons. It was
pointed out to them that something like the Lancastrian
objective might be obtained more cheaply in the form of an
orthodox crusade conducted by the bishop of Norwich in
alliance with the Flemish burgesses, who had just revolted upon
purely secular grounds against their Francophil and Clementist
count, Louis de Maele. This project would undoubtedly require
a money grant, but not upon so lavish a scale as the Lancastrian
scheme; moreover, the Flemings, who were hopelessly committed and had already asked for English help, were more
trustworthy[4] and useful allies than the king of the Romans. The
plan was known briefly as the "way of Flanders", and on the
whole did not commend itself to the lords at large, still the
recognised experts on military matters, any more favourably
than it did to the Lancastrians. Gaunt in fact now produced an
alternative scheme, of which the lords thought better. It consisted in giving national support on a more limited scale[5] to the

[1] The title of the emperor-elect, prior to papal coronation (which
Wenzel never received). Cf. Perroy, *Schisme*, pp. 152–3, 156–65.

[2] Clarke, *op. cit.* pp. 43–4.

[3] Bishop Braybrooke of London, a former keeper of the signet.

[4] Neither French, English nor Flemings had forgotten the battle of
Courtrai (1302), in which the Flemish pikemen had destroyed the
chivalry of France.   [5] £43,000 instead of £60,000.

dynastic ambitions of Gaunt himself in Castile and of his younger brother, Edmund of Langley, in Portugal. It was known as the "way of Portugal" and the excuse put forward for supporting it in preference to the "way of Flanders" was that Portugal formed an equally good Urbanist base from which to attack the Clementists (in this case the Spanish kingdoms) and that France, as in the Black Prince's day, might as well be threatened from the south as from the north.

In the end both courses came to be adopted in succession, beginning with the "way of Flanders", but for the time being the commons flatly refused to decide between them or to make a grant adequate for either; with complete constitutional correctness they pointed out that the decision on such matters of policy rested not with them but with the king in council.[1]

The "way of Flanders", if energetically and promptly taken, had a good deal to commend it. The effect of James van Artevelde's seven years of power in Ghent some forty years earlier had been to establish the tradition of democratic and municipal resistance to Flemish feudalism. Now in the next generation the old count Louis de Maele was being driven to depend more and more on the support of the new duke of Burgundy, Philip the Bold, brother of the French king, Charles V. Philip had married Louis's heiress, Margaret, and through him Louis was angling successfully for the support of France. Civil war, somewhat aggravated by the Schism,[2] had broken out again in 1379 when Louis, in return for a subsidy, had allowed the "poorters" or rich merchants of Bruges to begin a canal tapping the river Lys above Ghent, with the object of eliminating the Gantois middlemen from the corn

[1] N. B. Lewis, in *E.H.R.* xlviii, 364–94, has analysed the continuity of commons' personnel and policy, or absence of policy, in the parliaments of this year. Cf. Ramsay, *Revenues*, ii, 326 and Tout, *Chapters*, iii, 388. Perroy, *Schisme*, p. 223, notes that some even of the lords thought that both schemes were too dangerous a diversion of forces so soon after the Peasants' Revolt.

[2] Flanders was predominantly Urbanist but was much confused by its diocesan division between five bishops, all resident outside its borders. The count, of course, was Clementist, owing to his close connexion with the French: Perroy, *Schisme*, p. 167.

trade of Artois. The Gantois had used force to prevent the construction of this canal and had eventually revolted against their overlord. They were joined by other towns, including Bruges itself, where the craftsmen, as against the "poorters", were in sympathy with the men of Ghent. By the end of 1381 they had found an active leader in the younger van Artevelde, Philip, who was at once elected to the position his father had held, though he was young and without political experience. Louis thereupon closed the Bruges wool market, to the great loss, not only of the craftsman weavers, but also of the English wool trade. From this point the English had to choose between the count and his control of the Bruges market on the one hand and the Flemish weavers, with their vast consumption of English wool, on the other, and the difficulty of deciding which was going to be the winning side partly explains their hesitation.[1]

Louis began by trying to starve the Gantois into submission, but they broke out in despair and won the battle of Bever-houtsveld in May 1382; this gave them control of Bruges. Louis thereupon persuaded Burgundy and France, now ruled (in theory) by the young and feeble Charles VI, to intervene in force; the duke of Burgundy agreed to move as the prospective heir to Flanders, while the French king, or his advisers, may have felt some action necessary in order to impress the artisans of Paris, who had been showing sympathy with the Flemings.[2] Van Artevelde, on his side, naturally angled for an English alliance (from August 1382), making it a condition, which was ultimately agreed to, that the staple should be moved from Calais to Bruges.[3] He had no immediate success, since negotiations were still proceeding in October in spite of the prospect of French intervention and the further fact, which should have determined the English attitude, of the insurgent control since May of the vital market of Bruges. Their hesitation may have

[1] Perroy, *Schisme*, p. 173. But there was also the question of class feeling (below).

[2] H. Wallon, *Richard II*, i, 138 ff.: "c'était à Gand qu'il fallait frapper les mécontents de Paris."   [3] Clarke, *op. cit.* p. 40.

been increased by the recency of the Peasants' Revolt which, like the Maillotin rising in France, was thought to have points in common with that of Flanders. If so, this class feeling proved fatal. The French invasion started from Arras early in November 1382; the passage of the Lys was forced in the middle of the same month, whereupon the towns of western Flanders surrendered. A fortnight later came the decisive battle of Roosebeke, fought to protect Ghent and Bruges; van Artevelde was killed and Courtrai finally avenged. It has been said that Roosebeke "settled the whole question of popular revolts" and was perhaps for that reason not unwelcome, as Froissart suggests, to the English nobility. But it also lost England the control of Flanders, whose importance, not only as a wool market but also as a side-door into France and a safeguard to Calais, had long been appreciated, and with characteristic inconsequence, now that the war had been well and truly lost, the English made a belated and half-hearted attempt to take part in it. The attempt was in any case doomed to failure before it was ready to start,[1] for although even after Roosebeke Ghent was still holding out, there were further unconscionable delays and an unshakable determination to spend as little money as possible.

It was probably for this last reason of economy that the commons insisted[2] on accepting the bishop of Norwich's proffer to serve with 2500 men-at-arms, the same number of archers and a king's lieutenant, to be nominated by himself.[3] This force was totally inadequate, coming as it did so late in the day, for it was not until May 1383 that the bishop's crusade finally got under way. Moreover bishop Henry Despenser, though he chose a competent subordinate in the well-known English captain Sir Hugh Calverley and had himself served

[1] Tout, *Chapters*, iii, 388–9.
[2] Perroy, *Schisme*, p. 184, notes however that the commons were supported by Philip and Peter Courtenay, sons of the earl of Devon. Cf. Monk of Westminster, pp. 17–18. There was also a timely miracle (*Hist. Anglic.* ii, 84) which may have convinced some waverers.
[3] This was the post for which the earl of Arundel applied without success.

under the papal banner in Italy,[1] was not an effective soldier and would not listen to advice; his easy triumphs over half-armed and untrained peasants in 1381 appear to have turned his head. On the other hand it must be admitted that there was much sincere, not to say naïve, enthusiasm[2] among the rank and file for the Urbanist and crusading aspect of the expedition. Again, the sea communications between England and Flanders were guaranteed by the Flemish fleet cruising under Francis Ackermann,[3] which did something to mitigate the inevitable fiasco and to prevent it assuming the proportions of a disaster. By September all was over; the fatal substitution of Ypres for Bruges as the main objective had put the finishing touch to Despenser's incompetence and obstinacy, and he was in full flight for Gravelines and Calais, while his captains, led by Calverley, fought a skilful rearguard action to cover his precipitate retreat.[4] As a result the Urbanist cause had not profited while English commercial agents had been expelled from every important centre but Ghent and could only keep in touch with Ghent through Middelburg in Zeeland, whither the staple had been hastily removed. Finally, in December 1385, the English government had no choice but to acquiesce in the separate peace of Tournai negotiated between the Gantois and the house of Burgundy-Flanders.

It must have been the obvious breakdown of this foreign policy, long before it was conclusively demonstrated in the actual fiasco of the crusade, which brought the Lancastrians back to power, for Pole, as we have seen, became chancellor as early as March 1383. Since no one could accuse his faction of responsibility for what had happened he had a comparatively light task in his opening speech to the October parliament. The

---

[1] Perroy, *Schisme*, p. 176. [2] *Ibid.* p. 188, and *Hist. Anglic.* ii, 95.
[3] Perroy, *Schisme*, p. 189.
[4] There is a detailed account of the whole crusade in Perroy, *Schisme*, pp. 193–209. Wallon, *op. cit.* i, 168–94, exposes the much too favourable account of the bishop's prowess to be found in Walsingham. Cf. the less prejudiced Monk of Westminster, p. 26, who criticises Despenser and defends his captains.

Lancastrian policy was not yet one of peace but aimed rather at a more intelligent and vigorous prosecution of the war for, as Pole did not fail to point out,[1] the situation had now changed so much for the worse that there was a real danger of a French invasion of England, which did in fact all but take place in 1385 and again in 1386. He proceeded to renew Gaunt's arguments in favour of strengthening the prerogative of the crown; if the war was to be efficiently conducted the king, or his immediate advisers, must be allowed to assume responsibility and, what was more, obeyed. But once more, owing to personal feuds and the mutual jealousies of factions, among which by this time must perhaps be reckoned a new anti-Lancastrian court interest,[2] no agreement could be reached, and the session was principally spent in nicely apportioning the blame for the miscarriage of the crusade between Despenser and his subordinates.

What does seem to emerge from the confused history of the next few months is, on the one hand, a complete restatement of Lancastrian foreign and commercial policy and on the other a fresh grouping of parties, this time in three main factions instead of two. It will be simplest to begin with a brief mention of the new commercial policy of the Lancastrians, as expounded by Miss Clarke,[3] since that helps to explain the importance which the municipal politics of London suddenly assume from this time onwards in national affairs.

The alliance with the Urbanist Flemish democrats against Clementist France, which had for the time being commanded so much popular support, had been the policy not only of the clericals and the opposition generally but also of a powerful group of London victuallers interested in the financing of the wool trade. These had approved of the transfer of the staple from

[1] *Rot. Parl.* iii, 149; cf. Wallon, *op. cit.* i, 199.
[2] So Clarke, *op. cit.* p. 47, where she points out that Richard and his personal friends had been in favour of the crusade. H. L. Gray, *The Influence of the Commons on early legislation*, p. 256, puts Richard's first trace of independence in 1384; Perroy, *Schisme*, p. 390, not till the late summer of 1386. [3] *Op. cit.* pp. 40 ff.

Calais to Middelburg, probably because they thought it would assist them to supplant the more legitimately interested non-victualling gilds of London, whose centre of operations as far as the wool trade was concerned had long been established in Calais. Pole was committed to this party—he was in close alliance with the draper, John of Northampton, mayor of London in 1382—and he was therefore anxious to see the staple restored to its original position.[1] This would involve at least a truce with France, and that in turn fitted in with the strategic conceptions of the new Lancastrian foreign policy, as developed from the beginning of 1384.

The general idea of this policy, now that the Grand League of Urbanists had proved a failure, was to lull France into inactivity by a truce or series of truces until her allies, Scotland and Castile, could be struck down in turn, after which the war might be resumed with a better chance of success, or favourable peace terms might be obtained. From Gaunt's point of view this strategy had the further advantage of forwarding sooner or later his personal claims on Castile, which would be a bargaining counter of importance. To begin with it was not unsuccessful and, though it took a low view of the intelligence of the French government, this was not unjustified and on the whole the plan deserved success.

The first step was achieved when Gaunt in person managed to extract a short truce from the French at Lelighem, between Calais and Boulogne, in January 1384. The second stage, a somewhat hastily conducted raid against the Scots, also led by Gaunt in person in the spring of 1384, was not so successful. Negotiations for an extension of the French truce were resumed during the summer by Gaunt and his younger brother, Thomas of Woodstock, but by the November parliament it was known that these had broken down, since the French would not treat any longer without the cession of Calais and the English, not unnaturally in view of Gaunt's claim and their other intentions, refused to include Castile in the

[1] This was not, as a matter of fact, achieved until 1389.

projected peace. It now became necessary to proceed with the Lancastrian plan without having previously immobilised the French, on which the plan in theory had depended for its success. This was not perhaps so dangerous a step as it might seem, in view of French disunion and incompetence, faults at least as great on their side as among the English. None the less it did mean that by midsummer 1385 Philip the Bold of Burgundy had established himself as actual count of Flanders, that a large French army had been painfully collected at Sluys to threaten an invasion of England, and that the French admiral Jean de Vienne and other volunteers had been sent to Scotland to give technical advice and bring the Scots if possible across the border.[1]

Even at this stage, though not without some natural hesitation on the part of parliament, the Lancastrian plan was boldly pursued, and the extreme risk was taken of continuing to ignore French menaces and staking everything on a campaign in force against the Scots. Richard himself, now eighteen years old, took command; the court moved to York; and a final muster took place at Berwick, where it was found that over a third of the whole army consisted of Gaunt's men.[2] From Berwick Richard reached and occupied Edinburgh, but could not bring the Scots to action. Although he has been much blamed for doing so he was probably right in refusing Gaunt's advice to follow the example of his own spring campaign of 1384 and fling himself into the Highlands in a hopeless search for the enemy. The two campaigns had not been unsuccessful and it was unnecessary to repeat the risks which Gaunt had taken; the Scots had not been beaten in the field, but southern Scotland had been wasted so effectively that there was no more danger from the north for a matter of three years. In short the second stage of the Lancastrian plan had been successfully completed, and since the threatened French invasion had not materialised, the great risk taken had been justified.

[1] Tout, *Chapters*, iii, 395. See Wallon, *op. cit.* i, 239–40, quoting Froissart, for the comic discomfort of the French in Scotland.
[2] Armitage-Smith, *op. cit.* pp. 437–46.

The third stage and climax of the Lancastrian foreign policy was represented by the Castilian expedition, led by Gaunt in person, of 1386–9. It was, for more than one reason, a turning-point in Richard's reign. In the first place the conditions of 1385 were more or less repeated; once more a French army was massing for the invasion of England, but after the fiasco of the previous year it was much more easily decided by the English that this time they could afford to take the still greater risk of sending their main army to a distant theatre of war across the sea. But the brusque removal of the Lancastrian army which had bulked so large at Berwick in 1385 and of the personality of Gaunt immediately upset the balance of power in English politics and liberated forces which had hitherto been more or less under control. On top of this, some months after Gaunt had departed, the French threat suddenly became acute and the very wide-spread attack of nerves which resulted among the English, and is reflected in almost every contemporary chronicler, set in motion the train of events which began with the impeachment of de la Pole and ended with the merciless parliament. But this is to look too far ahead and deal with factors which have not yet been analysed; moreover, the great Castilian expedition of 1386 deserves further notice.

It is a little difficult to be persuaded by the argument of Miss Clarke[1] that the Castilian expedition was never intended to assert Gaunt's own claims to the crown of Castile, but merely to secure the alliánce of Portugal for England and the Urbanists and to bluff Castile, whose fleet was dangerous, into peace with England. Miss Clarke's general reconstruction of Lancastrian foreign policy, which has been largely followed in this chapter, is brilliant and convincing, but it seems unnecessary to credit Gaunt with such inhuman single-mindedness; moreover, his claim at this date was at least fourteen years old, for as far back as 1372 he had, with Edward III's permission, assumed the title of king of Castile and Leon and had been regularly addressed by it in England. It rested on the fact that in 1371 he

[1] *Op. cit.* pp. 45–6.

had married as his second wife Costanza, second daughter of Pedro the Cruel, while his brother, Edmund of Langley, simultaneously married Costanza's younger sister.

At the time of the marriages Pedro, though he claimed to be the rightful king, was not in possession of Castile, which was held by Henry of Trastamara, a bastard of Alfonso XI, but he had settled the crown on his daughters by Maria de Padilla in priority to his sons by other ladies and, the eldest daughter having retired to a nunnery and died, Costanza might plausibly be regarded as the heiress of Castile when Henry of Trastamara at last succeeded in defeating and killing Gaunt's unpleasing father-in-law. Usurper though he might be, Henry II proved too strong to be disturbed and until Henry's death in 1379 Gaunt's title had remained an empty claim.

The position was now complicated by the outbreak of the Great Schism. From this point Gaunt was able to conduct his claim to the throne under pretence of an Urbanist crusade, since Henry and his son were Clementist, but in the opinion of M. Perroy[1] this was only a hollow pretence, since the rights and wrongs of the Schism meant little in the Iberian peninsula and not only Castile but Aragon, Navarre and Portugal freely bartered their papal allegiances as seemed best to themselves. In May 1380 Portugal, which had all along recognised Gaunt's claim, agreed to a treaty with the English by which it should be actively asserted by both nations against Henry of Trastamara's heir, Juan I, in return for a marriage between Edmund of Langley's son Edward and the heiress Beatrice of Portugal. As has been seen, however, the "way of Portugal" did not then or for many years to come appeal to the English parliament, and an inadequate effort made by Edmund alone[2] in 1381–2 failed through lack of money and leadership. It also failed through Portuguese treachery, for in the autumn of 1382 the Portuguese suddenly made a separate treaty with Juan abandoning the

[1] Ch. vi, *passim.*
[2] Perroy, *Schisme*, p. 218, says that Gaunt wanted to go but that the Scottish situation was too threatening in these years for him to be spared.

English marriage for a Spanish one, and Edmund returned to England in November a disappointed man.[1]

Whatever the object of the Portuguese manœuvre may have been it resulted in a threat to Portugal, for Juan, having married the heiress Beatrice, proceeded to lay claim to the Portuguese throne on her father's death in 1383. The Portuguese, who had probably expected the treaty to work the other way, were scandalised by the proposal and in face of threats determined to resist by force. English volunteers, mainly archers, helped them to win the decisive battle of Aljubarrota in August 1385,[2] and when the English parliament met in October fresh from its qualified triumph over the Scots, Portuguese envoys appeared before it and begged for further help. This time parliament approved the support which Gaunt naturally gave to such proposals; so too did the king, perhaps because the new curialist party over-estimated its own strength so much that it was actually anxious to get rid of Gaunt in order to be able to pursue its own plans.[3] In the event the rather small sum of 20,000 marks was voted in support of what was predominantly a private expedition financed and manned by the Lancastrians; it sailed about 8000 strong, after an immense amount of pre-paration, in July 1386, and it may be convenient to dispose here and now of its later history.

In spite of the fact that Gaunt had taken with him his wife and three daughters, one of whom had just married his constable, Sir John Holland, who was also the king's half-brother, it is clear that the expedition was warlike in intention. Pope Urban supported it with bulls and a consecrated banner;[4] the English Lollards preached against it as they had preached against the

[1] This *volte face* by Portugal is perhaps another reason for the acceptance of Despenser's crusade in 1383 by parliament.

[2] Perroy, *Schisme*, p. 232, says this battle put an end to the Clementist hopes in Portugal. Prof. J. B. Trend tells me that it is still referred to as "*the* battle" by the Portuguese: there is a monastery (Batalha) dedicated to its memory.

[3] Perroy, *Schisme*, p. 233. This new court party is described below, pp. 111–17.

[4] *Ibid.* pp. 235–6.

crusade of 1383; and there was some real fighting in Galicia in the autumn of 1386 and in Leon early in 1387. Eventually, however, after a great deal of haggling, Gaunt consented to abandon both the Urbanist cause and his shadowy title to Castile in return for a considerable amount of cash down and the plighting of his two unmarried daughters, whom, as Miss Clarke points out,[1] he can hardly have brought with him for any other purpose, to the heirs of Portugal and Castile respectively. This, however, is not to say that his intentions had been entirely matrimonial from the start; M. Perroy points out that English intervention had at least definitely secured Portugal for Urban VI,[2] and Gaunt's motives were no doubt as mixed as most men's. English interests, his own especial claims, and Urban's cause probably all entered into them and he was prepared to use whatever means might prove the most successful in satisfying all three aims, nor can it be said that he entirely failed. From the point of view of English history the most material fact is that he had sent away his ships on landing in Portugal and was completely cut off, so that until Sir John Holland returned with a report in 1388 the only news which reached England concerning him was contained in a letter sent through Barcelona in October 1386.[3] This virtually complete elimination of the hitherto practically all-powerful Lancastrian interest for a period of over three years had a decisive effect in simplifying English politics into a relatively clear-cut struggle between curialists and magnates, for the understanding of which it is now necessary to turn back and trace the growth of parties other than the Lancastrian and to study the interlocking questions of administration and personal relationships in and after 1382.

The first factor to be reckoned with is the new queen of England,[4] whose importance, during her early years at any rate, has however been consistently exaggerated. Anne of Bohemia was the eldest daughter of Charles IV by his fourth wife, Elizabeth of Pomerania; she was a few months older than

[1] *Loc. cit.*   [2] Perroy, *Schisme*, p. 267.   [3] *Ibid.* pp. 241–2.
[4] Her marriage and coronation took place in January 1382.

Richard. According to her one biographer[1] "at fifteen or sixteen a blooming German girl is a very pleasing object", but judging by the effigy on her tomb, which appears to be a portrait, Anne was not beautiful. In compensation she is popularly supposed to have been "good", but the attribution of this quality to her rests on rather slender foundations.[2] It seems to be derived in the first instance from the many individual pardons granted at her nominal request to the rebels of 1381 not long after her arrival in England, but there is reason to believe that the far greater influence of the king's mother, Joan, princess of Wales, lay behind these pardons. It certainly lay behind Anne's equally nominal intervention to save Wyclif from the council of 1382, though in the former case at least the princess was willing that her young daughter-in-law, whose Bohemian train and poverty—she brought no dowry—were unpopular, should get the credit. It is in fact probable that these Bohemians were more important than the queen herself in English history; they help to account for the strong feeling against the court in 1386–8 and above all are almost certainly responsible for the tradition linking Wyclif with Hus. Richard could hardly have combined his rigid orthodoxy in religion with the great affection which he felt for Anne during their later years of married life if she had directly patronised the Lollards; on the other hand, certain members of Richard's own household were implicated without his knowledge or consent in 1394, and the same may well have been true of the queen's.[3] In short, there is little to justify the sentiment which has tended to collect round Anne's name; she is a plain and rather colourless figure who only comes to life for a few hours in the crisis of 1388 and again

[1] Miss A. Strickland, *Lives of the Queens of England*, i, 591–614. This particular biography has little merit, and contains at least three serious mistakes.

[2] There are, it is true, the official encomia of the chroniclers, at that time not unfriendly to the crown, on the occasion of her death in 1394, but these need hardly be taken seriously.

[3] For a recent (1939) summary of the whole question see R. R. Betts, "English and Čech Influences in the Husite Movement", *T.R.H.S.* series iv, vol. xxi, 71–102.

perhaps during Richard's quarrel with London in 1392. The feeling which Richard had for her was apparently of slow growth; it was perhaps transferred from that much stronger character, his mother, on her death in 1385; was deepened by the tragedies of the next three years, and finally brought to what can only be described as a pathological pitch in 1394.[1] But in 1382 it was still the princess of Wales who presided benignly over the two married children—for they were little more.

Outside the royal family there is little trace of any personal circle round Richard, other than that provided by household clerks and household officials, of whom there will be more to say later, before 1383. We know from Walsingham, however,[2] that up to 1385 he was much in the company of Thomas Mowbray, twelfth baron Mowbray, and from February 1383 earl of Nottingham. Mowbray was barely a year older than Richard and apparently an amiable enough young man of no particular distinction. Unfortunately he was the heir to great possessions and the heir expectant to still greater ones,[3] and this accumulation of baronial interests not unnaturally drew him slowly into thinking of himself as a magnate and peer of the realm rather than as a friend of the king. In 1385 he became the second husband of Arundel's daughter Elizabeth, and this completed the estrangement begun by Richard's open preference for his rival, Robert de Vere. Yet Richard never forgot his early friendship with Mowbray and there is no reason to suppose that the favours which were showered on him in and after 1389, in spite of his career as an appellant, did not represent a genuine attempt at reconciliation; they were barely affected by the final exiling of the duke of Norfolk, as he had then become, for Richard was certainly not normal in his last three years.

Richard's other close friend at this time, Robert de Vere,

[1] In the famous, but apparently only partial, destruction of the royal manor of Sheen in which she died.

[2] *Hist. Anglic.* ii, 156.

[3] The Bigod inheritance, held by his grandmother, Margaret Brotherton.

ninth earl of Oxford, was four or five years older than either
Mowbray or the king. He was distantly connected by blood,
and much more closely connected by marriage[1] with the royal
family, and seems to have been in continual attendance on
Richard from perhaps as early as 1381. His character is obscure
and negative, but, for reasons which cannot be determined,[2]
Richard's devotion to him knew no bounds. "Called the king's
kinsman, loaded with honours and marked out for a great
career in Ireland",[3] he seems to have been a handsome,
frivolous young man of more than ordinary incompetence,
both as a soldier and an administrator. His unpopularity must
have rested on the abnormal honours, including the first
marquisate in English history, conferred on him by the king;
no serious charge has been proved against him, and there is no
more trace of Gaveston's biting tongue in his few recorded
utterances than there is of Gaveston's humble origin.[4] On the
other hand his intrigue, just before the crisis of 1386, with one
of the queen's Bohemian women, Agnes Launcekron, gave
great offence to other magnates, notably to his wife's royal
uncle, Thomas of Woodstock, by this date duke of Gloucester,
more particularly because it was carried to the point of a
petition to the pope for a dissolution of his first marriage.[5] The
queen's attitude is doubtful, but it is by no means certain that she
did not protest, though vainly, against the whole affair.

Idle as de Vere may have been and uninteresting to all but
Richard it is important to remember that in singling him out as
his special friend and companion the king had had little choice.
Mowbray had deliberately chosen in 1385 to marry the daughter
of Richard's detested guardian, Arundel, and, Mowbray and de
Vere apart, the king was much the youngest of his circle; he

[1] Through his first wife Philippa de Coucy, grand-daughter of
Edward III.
[2] They were certainly not the scurrilous reasons of some contemporary
chroniclers, e.g. *Hist. Anglic.* ii, 148.
[3] Cf. Tout, *Chapters*, iii, 406–7.
[4] Ramsay, *Genesis*, ii, 181, thinks them similar.
[5] Monk of Westminster, p. 95.

came uncomfortably between the generations.[1] He could hardly associate safely with men of less than noble birth and though he had several clerkly confidants he was wise enough to keep them in the background—a precaution which still did not save many of them from suffering in 1388. For the heir to the tradition of the Black Prince, the would-be leader of chivalry, it was a difficult position, and Richard in the later phases of a sensitive adolescence is entitled to more sympathy than he has received.

From what has been said so far it is clear that the brains of the new court party are not to be found in the immediate circle of the king. Nor can they be looked for in the older offices of state, for the chancellor was the only great minister of distinction in this period, and Pole was a Lancastrian.[2] The treasurership of the exchequer was held from August 1381 to January 1386 by the colourless, if curially inclined, Sir Hugh Segrave, an old-established household servant of both the Black Prince and his son.[3] He was succeeded for a few months by John Fordham, bishop of Durham, another old household servant but one who had come to regard himself first and foremost as a bishop and a leader of the clerical party rather than a courtier. Walter Skirlaw, keeper of the privy seal from August 1382, was another of the same type; he was an experienced diplomat and canon lawyer, high in favour with the pope and frequently out of England. His sympathies were certainly with the court and he may be regarded as a valuable link during these years between Richard and the papacy. Yet he was never one of the intimates of Richard, who in 1386 unsuccessfully supported his secretary Medford against him as Fordham's successor in the see of Durham.[4] Two other offices were reckoned at this date to be

[1] Gaunt's son, Henry of Derby, was about the same age; his position will be considered later.

[2] Tout, *Chapters*, iii, 398–411, for this and most of what follows.

[3] *Ibid.* v, 217.

[4] Bishop Braybrooke of London, who was chancellor 1382–3, was perhaps a curialist, but had neither the tact nor the ability to retain his post for long.

among the five most important posts at the disposal of the crown: these were the stewardship of the household and the chamberlainship. The first was held from 1381 by Sir John Montague, brother of the second earl of Salisbury, with whom however he was constantly at law. An old soldier, who had fought at Crécy, he too was more of a professional official than a politician, though what politics he had were curialist and he was significantly anxious to extend the jurisdiction of the household court which he controlled.[1] Finally, the hereditary chamberlain of England was no other than de Vere, but the post was filled by deputies of small importance until he came of age in 1383, and even after that he was content to leave the real powers of the office to the vice-chamberlain, Sir Simon Burley.

With Burley and his chamber knights we reach the essence of the new court party. Burley was an old soldier of distinction, who had fought at Winchelsea and Nájera and had been a prisoner in France, but he was also a great deal more. He had been appointed Richard's tutor by the Black Prince and had helped to bring Anne of Bohemia to England. An old friend of the princess of Wales and in full possession of her confidence, he had always been on the best of terms with Richard and may have fostered in him that belief in the regality of which John of Gaunt himself and his Lancastrians approved. He is undoubtedly in this period the real power behind the throne, the architect, and perhaps the breaker, of the Lancastrian alliance, but he worked in such obscurity that little is really known about him.[2] It is clear, however, that he influenced Richard more than ever after his marriage through his mother and, later, through the queen, and Tout thinks[3] that his main work was to turn "the chamber into a special reserve of the court party, so

[1] Thus he condemned the Lancastrian ex-mayor of London, John of Northampton, to death in his court in 1383, when the two chief justices refused, though it is true the sentence was not carried out.

[2] His importance may be estimated by the struggle which raged over his life in 1388.

[3] Chapters, iii, 404.

that the chamber knights and squires could always be trusted to further the wishes of the sovereign" and to form "a reserve of workers for the king's cause".[1]

Burley was assisted in these objects by another old servant of the Black Prince, Sir Baldwin Raddington, who is now known to have been his nephew,[2] yet in spite of that was able to hold office as controller of the wardrobe through all political changes for the unprecedented period of sixteen years (1381–97). His tact and ability are attested by the fact that, though he was certainly quite as active as his uncle in the royal cause, he managed to survive the whole crisis of 1386–8, and this though he joined courageously in pleading for Burley's life during the merciless parliament. Like Burley he is noteworthy for helping to develop the military rather than the clerical side of the household. This he did to such effect that already by the summer of 1386 the royal bodyguard was able to spare a contingent, led by Raddington himself, to garrison Sandwich against the expected French invasion. On this occasion he even captured two French ships, which the chancellor, Pole, forced him to restore to their owners.[3] He was also the king's liaison officer with the new royal party which was rapidly springing up in London, led by the brave and capable, but violent, overbearing and unscrupulous grocer Nicholas Brembre, who had been chosen mayor in 1383. Altogether Richard had no more skilful or loyal supporter at any time than Raddington, and his retirement on a pension in 1397 was a serious, perhaps a fatal,

---

[1] Miss Clarke (op. cit. pp. 119–23) has thrown much doubt on the assertion of the Lancastrian chronicler, Knighton (ii, 294), that Burley also used his position to increase his private income from twenty marks to three thousand marks a year. The only grants that Tout was able to trace were the custody of Windsor castle for life and a two years' tenancy of a house near the great wardrobe. The list of Burley's forfeitures on his fall is not impressive and all the goods then described as his had been pawned at the time the inventory was made.

[2] See N. B. Lewis, E.H.R. lii, 662–9.

[3] In this incident Tout (Chapters, iv, 198) sees a possible explanation of the fact that Raddington survived Pole's fall; it may have meant that he was on bad terms with him, and therefore more congenial to Pole's enemies.

loss. Both the mildly Ricardian Monk of Westminster [1] and the extremely hostile Walsingham [2] join in a tribute to his character, and his pension was continued by Henry IV.

Another novel instrument of the prerogative in the years before 1386 is to be found in the development of the signet office and the secretary.[3] Before 1383 this latest and smallest of the king's seals was being used merely as a minor cog in the administrative machine, much as Edward III had used it after 1360. But in the secretaryships of John Bacon (1381–5) and Richard Medford (1385–8) there is a sudden jump in its importance and activity; thus the first six years of the reign are represented by a single signet file among the chancery warrants, but the next six years by sixteen. The reasons for this abrupt change are probably to be found in the growing officialisation of the privy seal under Skirlaw and the comparative lack of control which the curialists could exercise over it owing to his long absences from England, and again in the greater speed, secrecy and informality of signet procedure, whether used as a direct executive or merely to move chancery or the exchequer.[4]

In spite of this development the keepers of the signet, or secretaries, were still comparatively humble individuals. Thus John Bacon was a senior king's clerk who combined the office with one of the two chamberlainships of the exchequer and the keepership of the king's jewels. Richly rewarded with benefices and prebends, he was sent as one of two ambassadors to Urban VI in 1385 and died at Genoa. Although the signet had not been of much importance during his first two years of office it had been used to warrant the appointment of a chancellor [5] before the end of his term, and his successor, Richard Medford, a clerk of the king's private chapel, found his services in such constant demand that he was always kept in close attendance on the king, from the Scots expedition of 1385 to the time of his

---

[1] p. 274.   [2] *Hist. Anglic.* ii, 209.   [3] *Chapters*, v, 207 ff.

[4] One still extant warrant of 1386 bears the actual signature "Richard", and is thought by Tout to be "perhaps the first official document authenticated" by the sign manual.

[5] This had attracted adverse comment in parliament.

arrest by the appellants at the beginning of 1388.[1] Under him the signet reached its maximum activity, and it is significant that one of the most important opening moves by the baronial opposition in the autumn of 1386 was taken when a baronially appointed chancellor refused to accept a writ warranted by signet letter in favour of Sir Simon Burley. It is to the growth of this opposition that we must now turn.

Actually it was not the new court party which was in power up to July 1386, but the Lancastrian faction, working in increasingly uneasy coalition with the curialists, whose tendency was to stab it in the back. Accordingly the main objective in the first place of the orthodox baronial opposition was not the court, though they had little love for it, so much as the Lancastrian party; the court as such tended to be despised, or at any rate ignored. Arundel and the bloodier-minded magnates, men such as Thomas of Woodstock, duke of Gloucester, the dangerous and intriguing youngest uncle of the king, men like the grasping and ambitious, yet essentially timid, Thomas Beauchamp, earl of Warwick, all tended to join the clerical opposition to the Lancastrians and to their policy of at least a temporary peace with France. After all the trade of magnates of this type was war, and they grew fat on loot and ransoms, or at any rate hoped to do so.[2] The bishops too, being good Urbanists, were opposed to peace, at any rate upon Lancastrian lines, for it must be remembered that although Gaunt's alliance with Wyclif had long been formally abandoned, in popular opinion the party was still tainted by its once open associations with heresy.

The position of Gaunt's son Henry, earl of Derby, on the other hand, was more isolated and difficult; he had a foot in two camps, though not in the king's,[3] and was already giving

[1] He was released in June and nominated by the pope in November to the see of Chichester, on which he entered, after a long struggle, in 1390 and so passed out of politics. As early as 1386 Richard had tried to obtain the see of Durham for him in place of Skirlaw and he had already received quite as many prebends and benefices as Bacon.

[2] There is a good deal in Stubbs's theory of the moral degeneration of the English baronage as a result of the Hundred Years' War.

[3] They seem to have disliked each other from the first and to have met as little as possible.

signs of that cold judgment, shrewd sense of self-interest and
brilliant timing which were to serve him so well in later years.
His parental connexion must not be overstressed; he was now
about twenty years old and a magnate in his own right, having
divided with his uncle, Gloucester, the vast inheritance of
Humphrey Bohun, last earl of Hereford, Essex and Northampton.[1] Although for the moment he stood somewhat aloof,
this connexion alone was liable to draw him into the baronial
opposition for much the same reasons as those which were
attracting his contemporary, Thomas Mowbray, towards
Arundel. Finally, the youngest, ablest and most restless of the
bishops was another Arundel, Thomas, bishop of Ely, who
provided a natural link between the church and baronage;
his statesmanlike and subtle character was in great contrast with
that of his more irritable and dashing elder brother, yet he was
undoubtedly the more dangerous of the two.

There is no doubt that this little group of men and the powerful interests which they represented constituted a real danger to
the tottering Lancastrian-curialist coalition by the spring of
1386, but it was the premature ambition of the curialists and
their disloyalty to Gaunt which really played into the barons'
hands. The curialists had attacked Gaunt personally as early as
1384, while at the same time welcoming his peace policy—a
course which had done nothing to conciliate the official
opposition. A court programme of peace without Gaunt had
on the other hand brought over to the king the controlling
influence of the victuallers in London, where from this time
onward Nicholas Brembre was one of Richard's strongest
supporters. The relations of the victuallers with de la Pole are
somewhat obscure but, in spite of the support which he and his
faction had once given to their enemy John of Northampton, they
do not seem to have quarrelled with him openly by July 1386,[2]

---

[1] They had married the co-heiresses Mary and Eleanor respectively.

[2] This may have been due to Pole's failure to remove the staple from
Middelburg, where they wished to keep it, or possibly to the restraining
influence of those elements among their allies of the court (including
Richard himself) who were not personally hostile to Pole.

when John of Gaunt's withdrawal to Castile sapped the strength of the Lancastrians, and incidentally saved Derby from the difficulty, which he seems to have felt more keenly than might perhaps have been expected, of taking part in an attack upon his father.

Gloucester, Warwick and the Arundels at least were certainly in touch with each other from the beginning of the year, but even after Gaunt's departure had left Pole and the fag-end of the Lancastrians an inviting object of attack, they at first refrained from taking any action owing to the menace, already mentioned, of a great French invasion by an army concentrated at Sluys for the second time. This was so threatening in August and September that all party feeling had to be discarded and elaborate preparations made for national defence.[1] The end of September came, however, without a movement from the French;[2] on the contrary the English won several small successes at sea, while the government levies starved and pillaged in the neighbourhood of London. It was in the angry reaction from this unnecessary panic and its accompanying disturbance that there was summoned the so-called "wonderful"[3] parliament of October 1386, in which the time was obviously ripe for an opposition blow, and this was struck accordingly. It was struck, however, not against the curialists in the first instance but against Pole and his Lancastrian remnant, and it was only when Richard came hurriedly and amateurishly to the defence of Pole that the attack passed insensibly into an assault upon the court and upon what was afterwards known as Richard's first "tyranny".

[1] For these see *Hist. Anglic.* ii, 147–8 and the following commissions in C.C.R. 1385–9: (a) p. 60, special commissions of array to one captain in each county (this is very unusual) against the threatened French invasion (issued as early as March), (b) p. 261, special commissions to prevent the engrossing of arms and armour and the raising of their prices, apropos of preparations to resist the French (September).

[2] They were actually waiting for the duke of Berry and his contingent.

[3] This traditional name is based on a mis-reading of Favent, who meant it to apply to the February parliament of 1388, usually known as "merciless". See Miss McKisack's edition of Favent in *Camden Miscellany*, vol. xiv (1926).

CHAPTER V

The First "Tyranny"

IN theory the parliament of October 1386 was to have completed the Lancastrian programme by arranging for a grand assault on France now that the French allies, Scotland and Castile, had been temporarily immobilised; moreover, the existence of the French camp at Sluys seemed to offer every justification for much stronger counter-measures than had hitherto been taken. But in practice things did not work out that way; on the contrary, it was correctly assumed by the baronial opposition that the French danger, so long postponed, was over for the year and that the luxury of a domestic crisis might safely be enjoyed. In fact the French camp did break up about the middle of October, but even before it did so it became quite clear that, so far from voting any supplies of war, parliament was determined on the dismissal of the king's ministers and the impeachment of the chancellor. Both curialists and Lancastrians had hopelessly misjudged the situation.

The attack upon the ministers seems to have been intended in the first instance as a general indictment of the entire Lancastrian foreign policy, though it is difficult to see what the attackers, who were certainly not pacifists, could possibly have suggested in its place; theirs was not a constructive move. Moreover, it was so clumsily made that it almost immediately degenerated into a personal attack on de la Pole. The effect of this was curious, for the Lancastrian middle party, deprived of the support of Gaunt and his household, soon broke up and disappeared under the onslaught; Pole and the archbishop of York, Alexander Neville, leaning towards the curialists, and the king's remaining uncle Edmund, now duke of York, together with his nephew Derby and the earl of Nottingham, joining the opposition. Richard himself was personally outraged by the whole affair and plunged heavily into politics on his own account; he seems to have felt that the Lancastrian conception of the prerogative, on which he had been brought up, had been endangered by the demand for the dismissal of his two leading ministers,[1] and he accordingly refused to meet parliament. What was more, he sent the famous message from his manor at Eltham that he would not dismiss even one of his scullions at parliament's request.[2]

The extreme rashness of this message, which bears all the signs of youth and inexperience, makes it practically certain that it was Richard's personal contribution to the situation; it is inconceivable that Pole could have advised him to take so uncompromising a line. It was in no way modified by his offer to interview a deputation of forty knights at Eltham; on the contrary, the opposition immediately maintained that this must be a trap, by which the king meant to get all the best men in the commons into his hands.[3] Meanwhile, on the 13th of October, Richard made a third mistake in choosing this particular moment to appoint de Vere by charter duke of Ireland with unprecedented powers;[4] this could only be regarded as a deliberate challenge, associating the whole court party with the tottering Lancastrians. If so, it was immediately met by a parliamentary mission of two persons, namely the duke of Gloucester and the bishop of Ely, Thomas Arundel, who were sent to reason and expostulate with, and if necessary to threaten, the young king.[5]

Gloucester and the younger Arundel seem to have told Richard bluntly that he must hold at least one parliament a year

[1] The treasurer, John Fordham, was attacked as well as de la Pole.

[2] Knighton, ii, 215.

[3] Knighton, ii, 216. Walsingham, *Historia Anglicana*, i, 150, says it was exposed as such by Richard Exton, the "honest", i.e. hostile, mayor of London.

[4] This too was probably done at Eltham, though it is just possible that Richard appeared before parliament for the purpose and withdrew again: Tout, *Chapters*, iii, 412.

[5] Lodge and Thornton, *English Constitutional Documents*, pp. 23–4; Knighton, ii, 216–20.

and that a parliament which he did not attend in person was no parliament and could go home again after forty days.[1] The king is said to have replied[2] that this was open revolt and that he must get help from the French, but this alleged answer is improbable at this stage in the reign, when there was no effective peace party and Richard himself was still bellicose and patriotic; it is accordingly dismissed by Wallon[3] as opposition propaganda. If Richard said anything of the sort it is at least plausible that what he really suggested was the arbitration of the king of France, on the analogy of Louis IX's arbitration between Henry III and de Montfort, as expressed in the Mise of Amiens. In that event the famous threat which followed on the part of Gloucester and bishop Arundel would be merely a counter-appeal to history; if they had forgotten de Montfort's death at Evesham, had Richard forgotten the fate of Edward II? This, of course, was a precedent for revolution, not a legal precedent, for the suggestion that Edward's deposition had been carried out in some way in or by parliament was almost as baseless as the belief, with which the parliamentary envoys had tried to frighten Richard, that there existed some general statute authorising the parliamentary deposition of kings. None the less it was a precedent, and Richard gave way; his reply to it came nine years later when he sent pope Boniface IX a book of Edward's "miracles" and asked that this deposed king should be canonised, presumably in order that any outrage committed on him could never be made into an effective precedent again.[4] Meanwhile he reluctantly attended parliament, probably on the 23rd of October, which was the date of Pole's dismissal; made his enemy, the bishop of Ely, chancellor in Pole's place, and not

[1] This was a violent extension of the doctrine to be found in cap. xiii of the fourteenth-century *Modus Tenendi Parliamentum* (best text in Clarke, *Medieval Representation and Consent*, pp. 373–84). In this passage the unknown author of the *Modus* says that the king *nec se absentare debet nec potest*, unless he is ill, but there is no mention of forty days.

[2] Knighton, ii, 218.   [3] *Richard II*, i, 311.

[4] He may have first made this request as early as 1387: E. Perroy, *L'Angleterre et le grand schisme d'Occident*, pp. 301–3 and *Diplomatic Correspondence*, no. 95, pp. 62–3.

only substituted John Gilbert, bishop of Hereford, for Fordham
as treasurer but also John Waltham, keeper of the rolls, for
Skirlaw as keeper of the privy seal.[1] A petition of the commons
that the steward of the household should also be replaced *par
avis de son counseill* was, however, temporarily evaded, though
the king seems to have promised to take this step at a somewhat
later date.

There followed the impeachment of the fallen chancellor on
the sole precedent of 1376.[2] Dr N. B. Lewis has shown[3]
that the charges which were brought against Pole related to
"excessive usury, not fraud" and that the whole council, as the
lords recognised, had been equally to blame. Of the original
seven articles Pole was convicted only on three and these were
all on technicalities so that, though he was sentenced to forfeiture and imprisonment in Windsor castle, the whole episode
appeared such an open travesty of justice that his imprisonment
at least was merely nominal and soon ceased entirely.[4] Yet, as
Tout has noted,[5] there was little real vindictiveness so far about
the opposition, in spite of the triviality of the charges against
Pole and the threats against the king; Pole was the only victim,
and even in his case the earldom of Suffolk, which Richard had
conferred on him in August 1385, was actually safeguarded in
the sentence. In fact the main impression left is that the whole
incident had been staged as an excuse for getting rid of an
unpopular minister and that the real grievances, such as they
were, had not been touched. The most curious event had been
the king's blind attempt to rescue Pole; he had made the
most unfortunate use possible of his one weapon, the regality,
thereby showing, it is true, the personal chivalry, loyalty and
courage which the Peasants' Revolt had already proved that he

[1] Tout, *Chapters*, iii, 412–13.   [2] M. V. Clarke, *op. cit.* p. 244.
[3] *E.H.R.* xlii, 402–7.
[4] Through the good offices of Pole's younger brother, Edmund, who was
careful not to quarrel with the appellants, his heir, Michael, gradually
recovered most of his landed property during the next ten years though not
of course his moveables. See my article in *C.A.S. Proc. loc. cit.*
[5] *Chapters*, iii, 414.

possessed, but also a clumsy amateurishness in manœuvre and a complete lack of any true political sense.[1] The result was that by the end of 1386 the confused struggle for power had clarified into a straight fight between the king and his personal supporters on the one hand, representing a not entirely unhistorical theory of the prerogative, and on the other a powerful group of magnates who, although they were successfully dominating the commons, were merely anxious to confirm the precedents created by Edward's last years and Richard's minority and had as yet worked out no constitutional theory at all. Owing to Richard's impulsiveness the first round had gone so decidedly in favour of this opposition that from November 1386 he was saddled with the one thing which they wanted and he dreaded, namely, an all-powerful commission of government, appointed in parliament and modelled on those continual councils of the minority which his people had no reason to bless and he himself every reason to abhor.

But it is still important to stress the comparative moderation, even at this stage, of the opposition. The new commission consisted of the five great ministers and nine notables, and if it is true that the only potential supporter of the king was the archbishop of York,[2] it is equally certain that only three violent antagonists of Richard's were included, namely the two Arundels and the duke of Gloucester. The remaining ten members[3] could all be described as moderates and included some Lancastrians. The theoretic object of the commission was "to review and amend the administration",[4] but the wide

[1] It must be remembered that he was not yet twenty when the attack on Pole occurred.

[2] Richard was soon able to win him over by supporting him against his cathedral chapter and other diocesan enemies, notably the canons of Beverley. Cf. Hist. Anglic. ii, 152 and Knighton, ii, 233-4, who, however, says that Richard was unwilling to intervene at Beverley.

[3] The archbishop of Canterbury, the bishops of Hereford, Winchester and Exeter, the abbot of Waltham, the duke of York, lord Cobham, Sir Richard le Scrope, Sir John Devereux and John Waltham. Cf. Lodge and Thornton, op. cit. p. 67; J. E. A. Jolliffe, The Constitutional History of Medieval England, p. 470.   [4] Tout, Chapters, iii, 415.

powers given it for this vague general purpose[1] were wholly
abnormal. It was to be permanently resident in Westminster,
where it had full control of the great and privy seals and also of
the exchequer and finance in general; Richard's personal seal,
the signet, was ignored and he was forced to take an oath to
abide by any ordinances made by a bare majority of the commission and to denounce and punish all those who might advise
him to recall its powers. The one saving grace in the whole
humiliating business may have been the fact that the commission was as yet envisaged as a purely temporary expedient;
it was to last only from the 20th of November 1386 to the
19th of November 1387—a point which acquired some legal
importance when the time came for its powers to expire.

On the dissolution of the "wonderful" parliament Richard
was content for the moment to lodge a formal protest, saving
the prerogative and liberties of the crown against anything done
in that parliament. But he showed his rising resentment by
remitting the earl of Suffolk's fine and spending Christmas in his
company at Windsor, while early in the new year he took the
still more challenging step of deliberately breaking the promise
he had made to choose a new steward of the household by the
advice and consent of the council, that is virtually the commission, when Sir John Beauchamp of Holt, a strong curialist,
was appointed.[2] These signs of rebellion were, however, met
with resounding military successes by the magnates. Early in
1387 the earl of Arundel, who was again admiral, and Nottingham, making good use of the money which parliament had
denied the king but had now put at the disposal of the commission, defeated a great fleet of Flemings, Frenchmen and
Spaniards off Margate[3] and captured nearly a hundred ships full
of wine. By refusing to make any personal profit out of their
prize they acquired considerable popularity; for the whole year
wine was cheap in England and dear in the Netherlands;
moreover, the two earls, assisted by the earl of Devon, followed
up their victory by relieving and revictualling Brest, plundering

[1] C.P.R. 1385–9, p. 244.   [2] Tout, Chapters, iii, 416.
[3] This is the famous battle of "Cadzand": see D.N.B. "Arundel".

the country round Sluys, taking more ships and in general establishing a temporary command of the English Channel such as had not been known since Pembroke's disastrous failure in 1371.[1]

Richard's position was therefore very difficult. In addition to the inevitable sneers at the contrast between the new régime and the "carpet knights" of the chamber[2] he was hampered by his loss of control over the seals and the exchequer and by the purge of king's friends which the commission was initiating in various minor posts; it was, for example, at this time that Geoffrey Chaucer lost his two controllerships of customs.[3] Yet he was determined to continue his resistance, and it is clearly for this purpose that he left Westminster for the country on the 9th of February, after appointing various additional councillors of his own party whom he proceeded to take with him. The object of this move was clearly, as Tout has said,[4] to build up "a party, an administration and an army of his own elsewhere", since he had lost control of the central machinery at Westminster. As such "it can only be condemned on grounds of expediency",[5] for an itinerating court had the bulk of medieval precedents behind it and it was good doctrine that where the king was there was the government. Unfortunately Richard's exact itinerary is difficult to establish,[6] but it was clear that it was methodical and covered a good deal of ground. The most important points in it appear to have been York, which he reached in March and where he finally made sure of the support of archbishop Neville, Cheshire and north Wales (visited in July) and Shrewsbury and Nottingham (in August). The excuse put forward for the visit to the north-west was con-

[1] See the patriotic ecstasies of Walsingham in *Hist. Anglic.* ii, 153–6; he assigns some of the credit to the duke of Gloucester's enthusiasm and organising power.

[2] *Hist. Anglic. loc. cit.*

[3] *D.N.B. sub nom.* He retained two pensions; one from the crown, one from John of Gaunt.

[4] *Chapters*, iii, 418.   [5] Jolliffe, *op. cit.* p. 470.

[6] There is an interesting attempt to reconstruct it in detail in Tout, *Chapters*, iii, 418–20.

nected with de Vere's new duchy of Ireland, for which Chester was to be the point of departure, but the real reason undoubtedly had to do with the military preparations which de Vere, with Richard's connivance and encouragement, was already beginning to direct not against Ireland but against England. The council at Shrewsbury, held on the 21st of August, was the occasion of the first of Richard's two famous consultations of the justices about his legal position, but it was here too, according to Walsingham,[1] that he sounded the sheriffs, or some of them whom he had summoned for the purpose, about the possibility of raising the shires in his favour and, perhaps, of influencing the next parliamentary elections. The sheriffs, whose appointments in the previous autumn appear to have been entirely non-political,[2] returned unsatisfactory answers[3]—a thing Richard was not to forget and would provide against in his second "tyranny"; he was already beginning to learn from experience. Meanwhile, in the more famous council at Nottingham a week later, he caused to be repeated the questions which the justices had already been asked at Shrewsbury, and M. Perroy has recently shown[4] that this is also the approximate date to which we must attribute certain efforts made by Richard, on the respectable analogies of John, Henry III and Edward I, to win over the pope.

It is a matter of some interest to enquire how far these systematic travels in the summer of 1387 were really successful. The consultation of the sheriffs may have yielded no immediate results, but there are scraps of evidence which point in a different direction. The Monk of Westminster, for instance, repeats a story[5] of a royal *claviger* enlisting reservists with silver and gilded crowns in Norfolk, Suffolk, Essex and Cambridge.

[1] *Hist. Anglic.* ii, 161. [2] See my article in *C.A.S. Proc. loc. cit.*
[3] Cf. H. G. Richardson, *Bull. John Rylands Library*, April 1938, p. 43; he thinks the answers "apocryphal", but believes that they "reflect the obvious truth that even the king could not influence elections if he wished to strengthen himself in a quarrel with the magnates which he was not certain to win".
[4] *Schisme*, pp. 52–207. [5] p. 94.

He was arrested, no doubt by order of the commission, and there is no mention of any other similar agent, but as in the case of the sheriffs the abortive effort of 1387 becomes the fully thought-out system of 1398 and for that reason alone is worth mentioning. Active levies, as distinct from reservists, there is still less evidence for, though apropos of 1387 Tout repeats[1] a favourite charge made by Richard's enemies at the end of his reign, that he was aiming at a military despotism based on Cheshire, Wales and Ireland. It is fantastic to suppose that Richard raised, or ever could have raised, any troops worth having from Ireland, but even at this early date there is perhaps some substance in the charge as regards Cheshire and north Wales. Thus Tout has drawn attention[2] to the consolidation of de Vere's position as justice of Chester on the 8th of September 1387 and as justice of north Wales two months later, while there is the undoubted fact that de Vere did at that time raise an army in Cheshire, as the king himself notoriously did in after years—an army which on this occasion was decisively beaten by de Vere's fellow-magnates before the year was up at Radcot Bridge. Further than this, we have the very probably true assertion of the Monk of Westminster,[3] a not unfriendly authority, that Richard himself, even at this early date, brought back with him from this region the nucleus of that bodyguard of Cheshire archers and Welsh pikemen which is so famous later in the reign. Nor must we forget the extremely efficient chamber knights and squires under Burley and Raddington, of whom Burley at least appears to have been with the king, so that by the autumn of 1387 the red and white colours of Richard may have clothed at least the embryo of a royal military force quite apart from de Vere's levies, even though there was as yet no livery of the white hart and, which is even more important, no money to retain these forces for long.

For in 1387 the absence of an administration and the financial means to maintain an administration was Richard's fatal deficiency. He had in effect only his immediate household with him and this was quite inadequate in view of the traditional

<hr>

[1] *Chapters*, iii, 421.   [2] *Ibid.*   [3] *Loc. cit.*

hostility which household methods of government now aroused. Secretary Medford and his slighted signet were a poor substitute for the great and privy seals; there was again no real financial organisation possible for the royalists, except for the now helpless clerks of the wardrobe. The "council" with Richard could consist only of the steward, the vice-chamberlain and what bishops, lords and judges the king could momentarily attract to it on special occasions, notably at Shrewsbury and Nottingham. Even pope Urban seems to have realised something of the essential weakness of Richard's position, judging from the comparative failure of royalist intrigues at the papal curia that summer.[1] Nothing was really left to Richard except his legal rights.

These, on the other hand, were of the highest importance to him, both then and later, and the exchange of question and answer with his justices deserves detailed examination. At Shrewsbury there seem to have been present from the king's bench Tresilian, then sole justice of that bench; from the common bench Bealknap (chief justice), Holt and Burgh, and from the exchequer chief baron Cary. Little is known of this interview or why a second one was necessary at Nottingham, but a possible explanation is that the king's questions were propounded on the first occasion, held over for a week, and then formally repeated so that considered answers might be given. There was, however, one important change in personnel between the two meetings, which militates to some extent against this theory; at Nottingham upon the 25th of August Fulthorp of the common bench replaced Cary.

The gist of the ten questions[2] prepared for Richard by one of

[1] Perroy, *Schisme*, pp. 301–3.
[2] (1) Was the late commission derogatory to the royal prerogative?
   (2) How should those be punished who procured its appointment?
   (3) And those who incited the king to consent to it?
   (4) And those who constrained him to have it appointed?
   (5) And those who in general interfere with the royal prerogative?
   (6) Ought parliament to discuss first the matters defined by the king, or those determined on by themselves?
   (7) Can the king dissolve parliament at his pleasure?

his serjeants-at-law lies in the main point whether or no the commission had impeded him in the exercise of his prerogative and whether it was therefore treasonable. The reply was categoric, in the sense that all the judges gave the answers expected of them, though according to Knighton,[1] Bealknap at least had to be forced to do so; the fact that they all[2] claimed to have answered under duress when on trial for their lives a year later is of little significance, since there is no evidence that they were actually in danger in 1387 and no doubt that they were in very grave danger, from the other side, in 1388. Apart from this Wallon[3] has suggested that there is other reason to doubt that the original answers were given under constraint. Thus the rolls of parliament[4] show that the questions and answers were the same at both Shrewsbury and Nottingham, but in that case if the justices were successfully constrained at Shrewsbury, what need was there to constrain them again at Nottingham? If, on the other hand, they answered freely at Shrewsbury there can have been no need to constrain them to make the same answers a week later. Altogether it would seem probable, though by no means certain, that the justices answered freely in the first instance, and that the replies were so unexpectedly favourable that, for the sake of added weight and solemnity, and possibly also to evade the charge that they had not had time to consider their judgment, they were invited to repeat their opinion at Nottingham. But if the justices' answers were not, in Taswell-Langmead's phrase, "servile", were they "sanguinary" and

(8) Should the king, or should parliament, punish justices and other royal officials?

(9) How should he be punished who moved for the production of the statute relating to the deposition of Edward II?

(10) Whether the judgment on the earl of Suffolk was wrong and revocable?

The questions are given in detail by the Monk of Westminster, pp. 99–101, and by other chroniclers. See also Lodge and Thornton, *op. cit.* pp. 25–6.

[1] ii, 237.

[2] With the exception of Tresilian, who had already been condemned and executed.

[3] i, 327.   [4] iii, 238.

"unconstitutional for the most part, even as the constitution was then understood"?

We must, of course, in the first place be very chary of using the words "constitution" and "constitutional" with reference to the fourteenth century; they imply a degree of self-conscious theorising and a rigidity of institutional growth which had not yet been attained, and their terminology in any case is that of a later age. As Mr Lapsley has said,[1] "there was no constitution to be broken [in 1341], only precedents pointing in different directions"; and it may be doubted whether what was true of 1341 is not almost equally true of 1387, or even of 1399. It is, none the less, legitimate to ask, as Tout does,[2] whether the view now accepted by the justices was not in fact a new and more extreme view of the royal prerogative and more explicitly stated than it had ever been before. Such an interpretation seems, however, very hard to maintain, for while it may be admitted that the joint opinion of the justices overrides the precedents of Edward III's last years and Richard's own minority it can hardly be said to be in conflict with the general policy and claims of any previous king of England and, as Miss Clarke has pointed out,[3] it merely repeats and amplifies the views of the prerogative put forward by Gaunt in 1377. Tout is on still weaker ground in holding that the opinion, whether freely given or not, was clean contrary to "parliamentary supremacy and the idea of law", for if by the first part of the phrase is meant the idea of parliament as a separate institution being ultimately supreme over (among other things) the crown as a separate institution, it is highly doubtful whether any contemporary could have accepted either the separation or the supremacy,[4] while the latter part of the phrase—"the idea of law"—is so general as to have little meaning apart from the

[1] *E.H.R.* xxx, 215.
[2] *Chapters*, iii, 424. Chrimes, *English Constitutional Ideas in the Fifteenth Century*, p. 42, agrees with him.
[3] *Op. cit.* p. 52.
[4] Cf. B. Wilkinson, "The Deposition of Richard II and the Accession of Henry IV", *E.H.R.* liv, 215–39.

anachronistic parliamentary content that has just been given to it.

The fact is that the famous opinion represented little more than a royalist reaction against the aristocratic encroachments of the previous fifteen years, and the main point is surely that Richard took the trouble to get a legal opinion at all; a notable alliance was in fact being attempted between the crown, the rudimentary "civil service" and the common lawyers against the aristocracy's general strike. "The rule of law", whatever that may have meant precisely at the time, was as much on the king's side as anybody's; he had older and more numerous precedents. This is still true, even though it may be admitted that Professor Tait is right in pointing out[1] that "so uncompromising an assertion of royal prerogative was bad policy" at that particular moment, that it prematurely drove Richard's opponents to bay and rallied the commons around them.[2] The reason for this, however, lies much less in the general nature of the opinion than in the fact that it represented an attempt to go behind the very narrow definition of treason—a definition which deliberately excluded the offence of "accroaching the royal power"—contained in the carefully drafted treason statute,[3] aimed at general appeasement in 1352. Here again at first sight it may seem "unconstitutional" for the king's justices deliberately to disregard a thirty-five year old statute of the realm but, as Chrimes has pointed out,[4] "the modern doctrine of the absolute authority of statutes does not appear until the very end of the fifteenth century",[5] and in any case the justices were merely finding a true bill for a treason trial,[6] not passing sentence. There seems therefore on all counts to have been

[1] D.N.B. "Richard II".

[2] Mr Lapsley agrees that throughout his whole reign this was Richard's most typical mistake.

[3] Lodge and Thornton, op. cit. pp. 21–2.   [4] Op. cit. p. 49.

[5] Professor Plucknett would put the transition from free to strict interpretation a century earlier (Concise History of the Common Law, pp. 294 ff., summarising his own Statutes and their Interpretations in the Fourteenth Century). But see Chrimes, op. cit. p. 290.

[6] Wallon, op. cit. i, 504.

nothing remarkable in their decision if allowance be made for the extreme recency of parliamentary-aristocratic precedents,[1] for the natural conservatism of common lawyers and for the relatively small respect felt by fourteenth-century justices for the letter of statute law.

But at the same time it cannot be sufficiently emphasised that whatever sort of a case can be built up in theory for Richard's action, the whole episode was a political mistake of the first magnitude and has furnished a handle for his enemies ever since. He does seem, it is true, to have made some attempt to keep the story of the two interviews from the commission for the time being, but it was almost immediately betrayed to the duke of Gloucester by one of the witnesses, Robert Wickford, archbishop of Dublin[2]—a fact which seems to have done more than anything else to put an end to the comparative moderation which the commission had so far shown, and to precipitate a civil war and a proscription. The reason for the alarm felt by the magnates when Wickford's report reached them lies precisely in the fact already mentioned, that the original statute of treasons had been part of the compromise effected by Edward III between the great men and the crown; it was, moreover, retrospective, put an end to all the attaints and forfeitures of Edward II's reign, settled the present title of such men as the earl of Arundel himself, whose forbears had been implicated in rebellion, and finally defined treason so narrowly for the future, even private war being excluded as well as "accroaching" the royal power, that it had come to seem an offence hardly ever likely to recur.[3] Thus in all the troubles of the past fifteen years the dangerous word *treason*, with all that it implied of forfeiture, hanging, quartering, disembowelling and attainted blood, had not been used on either side, and indeed, or so it was hoped,

[1] Cf. Jolliffe, *op. cit.* p. 431 n.; the next year the commons were to claim that the twelve-year old process of impeachment was among the "ancient ordinances and liberties of parliament".

[2] Monk of Westminster, p. 103.

[3] For a discussion of the whole subject see Miss Clarke's admirable essay in *Fourteenth Century Studies*, pp. 115–45.

could not lightly be used or bandied about any more. Yet here was Richard going back on that in 1387, and with judicial authority; indirectly threatening the very title of some magnates to the lands they held and reintroducing for all of them the old uncertainty and danger. It is hardly surprising that the leaders of the opposition, whose consciences may in any case have been none too clear, felt that the days of *sauve qui peut* had returned and that it was essential to get in the first blow.

Thus when, early in November 1387, Richard had come back to the neighbourhood of London there is little doubt that it was the leaders of the opposition who took the first steps towards war. The duke of Gloucester and the earl of Arundel rejected an invitation to meet the king at Westminster and, together with the earl of Warwick, raised a small private army, which by the middle of the month they had concentrated at Waltham Cross.[1] Walsingham justifies this action of the leading magnates by what Tout calls "a campaign of mendacity ... against the king's supporters"[2]—a campaign which probably reflects the excuses put forward by the rebels at the time. He begins by saying that in any case Richard had been the first to try to raise troops, even if he had met with no success, and hints that this alone would have justified baronial action. The charge is probably a conflation of the stories circulating about de Vere's levies in Lancashire, Cheshire and north Wales and the unhappy *claviger* in East Anglia with the undoubted fact of certain advances made by Richard to the Londoners, advances which had not yet been decisively rejected. There is therefore some truth in it, but not much, because Richard does not seem to have brought any of de Vere's levies south with him or to have realised that he needed an armed force until he found himself opposed by one.[3]

Secondly, and somewhat inconsistently, Gloucester at least is represented as being still conciliatory at heart, but the earl of

---

[1] Walsingham (*Hist. Anglic.* ii, 163) includes Derby as raising troops, which is probably correct, but he was not with the other three at Waltham Cross.   [2] *Chapters*, ii, 425 n.

[3] *Rex vero stupefactus*, Monk of Westminster, p. 106.

Suffolk is said to have deliberately inflamed Richard's relations with him[1]—a statement which seems most improbable on all counts. The Monk of Westminster adds to it[2] the still wilder story that de la Pole simultaneously advised Richard to assassinate the earl of Warwick, perhaps the least dangerous of his immediate enemies; and Walsingham returns to the charge with a similar story about Richard trying first to arrest and then to murder Arundel.[3] The significance of all three legends is obviously that they put the king in the wrong and provide the best possible excuse for the action taken by the duke and the two earls.

Turning to wider issues, Walsingham then accuses Richard of planning to bargain with the French, on the pretext of a pilgrimage to Canterbury, for the sale of Calais, Guines and other English possessions overseas, presumably in return for help against the rebels.[4] Elsewhere[5] he claims that a messenger was actually taken by the patriot lords at the end of 1387 together with a document proving the whole story and that Gloucester was thus enabled to prevent Richard going. The Monk of Westminster repeats the story,[6] though in a more innocent form; he says nothing about the pilgrimage to Canterbury and emphasises the fact that Richard was to keep Aquitaine at the price of doing homage for it, while the object of the negotiations was simply to effect economies which would make a reduction in taxation possible. However, all these incoherencies are probably no more than echoes of previous gossip about foreign policy more than a year old; similar charges were made during the last years of the reign and need hardly be taken seriously, since no fourteenth-century English government could afford to give up Calais or ever seriously contemplated doing so.[7]

[1] *Hist. Anglic.* ii, 162–3.   [2] p. 105.   [3] *Loc. cit.* pp. 163–4.
[4] *Loc. cit.*   [5] *Hist. Anglic.* ii, 170.   [6] p. 103.
[7] Tout, *Chapters*, iii, 425, quoting *Hist. Anglic.* ii, 159–60, also connects with this first fortnight in November 1387 the charges of Lollardy against the king's household knights inserted by Walsingham a little earlier in his narrative. These have been rebutted in detail by W. T. Waugh, *Scottish Hist. Rev.* xi, 55–92.

These passages in the chronicles probably reflect contemporary special pleading designed to excuse Gloucester, Warwick and Arundel for having taken the initiative and forced the king's hand. There is little doubt that Richard was taken by surprise and temporarily helpless, and on top of this the propaganda of his enemies was so effective that the moderate majority on the commission, hitherto not ill-disposed, now forced him to receive the rebel leaders, together with a substantial bodyguard, at Westminster (November the 17th), while by the end of December, if not earlier, the Londoners had also changed sides and definitely refused to help him.

Meanwhile, archbishop Neville, de Vere, Suffolk, Tresilian and Brembre had been formally appealed of treason by Gloucester, Warwick and Arundel (not as yet by Derby and Nottingham) on two separate occasions, once at a preliminary meeting with the commission at Waltham Cross on the 14th of November, and again before the king at Westminster on the 17th. This was their real reply to the opinion of the justices; if the old, lax conception of treason were going to be revived, it was vital for them to make the first use of it, and now they had caught the king by surprise and had succeeded in doing so. The question none the less arises why the appellants, as they may now be called, followed Richard in raising this cry of treason which they could not legally maintain, instead of merely referring the justices to the statute of 1352, or alternatively, if they were going to ignore that statute themselves, why they did not get it legally repealed, as they could undoubtedly have done, by forcing Richard to call a parliament.

The most satisfactory answer to this problem has recently been put forward by Miss Clarke.[1] In the first place the narrow statutory definition of treason was of advantage to the magnates in ordinary times as individuals, since if it protected the king's ministers against them it also protected the magnates against the king. Secondly, the narrow definition was of advantage to them as lords whose tenants were constantly getting into the

[1] *Loc. cit.*

sort of trouble, notably private war, which before this statute was made might have been construed as treason to the crown; the point being that a subtenant convicted of treason lost all his lands and goods for ever to the king, while one convicted merely of felony lost them only for a year and a day to the king, after which they reverted to the immediate lord. The statute of 1352 had therefore much to commend it on general grounds as long as crown and magnates were on good terms, but it was awkward in a crisis when there were in the air charges of treason which could hardly be substantiated within the narrow terms of this statute. Thus to invoke the statute in 1387 would no doubt have protected the appellants—it depends on how much weight parliament, if summoned, would have attached to the opinion of the justices—but it would have given them no power of aggression against the king's advisers. At the same time the appellants were unwilling to get it repealed owing to its value in normal times and also owing to the fact, already mentioned, that the whole status of Arundel and others as peers of the realm depended on the retrospective action of the statute in condoning certain offences of their ancestors committed between 1321 and 1331.

Hence the statute was simply ignored by both sides in 1387–8, but it remained a submerged obstacle which accounts for the mysterious surface swirl of political currents in this period. More, this single fact alone—and, as will be seen, there are other facts—is enough to discredit the theories found in many histories about the working out of the doctrine of the supremacy of parliament in 1388 in answer to the supposedly new royalist theory of the justices in 1387. In place of this alleged constitutional development we are left simply with a group of puzzled and vindictive men, anxious to recover their powerful position in the state by somehow convicting the king's friends of treason, statute or no statute, and, what is more, if possible without reference to parliament at all.

The truth of the last statement becomes clear when we consider the nature of the original appeal. Thus it was almost

certainly the intention of the first three appellants[1] to lodge
their appeal in the household court of the constable and
marshal of England, known as the *curia militaris*; the duke of
Gloucester, in particular, happened to be constable himself at
that date and had written a treatise on his duties, which he is
known to have taken very seriously. This may be seen from the
fact that "appeals of treason" were unknown to the common
law, whereas in the *curia militaris* suits were commonly begun
by appeal, whether of treason or other offences, conducted
according to the civil (or Roman) law and, if the evidence was
thought insufficient, settled by the judicial battle.

Richard's answer to the appeal, on the other hand, was to
make his first really intelligent move in the whole crisis by
referring the matter to parliament. This had the immediate
effect of gaining time, for the magnates dared not reject the
reference, and it is a fact that during the ensuing interval
archbishop Neville and de la Pole were able to escape abroad[2]
while de Vere and his private army were given a chance of
rescuing the king. Besides this, there was another chance—that
parliament might not be hostile. Richard, as the event proved,
had some supporters in the lords, and as regards the commons
the first writs he issued (on the 17th of December) particularly
laid down that the members returned were to be *in debatis
modernis magis indifferentes*; he could not foresee that the
appellants would force him to cancel these writs, which in any
case might not have been very effective without previous
preparation of the shrievalty, and that the temper of the
commons would in fact be what it afterwards became. Meanwhile, de Vere was in arms and marching down the Severn
valley.

According to the Monk of Westminster[3] the first thought of
the magnates, when news came of de Vere's rising, was to

[1] They were only joined by the earls of Derby and Nottingham somewhat later, when de Vere had levied private war against them.

[2] Tresilian concealed himself in Westminster, while Brembre remained
openly in London, where he boldly continued to work for Richard's cause
until arrested at the end of the year.   [3] pp. 109–10.

dethrone Richard outright; he adds that Warwick stoutly resisted this proposal and persuaded them, which was only common sense, to begin by making certain of defeating de Vere. The story is not improbable in itself but for the mention of Warwick as the leading figure; Derby is much more probable. As Wallon points out,[1] he as Gaunt's son stood to gain nothing by the substitution of his uncle for his cousin on the throne, nor could he claim it for himself while his father was alive, and the line attributed to the rather dim figure of Warwick is just the line one would have expected Derby to take. It is quite clear at any rate that both he and the earl of Nottingham were now shocked for perhaps the first time into active support of the appellants, subsequently associating themselves with their appeal, and it was actually Derby, and not Warwick, who played a decisive part in the ensuing campaign.

The campaign itself has been brilliantly reconstructed from the conflicting accounts in the chronicles by Mr J. N. L. Myres,[2] who describes how de Vere, in his attempt to pass from the Severn to the upper Thames, marched with all his usual incompetence into a trap neatly laid for him at Radcot Bridge. He himself managed to escape, and ultimately to leave England, but the entire army on which Richard had relied was hopelessly dispersed. Adam of Usk, then teaching at Oxford, describes[3] how he saw the army of the appellants march triumphantly through Oxford on their way to London after this battle; they were headed by Warwick and Derby, Gloucester leading the main body, and Arundel and Nottingham the rearguard. On their arrival they encamped at Clerkenwell, while Richard took refuge in the Tower.

From this point onwards the conduct of the opposition was frankly revolutionary, for since the legal expiry of the commission's powers on the 19th of November the appellants' action had become simply an exercise of superior force.[4] No

---

[1] *Op. cit.* i, 338.
[2] *E.H.R.* xlii, 20–33.
[3] *Chronicle*, ed. E. M. Thompson, pp. 5–6.
[4] Wallon, *op. cit.* i, 329.

notice was taken of the legal expiry of the commission and from
the 31st of December acts of state were warranted *per concilium*,
which in fact meant warranty by the defunct commission,
while at least one member, the now renegade Skirlaw, was
added to it by the appellants without any authority whatever.[1]
They were, however, determined to regularise their position
in one way or another, in parliament or out of it, and their
partially successful efforts to conceal the revolution which
was taking place distort the history of the ensuing year.

[1] Tout, *Chapters*, iii, 428.

CHAPTER VI

The Appellants

THE battle of Radcot Bridge merely set the seal of successful violence, or successful opposition to violence, on the mastery which the appellants had already asserted at Westminster. This mastery is first seen in relation to London, but it was quickly extended to the coming parliament and the remaining fragments of curialist administration. London, thanks to Brembre, had received Richard tolerably well in the autumn of 1387 and had promised him, if not active support, at least protection.[1] But the propaganda of the opposition lords,[2] in conjunction with resentment at de Vere's rising, had taken effect, and during December majority opinion in the city passed rapidly from a neutrality friendly to Richard to a fairly close alliance with the appellants; they for their part naturally did all they could to keep the non-victualling gilds opposed to Brembre in power. Thus there exists the record[3] of an explanation made by the lords to the citizens in the Guildhall on their arrival at Clerkenwell, while in January 1388 came an attempt on their part, also in the Guildhall,[4] to reconcile the quarrels of the crafts. The fruit of this policy is seen in the use made of the London gilds during Brembre's trial before the merciless parliament, but apart from that use, which had probably not been anticipated, it was of course vital for the appellants to obtain the support of London; Richard had taken refuge in the Tower, and with the help of the Londoners, if that had been available, might have defied his enemies until their rather unstable coalition had broken down.

The final purge of the administration, which accompanied these measures, was preceded by yet another renewal of the

[1] Monk of Westminster, p. 104.

[2] Knighton, ii, 246–7, records a very interesting letter which they addressed to the Londoners.

[3] Monk of Westminster, p. 114.   [4] *Ibid.* p. 117.

appeal, made on the 28th or 29th of December in the king's presence in the Tower; it is interesting for a sidelight it throws on the policy of Derby and also because for the first time all five appellants took part. On this occasion, according to the Monk of Westminster,[1] Richard was not only invited to surrender the "traitors" but definitely threatened with deposition. Knighton does not mention this but does say[2] that the king was persuaded to submit by Derby, who drew him to the window and showed him the mob of appellant supporters outside. He adds that Derby and Nottingham subsequently stayed the night with Richard at his own request[3] and that the arrests were made next day, though he appears to put these events a day or two too early. Galbraith and Clarke[4] go further, and by combining a note in the continuation to Higden's *Polychronicon* with Gloucester's confession, made in 1397, and with hints in other chronicles, such as Favent's, arrive at the conclusion that Richard may have actually been "deposed", whatever that may mean exactly, in the Tower for the last three days of December, but was restored again by the 1st of January owing to the protests of Derby and Nottingham, with the result that the whole affair was afterwards hushed up. However this may be, the whole episode clearly illustrates the middle course pursued by Derby at this date; it was, as has already been suggested, obviously not to his interest that Gloucester should go to such extremes against Richard while Gaunt was out of England and, it may be added, while the fourth earl of March, another possible heir to the throne, was alive.

Meanwhile the arrests to which Richard undoubtedly consented went far beyond the five chief victims, four of whom had already escaped. The Monk of Westminster[5] gives a fairly complete list; it includes Simon Burley, whose office of vice-

---

[1] p. 109.   [2] ii, 256.

[3] Walsingham, *Historia Anglicana*, ii, 172, agrees, omitting Nottingham.

[4] "Deposition of Richard II", reprinted in M. V. Clarke, *Fourteenth Century Studies*, pp. 53–98.

[5] pp. 115–16. Cf. Tout, *Chapters*, iii, 428–30.

chamberlain was left vacant, the steward, Sir John Beauchamp, who was replaced by Sir John Devereux, a member of the commission, and the justices who had appeared at Shrewsbury and Nottingham. Six of these were deprived and later sentenced and two new chief justices were appointed, Clopton for the king's bench and Charlton for the common bench; by the end of April there was also a new chief baron of the exchequer. Besides this, the chamber lost a number of knights and minor officers, such as Berners and Salisbury, while others, such as Aubrey de Vere, the uncle of the duke of Ireland, and Abberbury, though not arrested, were driven from the court. Peter Courtenay's appointment as the new chamberlain,[1] in place of Robert de Vere, seems to have been a concession, since he was agreeable to the king. Finally an attack was made on a number of confidential king's clerks; Medford, the keeper of the signet, was arrested and the office of secretary left vacant, while bishop Rushook, Richard's confessor, Nicholas Slake, the dean of his chapel, and Richard Clifford, one of his chaplains, were also taken into custody. This concludes the list of changes in the administration, but what was not changed is almost equally significant; thus there were no changes in the wardrobes, which appear to have lost all political importance by this date, and no changes in the three great offices of state with the sole exception of John Lincoln, one of the chamberlains of the receipt of the exchequer, who was arrested apparently because he had been present at Nottingham during the summer. The reason for this moderation is to be found in the fact that Richard had not ventured to attack the great officials nominated in 1386, and the permanent staffs, apart from John Lincoln, appear to have become largely non-political.

The stage was now set for the great scene, namely the merciless parliament, which sat from the 3rd of February to the 4th of June 1388. Its session marked the culmination of the first great crisis of the reign and as such the main authorities on which our knowledge of it depends need some words of criticism and appreciation, but before dealing with them it may be as well to

[1] Monk of Westminster, p. 178.

consider the composition of the parliament and the theory that it may have been packed in one interest or the other.

It has already been suggested that the idea of calling a parliament at all to settle the questions in dispute originated with Richard and not with the appellants; it is therefore to the crown that we must look in the first instance for any attempt at packing, and here the little evidence available seems at first sight to suggest, not that Richard packed, but that he made certain efforts to avoid packing by the other side. Thus, as regards the lords, it is clear that all the magnates of any party, including the accused, had been summoned; it was an exceptionally well-attended parliament, and in what follows it is noticeable that the lords, taken as a unit, are on the whole comparatively moderate in tone. As regards the commons, the only possible packers could have been the local magnates and the sheriffs, and it is very difficult to say how far either force could have been widely successful in such an aim in 1388. There is some evidence that a few knights friendly to, or in the pay of, the appellants were returned, but probably not in sufficient numbers to affect the whole assembly, and there appears to have been no special interest taken by any great man in the boroughs, such as is found in the fifteenth century. For packing on the king's part some preparation of the shrievalty, such as actually did take place in the late autumn of 1397, though its object cannot then have been parliamentary,[1] would have been required, but there is no evidence whatsoever that Richard or anyone else effected any manipulations of this kind in the shrieval appointments of the autumn of 1387.[2] All he did was to issue the famous writs asking for the return of knights *in debatis modernis magis indifferentes*, which suggests that he had taken no precautions himself and was perhaps afraid that the other side had taken theirs. It was the appellants who forced him to cancel these writs, which were unprecedented in form, and issue new ones of a normal nature on the 1st of

---

[1] Because the "special" sheriffs were not appointed until *after* Richard's last parliament had met—a point which Tout misses.

[2] See my article in *C.A.S. Proc.* xxxvi, 1–34.

January, and although this may help to explain the subsequent temper of the commons it does not necessarily follow that while the king was pleading for impartiality the magnates were influencing the elections, for, as Mr H. G. Richardson has shown,[1] there was a long-standing tradition that the county court's freedom of choice, if it wished to exercise it even in an apparently partisan direction, should be respected. The implication is that there may have been a genuinely hostile feeling towards the court among the minor gentry and perhaps some burgesses in 1388—a feeling for which it is much more difficult to account at that time than in 1399 but which cannot merely be explained away by any facile assumptions of "packing". For the whole trend of modern research, notably that of Mr H. G. Richardson, suggests that "packing" in the later sense was as unknown as the word itself in the fourteenth century, and the unrestricted use of it is yet another instance of the unfortunate effects achieved by importing into the Middle Ages practices and terms which belong in fact to later history.

The record of what was actually done in this parliament, packed or unpacked, depends chiefly on the incomplete and partisan parliament roll,[2] which appears to have been copied and circulated after the event as appellant propaganda, to be inserted in brief in several chronicles. But there are also certain other sources of value, notably a political pamphlet, written by an eyewitness, Thomas Favent,[3] and also some additional material, put together from an independent standpoint and added to the long and rather confused account given by the Monk of Westminster.[4] Thomas Favent was probably a clerk in the diocese of Salisbury, or perhaps a member[5] of the household of an appellant magnate, it is not known which. Miss McKisack in the introduction to her edition has made out a good case for the theory that his pamphlet was written almost immediately after the rising of the merciless parliament, whose proceedings

---

[1] "The Parliamentary Representation of Lancashire", *Bull. John Rylands Library*, vol. xxii.   [2] *Rot. Parl.* iii, 228–56.

[3] Edited by M. McKisack, *Camden Miscellany*, vol. xiv.

[4] pp. 118–83.   [5] Tout, *Collected Papers*, ii, 173–90.

it exalts and justifies, insisting on their legality and "fullness". The new matter in it is mostly detail of secondary importance, but the parliament is described with a vividness which perhaps surpasses even that of the *Anonimalle Chronicle's* account of the Good Parliament,[1] and furthermore the mere existence of this pamphlet, taken in conjunction with the undoubted priming of the other chronicles, is of interest for, as Tout has shown,[2] it betrays a consciousness of what might now be called a "public opinion", which is something new in England, together with a developed sense of the kind of propaganda necessary to foster and control it.

The Monk of Westminster, however, is the most valuable of the chroniclers of the merciless parliament, and this for two reasons. He is the least biased, and he adds to his own very full account the contents of an anonymous French pamphlet, which was probably written for the occasion and contains special information of its own about the trials, notably Brembre's. On the other hand a careful reading of his own rambling recapitulation of the whole affair makes it clear that he was left bewildered by the story of what was done in 1388. He has no considered or digested view of his own but, though he sets it all down, he is evidently not quite convinced by the appellant propaganda against a king whose affection for the church, particularly the monastic house of Westminster, was so well known and whose policy towards the Lollards and questions of sanctuary, then very acute, was so sound. Accordingly, he seems to have some sense that there is a flaw somewhere in the appellant case, though he cannot put his finger on it. It is unfortunate that the one contemporary[3] who had the

[1] Favent has long been known in the rough translation of 1641, which however was represented as being an original composition of the time of Charles I with application principally to the politics of that day. In this dress it deceived Wallon and other historians of Richard II. The importance of Miss McKisack's discovery of the original Latin text is to show that, though still propaganda, it is at least a contemporary piece of propaganda and that its detail can be trusted more than at one time used to be believed.

[2] *Loc. cit.*

[3] Contrast Walsingham (*Hist. Anglic.* ii, 173–5), who adds nothing in his very short account and is wholeheartedly hostile to the court.

will, and perhaps the opportunity, to find out the truth about the events of 1388 either had not the courage or had not the intellectual power to do so. Even so, we can to some extent read between the lines.

The parliament met on the 3rd of February 1388 in the White Hall of Westminster palace, and this time there was no question about the king's personal presence, as there had been in 1386. Favent gives a vivid picture of the scene—the king on his throne, the higher clergy on his right, the lay magnates (excluding the appellants) on his left and the chancellor, bishop Arundel, sitting on the woolsack in the centre with his back to the throne. Then came the dramatic moment: the doors were flung open and, triumphant in cloth of gold,[1] the five appellant lords marched arm in arm into the hall, as if to emphasise that unity which they did not possess. After a brief speech by the chancellor the appellant case was opened by Sir Robert Pleasington, a former chief baron of the exchequer who had been deposed in favour of Cary in 1386; he declared their innocence of treason and renewed the appeal on their behalf. It is probably at this point that we should insert some prefatory words in Knighton's version,[2] to the effect that the commons' action was primarily directed against certain general wrongs done to the realm, to wit that law had been unequally administered and extortion practised, that taxes had been unfairly assessed and the proceeds not spent as the grantors had intended and that the national defences had been allowed to fall into a state of decay and insufficiency. Redress was therefore demanded before it was too late to apply a remedy, and this redress was to be something as follows. In the first place right and justice were to be administered to the poor as well as to the rich. Secondly, the honour of the crown was to be upheld through the provision of better advisers, by whose counsel the taxation that was ruining the country and the intolerable expenses of the war might be respectively remitted and diminished. Thirdly, a small

[1] Cloth of gold was apparently the orthodox attire for magnates; one of Gaveston's offences had been the wearing of the royal purple instead of cloth of gold.
[2] ii, 266–70.

commission with wide powers was demanded to carry out these measures; so would the crown be honoured and the people kept in peace. It is, of course, possible that the whole of this passage, which is just as appropriate to the situation as it existed in 1386, has been transferred by Knighton in error from the annals of that year but, if not, the demand made by the appellants at the outset for another commission is most significant of their ideal of government.

Next a clerk of the crown,[1] Geoffrey Martin, a civil servant of long standing who had hitherto played no part in politics, read aloud in French the preamble and thirty-nine articles of the appeal itself. Most of these related to the events of 1387 only. Thus the youth of the king had been taken advantage of (1-4) by bad advisers, who were also personally corrupt (5-7, 10, 13, 23). Special attention was drawn to the regal position bestowed upon de Vere in Ireland (11) without either Irish or English consent. Furthermore, the king's advisers were not only incompetent (8) in the matter of national defence but were ready for positive treachery (29-32). At home they had tried to keep the king from attending parliament (16) and council (i.e. the commission) (21) appointed for his own and for the nation's good (17), and they had persuaded him to take legal opinion against the council (18, 25, 27). They had also perverted the law in other ways (9, 12), de Vere being specially guilty as justice of Chester (22). They had retained reservists (19, 20), developed the military side of the household (24) and tampered with the loyalty of London (33-5). They had also led the king to appoint special sheriffs in order to pack the commons

[1] See Tout, *Chapters*, iii, 444, for a full account of this clerkship, also of the clerkships of parliament and of the commons. (There was more than one clerk of the crown.) These clerks were all drawn from chancery, and from about this date tend to take their political colour more and more from the head of their department, the chancellor of the day. Hence it is not surprising to find that Geoffrey Martin, although originally connected with the Black Prince, like Burley and other royalists, was something of a hero to Favent and was rewarded with grants from the earl of Suffolk's forfeitures by the Cambridge parliament later in the year—so was the clerk of the commons.

(36).[1] They had plotted against the duke of Lancaster (*sic*) and other nobles (26), had injured many patriotic magnates (14, 15, 28) and had finally brought about civil war in the military operations of de Vere (37–9). Hence the archbishop of York, the earl of Suffolk, de Vere, Tresilian and Brembre were formally appealed of treason, for the fourth and last time.

The influence of the earl of Derby may perhaps be seen in certain articles of the appeal, first and foremost in the correct attitude adopted towards Richard himself. Suffolk, de Vere and the archbishop of York were specially accused of having "degraded the royal prerogative" by making the king swear to obey their orders, although in fact the coronation oath was the only oath he should take and he ought to be "free-er" than his subjects. This fiction of bad advice was now consistently kept up and there was no hint of attempted deposition. Secondly, but more doubtfully, the same influence may be seen in the rather absurd reference to the absent Lancaster, to which however the obscure events of 1384–5 may possibly have lent some colour. This reference may have been intended to keep Gaunt out of the way, should any news reach him, by suggesting both that he himself was or had been in personal danger and that his cause was none the less being loyally upheld. It may also have been meant to rally the still considerable Lancastrian interests in the country to the appellant cause, much as Richard attempted to rally them eleven years later after the great sequestration by specifically renewing the numerous grants and pensions to retainers with which the estates were charged. Apart from these speculations the articles of the appeal of 1388 have little interest; they represent some clever special pleading, which made the most that could be made out of the rebel magnates' case, but that is all. The only entirely baseless ones were probably nos. 8, 26 (perhaps) and 29–32, and even these were good propaganda for the age.

[1] This charge has already been examined and dismissed, *ante*, pp. 144–5. For a detailed discussion of the evidence see my article in the *C.A.S. Proc. loc. cit.*

N.B. The numbering of the articles has been taken from the Monk of Westminster, pp. 119–40.

No sooner had the appeal before parliament been made than a very natural doubt arose as to the legality of the whole procedure. The precedents, two at most, were not only scanty but obscure,[1] and it is therefore not surprising to find that when various judges, serjeants, sages in the law of the realm and sages in the civil law[2] were asked about its legality, they all replied that it was illegal both by civil law and by the law of the land (and therefore in fact meaningless) to "appeal" anyone of treason before parliament. The reasons for this answer are no doubt to be found in part in the perfectly clear treason statute of 1352 and in the fact that none of the offences alleged in the articles of 1388 could possibly be brought under that statute, but there was a real difficulty about procedure and competence as well. What is important to stress is the fact that this answer must have been made, as Tout has pointed out,[3] not by the Ricardian justices, who were all under arrest, but by the justices newly appointed by the appellants themselves, notably Clopton and Charlton, the chief justices of either bench. To talk of these lawyers, as Tout himself then curiously proceeds to do, as being "faithful to their royalist bent" is patently absurd; they were not royalists and there was a real legal difficulty.

The difficulty was solved, or rather overridden, by the appellant party in the lords, who persuaded that body to declare that the high crimes alleged in the appeal could in fact be dealt with in parliament "by the law of parliament", that is, as parliament wished, and secondly that, with the king's assent, the lords of parliament were themselves the proper judges in such cases and that they were not bound by either the civil law or the law of any other inferior court, since all other courts were merely executors of the laws of the realm and of the ordinances of parliament. Thirdly, they declared that the appeal was in order and that they would proceed to deal with it themselves. Further, the declaration appears to disallow any hearing in the

---

[1] Miss Clarke does her best to elucidate them, *Fourteenth Century Studies*, p. 134.

[2] Lodge and Thornton, *English Constitutional Documents*, pp. 156-7.

[3] *Chapters*, iii, 432.

curia militaris—"it is not the will of parliament nor of the king and lords that the realm should be adjudged by civil law".[1]

Tout, following a long historical tradition, makes much of this famous declaration.[2] He believes it represents the first clear statement of a parliamentary theory of the constitution, worked out in answer to the royalist theory stated at Nottingham. He notes that "the declaration that parliament, as the law maker, could override the executive officers of the law involved an assertion of the ultimate sovereignty of parliament which, after a lapse of centuries, was to become the received theory of the English state". Again, he holds that this declaration contains "the first adumbration of the 'house of lords' as the supreme law-court, including the further consequence of judgment by legislative act, which was to prepare the way for acts of attainder".

These are weighty words, but the doctrine they expound has been severely damaged by the recent criticisms of Miss Clarke. It may be true that this deep consciousness of profound constitutional issues and developments was really present in 1388, but the facts are equally, perhaps more easily, susceptible of a more practical and cynical interpretation. Few would deny that after Radcot Bridge the appellants were out for blood, yet the whole course of subsequent events shows that from the first they had difficulties with their own legal advisers and also with a moderate majority in the lords. They seem to have failed to induce that majority to approve a hearing before the *curia militaris*—the realm was not to be adjudged by civil law, and there was no reason for these moderates to reject the king's reference of the appeal to parliament. But the appellants were not going to leave it at that; they were desperate men, and they were prepared to cut the knot by playing on the lords' natural vanity to persuade them to ignore the lawyers' attempts to restrict the jurisdiction of parliament by accepting cognisance of the appeal and declaring law of their own making to be supreme.

[1] Lodge and Thornton, *op. cit.* p. 158.
[2] *Chapters*, iii, 432–3.

The logical result of this attitude would have been to make a statute *ad homines* in due form, declaring their opponents guilty of treason and subject to its penalties. This, as Tout says, is attainder, the common practice of the fifteenth century. But attainder means declaring a man guilty by act of parliament, without due process of law, which is so obviously unjust that opinion in the fourteenth century, not yet so embittered and sanguinary as it became during the Wars of the Roses, was not yet ready for it. The appellants were, moreover, undoubtedly divided among themselves, Derby and Nottingham holding back from the other three, while the other lords of parliament required most careful management. Hence the appellants shrank from the cruel logic of attainder, and found themselves in another impasse as the result. The only way out of this impasse, short of giving way entirely, was the arbitrary establishment of the short-lived, bastard procedure known as the "parliamentary appeal of treason". It should be noticed in the first place that this procedure had been declared illegal by the appellants' own lawyers, and secondly that it never received the only possible sanction which might have legally overridden their decision, namely that of a parliamentary statute. Hence it was in fact little better than lynch law, and this had two results. The first of these was the short life of the process—it was used only in 1388, 1397, and 1398 and was abolished in the first parliament of Henry IV. The second was the absence of any known rules when difficulties arose; no one knew what to do when there was a hitch in the proceedings, because all laws had been thrown overboard. This constantly crops up in the trials.

So far then from the decision of the lords of parliament to hear the appeal of 1388 being, as Tout and other historians say, the first assertion of the ultimate sovereignty of parliament, that decision represented no more than a muddled compromise into which well-meaning men were driven by unscrupulous ones. This can be illustrated by three points taken from the last activities of the parliament. Thus its complete failure to understand the true doctrine of parliamentary supremacy, which must imply that any given parliament is competent to reverse the acts of its predecessors, was shown by a futile attempt to bind all future parliaments not to revoke what it had done. Secondly, the same point was driven home by a still more naïve declaration that no future parliament was to imitate its actions. This reluctance to let its acts run as precedents was partly, but not wholly, due to the fear of future revenge should the king's party ever come back into power; it is, however, to be explained not only by that consideration but once more by reference to the statute of 1352. Both that statute (implicitly) and the statute of Westminster III[1] (explicitly) had laid down that forfeiture for treason was not to affect entails, but the appellants were determined that on this occasion (only) the forfeitures they inflicted on their victims should none the less extend to entailed properties—a policy imitated in acts of attainder during the fifteenth century. The justices were accordingly informed that in this respect, as in other major issues, they were to disregard statute law, but only for the time being; to break any inconvenient statutes now but to interpret them strictly for the future. The contempt shown by this parliament for its own semi-legislative, semi-judicial activities as an institution could hardly have been carried further, but it may be added, thirdly, that even when it legislated in proper form it provided for the immediate breaking as well as for the subsequent observation of one of its own statutes. The statute was one made, apparently as an afterthought, at the extreme end of the parliament in order to clarify still further the delicate question of a raid upon estates tail which was to be not only unprecedented but unrepeatable. It actually attempted to minimise the departure from tradition by specifically protecting dower and estates tail from forfeiture in all future crises, but not in the existing one. No further comment is necessary on the "principles" of the merciless parliament;[2] it will be enough to watch them working in the trials of its victims.

[1] Of 1285—in its famous first clause *de donis condicionalibus*: Stubbs, *Select Charters* (9th ed.), pp. 462-3.
[2] For a general analysis of the confused ideas about parliament at this date cf. S.B. Chrimes, *English Constitutional Ideas in the Fifteenth Century*, pp. 66-141.

Of the five chief victims only Brembre was in custody to begin with, so the four absentees were sentenced first. After accepting cognisance of the appeal the lords deliberated for ten days, as well they might, apparently upon the law of treason as well as on the guilt or innocence of the accused. In the end they declared to be treason fourteen out of the thirty-nine articles of the appeal; it is not known which, but it does not greatly matter since in actual fact it is impossible to bring more than eight[1] or nine at most under the statute of 1352, so that the lords in any case went well outside the statute. The four absentees were then promptly condemned to death, with the exception of the archbishop of York who was dealt with later by the pope[2] at the appellants' request. It is worth noting that neither king nor commons formally assented to these proceedings by the lords; the process was purely arbitrary and neither legislative nor judicial, since the absence of the accused was in itself contrary to fourteenth-century notions of law.[3]

On the 17th of February Brembre was brought up for a more formal trial and, owing to the physical presence and courage of the accused in repeatedly denying jurisdiction,[4] difficulties at once arose concerning the correct procedure. To begin with, Brembre was denied counsel "by law of parliament". This was a meaningless phrase; such denial was counter to the common law and not justified by any statute. In this instance "law of parliament" therefore simply meant "will of parliament". Secondly, he was denied both a copy of the articles of appeal and time to prepare his answer;[5] this, though unjust according to modern ideas, was more in accordance with the practice of the fourteenth century; in fact it was not finally determined that a prisoner must have a copy of his indictment until 1695.[6] He therefore merely pleaded "not guilty" as each article was read aloud to him and in support of his plea offered battle. More

[1] Nos. 22, 29–32, 37–9.   [2] By translation *in partes infidelium*.
[3] M. V. Clarke, *Medieval Representation and Consent*, ch. ix, p. 180. Cf. Tresilian's protest, Monk of Westminster, pp. 167–8.
[4] Monk of Westminster, pp. 166–7.
[5] *Ibid.* pp. 148–9.   [6] Miss Clarke, *loc. cit.*

than three hundred gloves were cast against him, but none the less trial by battle was withheld on the ground that it lay only where there were no witnesses.[1] Finally a committee of twelve lords, including the duke of York and the earls of Kent, Salisbury and Northumberland, was appointed to investigate the charges made against Brembre, but these, to the extreme annoyance of the appellants, unexpectedly reported that he had done nothing worthy of death.[2] Serious disorder was in fact only averted at this point by the sudden news that Tresilian had been taken; Brembre's case was temporarily suspended and the execution of Tresilian—he had of course already been condemned in absence—followed.

Tresilian had certainly been in hiding near Westminster palace the whole time, though Knighton, Favent, Froissart and the Monk of Westminster all tell the story differently. Favent's story of the *tremescens paterfamilias* who was reluctantly concealing him in his house is the most picturesque; the Westminster chronicler adds the important details[3] that he was able to take sanctuary in the abbey before his arrest and that only the duke of Gloucester in person would take the responsibility of laying hands on him there. In any case he was dragged off to his death, protesting as he went not only against the violation of sanctuary[4] but also against the illegality of the whole process which had already condemned him.[5] The first protest seems to have been ignored at the time, though both bishop Arundel and Wykeham argued rather dubiously *ex post facto* that such arrests were justified;[6] the second was answered on the spot (*confestim*) by the statement that the *factum sive judicium parliamenti* was irrevocable.[7] It seems legally doubtful whether this reply meant anything at all, though the very hesitation of the

[1] Probably an echo of practice in the *curia militaris*.
[2] Monk of Westminster, p. 167.
[3] p. 167, queried unnecessarily by Tout, *Chapters*, iii, 433 n.
[4] In which the Westminster chronicler (pp. 173–5) was certainly on his side—*violenter funestis manibus abstraxerunt*. He praises Richard later for taking the orthodox view.
[5] Monk of Westminster, p. 168. [6] *Ibid.* p. 174. [7] *Ibid.* p. 168.

appellants as to whether Tresilian's condemnation had been a *judicium* or a *factum* is illuminating. However, legally or not, the ex-chief justice of the king's bench was promptly drawn on a hurdle to Tyburn and hanged; and the opposition having tasted blood at last, turned with renewed excitement to the harrying of Brembre.

Since the lords had virtually acquitted the ex-mayor of London the appellants bethought themselves of his enemies among the gildsmen. There were many libels current about him in the city at this time; thus Walsingham says[1] he had planned to change the name of London to Petty Troy, of which he himself was to be duke, and adds that he had already drawn up proscription lists for some thousands of his fellow-citizens. Knighton repeats the legend,[2] fixes the number of the pro-scribed at 8500 *et plures*, and says that Brembre had gone so far as to prepare a special axe and block, on which he himself suffered in the end. It was a clever move on the appellants' part to attempt to capitalise local fears and local hostility, but it is hard to see what legal force they thought they could extract from the opinion of an *ad hoc* assembly consisting of two repre-sentatives from every major gild and mistery in London. In any case, according to the Monk of Westminster and Favent, this body gave and could give no decisive answer;[3] it naturally replied according to the party line in London politics, the victualling gilds for Brembre and the non-victualling against him, so that the ends of justice, or injustice, were not helped. At this point the appellants, getting desperate, applied to still another *ad hoc* assemblage for a verdict on Brembre, namely to the mayor and aldermen and the recorder of London.[4] These replied cautiously that he was on the whole more likely to be guilty than not and the recorder, when pressed, admitted further

---

[1] *Hist. Anglic.* ii, 174.   [2] ii, 293.

[3] Miss Clarke, *Fourteenth Century Studies*, pp. 139–40, notes that eleven extant petitions against Brembre on the part of the non-victualling gilds should probably be assigned to this occasion. The counter-petitions of the victuallers have been significantly "lost".

[4] Monk of Westminster, p. 168.

that if he were in fact found to be guilty and if the offence were really treason the penalty would be death. This remarkable opinion was actually good enough for the now impatient appellants and Brembre duly suffered the same fate as Tresilian, making or not making an edifying end according to the bias of each chronicler. It is hardly necessary to emphasise any further the state to which the parliamentary appeal of treason had reduced the conception of justice; it is equalled only by the political indecency of attempting to exploit the London factions, and the one encouraging feature to offset it was the survival of a strong neutral party in the lords.

These difficulties offered sufficient reasons in themselves for the total abandonment of the process with the second batch of victims.[1] The method used this time was impeachment and the forms of common law were more or less observed; thus though no witnesses were called, that remained good common law procedure until the sixteenth century,[2] and the accused were at least allowed to hear specific charges and to speak in self-defence. They consisted of Burley, Beauchamp and two other chamber knights, of John Blake, the royal serjeant-at-law who had drafted the questions to the justices in 1387, Thomas Usk, under-sheriff of Middlesex and former clerk to Brembre's rival, John of Northampton, whom he had betrayed to the curialists as long ago as 1384, the remaining justices of 1387, and bishop Rushook of Chichester, the confessor of the king.[3] Of these Blake and Usk were taken first. The charges made against them are not specified by the record, but their nature may be easily guessed; Blake for long refused to plead in the hope of avoiding forfeiture for the sake of his heirs, but in the end both men answered severally to the charges and in the first week of March 1388 both were condemned and executed.[4] Next day

[1] Tout, Miss Clarke and others on the other hand suggest that the change was merely due to the lower rank of the accused.

[2] W. S. Holdsworth, *History of English Law*, i, 234.

[3] Lodge and Thornton, *op. cit.* p. 157.

[4] Monk of Westminster, p. 150. Usk obstinately declared his innocence to the end, *ibid.* p. 169.

the bishop of Chichester and the justices came up for trial, but
they escaped comparatively lightly. Thus when the bishop
was impeached before the prelates and other lords of *certainz
pointz de treson* his fellow-bishops came to his support and
secured the adjournment of his case, although all his property
was confiscated and his temporalities, like those of archbishop
Neville, declared forfeit to the king.[1] On the same day (the
6th of March 1388) the justices of the previous year were
sentenced to be drawn and hung and lose their property, but
once again the prelates came to the rescue, incidentally averting
a second attack upon the bishop of Chichester, and eventually
their lives were spared though they were each exiled to a
distant part of Ireland.[2] To say with Tout[3] that "thus the
'Merciless Parliament' first began to show a touch of mercy"
seems inapt; for the commons, now unleashed in the congenial
process of impeachment, were clearly out for blood of their
own baying and, if Favent is to be believed, not only the higher
clergy but Gloucester, Warwick and Arundel themselves endeavoured to restrain them. This restraint was successfully
exercised in the case of the bishop and the justices;[4] it met
with less powerful support in the case of the four chamber
knights and was correspondingly less availing.

There was a short interval in the trials during the second
week of March, in the course of which the earl of Arundel

[1] Monk of Westminster, pp. 148, 170.
[2] Walsingham, *Hist. Anglic.* ii, 174 and Favent, p. 23.
[3] *Chapters*, iii, 434.
[4] Favent seems particularly well-informed about the trial, punishments
and allowances of the justices—so much so that he may have had access to
official records, perhaps through Geoffrey Martin. For their ultimate exile
to Ireland see also Monk of Westminster, pp. 179–80—Knighton, ii, 296,
adds that their wives and children were not allowed to visit them, and that
their allowances varied between £20 and £40 a year and their bounds
between circuits of two and three leagues, which were not to be broken on
pain of death. Rymer, *Foedera*, vii, 591 (8 and 12 July 1388), shows that
Bealknap and Sir J. Holt were banished to Drogheda; Sir Robert Fulthorp
and Sir W. Burgh to Dublin; Sir John Cary and John Lokton, serjeant-at-
law, to Waterford. The bishop of Chichester was translated to Kilmore
(Tout, *Chapters*, iii, 436).

obtained a half-subsidy for the prosecution of his naval plans,[1] but on the 12th proceedings were resumed, this time against Burley, Beauchamp, Salisbury and Berners.[2] There had already been drawn up sixteen articles of accusation against these four knights of the chamber,[3] most of which were simply rehearsals of the charges contained in the original appeal,[4] together with a special charge of "counselling, aiding and abetting" the five principal offenders. There was, however, quite clearly, a special animus against Burley, who was accused of having illegally obtained the constableship of Dover castle (4) and of having caused the mayor of Dover to promise Richard, when at Sheen, that the Cinque Ports would be defended in his interest by a thousand men (11).[5] He was also accused as constable of Windsor (5) of having let de la Pole escape, which was probable enough, and of having advised the king (7) to support many foreigners, notably Bohemians, about the royal person to the great impoverishment of the realm. This last was an ingenious perversion of the fact that Burley had certainly allied himself closely from the first with queen Anne and her following, and relied for its effect on the known animus against the queen's Bohemians,[6] but all these details were really beside the point, for what everyone, friend and enemy alike, knew was that these four knights, especially Burley, had in fact formed the heart of the royalist stronghold in the militarised chamber of 1386-7 and had been hand in glove throughout with the five who had already suffered, and this was the real charge against them.

This being so, the three leading appellants and the commons clamoured steadily for their condemnation,[7] but it took them some time to get their way because the opposition to so much

[1] Monk of Westminster, iii, 152.

[2] Since Favent, p. 20, and *Rot. Parl.* iii, 241 agree on this point, it is better to reject the Monk of Westminster's assertion that Medford, Slake, Lincoln and Richard Clifford were arraigned with them. Cf. Tout, *Chapters*, iii, 434 n.

[3] Monk of Westminster, pp. 141-7.   [4] E.g. nos. 1-3, 6, 8-10, 12-16.

[5] The first of these two points was a technicality but there may have been something in the second.

[6] E.g. in Walsingham, *Hist. Anglic.* ii, 97.   [7] Favent, p. 21.

judicial murder, which had existed in the lords from the beginning, was now gathering force. The three other knights and Burley, who was ill and had to be supported on the arms of two friends, were twice called and twice remanded to the Tower, and it was not until the 5th of May after a long and dramatic battle for their lives that they were finally condemned and executed.[1] The impatience of the commons all this time was particularly remarkable; the death-sentence was demanded by them as early as the 13th of April as soon as parliament met again after an adjournment. Their point of view is undoubtedly reflected in the bitter gibes of Walsingham,[2] who goes out of his way at this point to load Burley with charges of every kind, from high treason to adultery. On the other side feeling was equally strong—from Richard himself, who risked his throne again in his three weeks' opposition, and his queen, who is said to have knelt at Gloucester's feet for Burley's life,[3] to the controller of the household, Baldwin Raddington,[4] to whom, as a noted royalist himself, the risk was particularly great. Even outside the household the old knight had no less powerful supporters; both Derby and Nottingham are said to have been on his side, while the duke of York felt so strongly that he quarrelled with his brother Gloucester[5] in full parliament over Burley's fate and, accompanied by John, lord Cobham, as a representative of the other moderate lords, went to reason with the commons on his behalf; but nothing availed him. In the end all that Richard himself could do for Burley was to save him from drawing and hanging; on account of his ancient service with the Black Prince and as a knight of the Garter he was merely beheaded.[6] A similar privilege was accorded to

[1] Monk of Westminster, pp. 152–3, 177–8.

[2] *Hist. Anglic.* ii, 174. Cf. *Anonimalle Chronicle*, p. 136.

[3] It is tempting to suppose that this famous occasion marks the point at which Richard's affection for his dead mother was first definitely transferred to Anne.

[4] Now known to have been Burley's nephew: N. B. Lewis, *E.H.R.* lii, 662–9.

[5] Walsingham, *loc. cit.*, says it was Derby who quarrelled with Gloucester. Both stories may be true.   [6] Monk of Westminster, pp. 155–6.

Beauchamp and Berners when their time came, but not to Salisbury, who was suspected of being a French agent.

After this orgiastic climax the commons and their three principal leaders seem to have relaxed the tension of their enmities, though parliament was not dismissed until the 4th of June. Thus all the remaining offenders were released under surety—this included the chamber knights Trivet, Elmham and Dagworth as well as the clerks Medford, Slake, Clifford and Lincoln[1]—and nothing more seems to have been done about any of them, while parliament turned to innocuous discussions of administrative reform and the still more congenial task of distributing money grants, honours and appointments among the leading figures of the successful party.

Household reform, in spite of several petitions on the subject, was rather surprisingly neglected; apparently it was felt that the separate households of the king and queen were both so completely under appellant control as a result of the proscriptions that no new ordinances for their governance need be made. But departmental reform was another matter; there were numerous petitions for the purge of chancery, exchequer and the law-courts, as well as of the household; the appellants had seized power after all as a reforming body, and it was necessary not only to confirm chancellor Arundel's conduct in rejecting warranty by signet since 1386, to appoint a new council or commission, and to provide the holding of another parliament later in the year, but also to carry out a survey of the administrative machine and to attend to its more obvious defects. The survey in question seems to have been made by Thomas Arundel himself, bishop Gilbert, the treasurer, and John Waltham, the keeper of the privy seal; at any rate something of the sort is the most probable cause of the important chancery ordinances of 1388-9, which afford the first clear picture of the internal organisation of the medieval chancery and its staff now something like 120 strong.[2] No other reforms

---

[1] Ibid. pp. 181-2.
[2] Text in B. Wilkinson's appendix to his *Chancery under Edward III*; detailed commentary in Tout, *Chapters*, iii, 443-9.

seem to have resulted; nor do the remaining petitions of the parliament need any further comment. The attempts to control the creation of precedents and to bind future parliaments by means of various oaths,[1] pardons, declarations on the law of treason and so forth have already been mentioned.[2] On the other hand the grants are interesting.

Of these the most striking is the prodigious sum of £20,000, or considerably more than half a subsidy, now voted to the appellants personally "for their great expenses in procuring the salvation of the realm and the destruction of the traitors".[3] We are not informed precisely how it was allotted, but the mere fact of the grant, which must presumably be related to the campaign of Radcot Bridge, is a curious comment on a clique which had seized power in the interests of economy and goes far to explain that widespread disillusionment with appellant rule without which Richard could hardly have reasserted his power a year later. Compared to this the grants made to the state were adequate, but not generous—the appellants had to justify their claim to war efficiency without either surrendering their own spoils or pressing the commons too hard. The wool duties and tunnage and poundage were prolonged at the existing rates, while the half-subsidy already voted was supplemented by a whole one voted at Cambridge in the autumn of the same year.[4]

Of the new honours and appointments the most significant were those which were intended to buy the support, or at any rate the silence, of Gaunt and his friends. It could not be assumed that the duke of Lancaster would never return to England or that, when he did so, he would necessarily approve of what had been done. Meanwhile his constable, Sir John Holland, the king's half-brother, who had come home to report progress in Spain, had been a dangerous witness of the appellants' activities since the beginning of April and it was necessary

---

[1] A special oath of loyalty to the new régime was administered in the shire-courts as early as March 1388: *C.C.R.* 1385–9, p. 405.

[2] Monk of Westminster, pp. 158–65.

[3] *Ibid.* iii, 154.   [4] Ramsay, *Revenues*, ii, 357.

to stop his mouth. He was therefore not only created earl of Huntingdon[1] but given the abnormally large pension or allowance of 2000 marks per annum to sustain the title; this allowance for an earl contrasts sharply with the 1500 marks granted to the king's younger uncles when they became dukes three years before.[2] Meanwhile, when it was learned from Sir John Holland that Gaunt's claim to Castile had now been finally abandoned and that he was preparing to come home, it was hastily decided to appoint him king's lieutenant in Aquitaine (May 1388)—a post of great honour and responsibility and perhaps some profit—"by the assent of our council in this our present parliament". Tout[3] calls these two acts "riveting Richard's fetters with the Lancastrian and Holland influence", and there is in fact little doubt that both appointments were in the nature of bribes, neither of which, however, was ultimately effective.

On the other hand, the commons' petition for a new council does not seem to have been granted. True, according to the Monk of Westminster,[4] one of the last acts of the parliament was to appoint the bishops of Winchester and London, the earl of Warwick, John, lord Cobham and Gaunt's friend Richard le Scrope of Bolton to attend continually on the king, but these were warders rather than councillors and the real government lay in the hands of the five leading ministers, the appellant lords and what was left of the commission of 1386; thus Tout points out[5] that the thirteen witnesses of the new earl of Huntingdon's charter included eleven members of the commission, which it may therefore be assumed was still existing and functioning as a unit. Apparently the commons acquiesced in this state of affairs and even now the commission's legal title was not, as it could so easily have been, renewed.

Before we pass to the use made by the appellants in the ensuing year of the powers so dubiously acquired there are still two points which deserve mention. The first of these is the fate

---

[1] Monk of Westminster, p. 172.   [2] H. Wallon, *Richard II*, i, 373.
[3] *Chapters*, iii, 437; E. Perroy, *L'Angleterre et le grand schisme d'Occident*, pp. 254–5, agrees.   [4] p. 178.   [5] *Chapters*, iii, 438 n.

of the condemned prelates, which is of some interest for the light it throws on relations between England and the papacy. Thus although Urban might have been described up to this year as mildly royalist where England was concerned, the continuance of the Schism forced him to accept the change of government without comment and even to assist it by the elimination of Neville and Rushook and the promotion of Arundel, Skirlaw and John Waltham; he may have been consoled in this course by the heavy fees and *dona* payable at each stage in the necessary series of episcopal translations. These were as follows. Neville, now an exile in Brabant, was translated from York to the Avignonese see of St Andrews, which was tantamount to translation *in partes infidelium*, and his place was taken by Thomas Arundel, who vacated Ely. Rushook was sent from Chichester to the distant and impoverished see of Kilmore in the province of Armagh, of which in any case he was unable to obtain possession, so that he had to take refuge at Cork, where the spring parliament of 1390 gave him £40 a year on which to live.[1] Skirlaw was given Durham, whose more loyally Ricardian bishop, Fordham, was degraded to the poorer see of Ely, while Ralph Erghum, the former chancellor of Gaunt, received Wells, which was vacant, leaving Salisbury for Waltham. Favent, alone among the authorities, says that these changes formed the topic of heated debate in parliament on the ground that they were unreasonably complicated and that the complication was designed deliberately to repay the pope in fees for the loss of half a tenth which he had just tried without success to collect from the English clergy.[2] Actually the translations complete the appellant programme and do not appear to have been much more numerous than was necessary, though it is true that they were certainly of financial benefit to the curia.[3]

[1] Perroy, *Schisme*, p. 97. He points out (pp. 98–9) that at this date Ireland was largely Clementist.

[2] The Monk of Westminster seems to admit the charge (pp. 178–9) but lays the blame rather quaintly not on the pope but on the English clergy themselves, who, he says, evaded the tax by *provoking* the pope to order this general post among the English bishops.

[3] *Cal. Pap. Reg. Let.* iv, 268–9.

The one remaining point of interest about the merciless parliament is the fact that when, as usually happened at the end of a parliament, many bills and petitions were still left un-answered at its close, an *ad hoc* committee of certain lords was given full parliamentary powers to remain behind and deal with them, thus enabling the rest of the parliament to go home. There was nothing very new about this, but the matter is of some importance in view of the outcry raised against Richard by historians for adopting a similar device at Shrewsbury ten years later, when much is made of the "parliamentary com-mittee of 1398" as if it were something totally unprecedented.[1]

Meanwhile, it is more important to consider whether the appellant revolution of 1388, if not justified in its means, was at least justified in its works. The appellants had seized power as a "national" and patriotic party; they should therefore be judged in the first instance by the success or otherwise with which they carried on the war. As regards France and Flanders there were at first some sporadic attempts to carry out the aggressive policy which they were supposed to represent. The net result, however, was astonishingly small and did little or nothing in itself to justify the change of government. The fact is that in spite of all their war talk the appellants, with the solitary exception of the duke of Gloucester, seem to have intended from the start[2] to carry on their predecessors' peace ne-gotiations with the French and Flemings, and though this line of policy was not unreasonable it would be easier to share Tout's admiration for the appellants' sense of continuity[3] if they had not made the misconduct of foreign affairs, and especially the opening of peace negotiations, one of the principal accusations

[1] Richard's forging of the parliament roll to extend the 1398 committee's powers still further was of course unprecedented, but that is a different matter.
[2] Perroy, *Schisme*, p. 354 (cf. *Diplomatic Correspondence*, p. 201), shows that the council were seventeen to one against Gloucester on the point. Cf. *C.P.R.* 1385-9, pp. 502-3. The Monk of Westminster (p. 214) sees Clemen-tist machinations at the back of these peace proposals and rejoices that Urban's firm attitude saved the situation, but Perroy shows that the French were even less ready for peace at this period than the English, many of whom, outside the council, supported Gloucester. [3] *Chapters*, iii, 439.

against their enemies. They even used the same negotiators; thus Skirlaw was as prominent as he had been under the old régime, while the colleagues given him by the appellants included experts from the king's household and chamber, one of whom, Sir Nicholas Dagworth, had actually been singled out for attack in the merciless parliament.

As regards Scotland the appellants had said comparatively little in the articles of accusation[1] and remained extremely dilatory; thus they made no effort to induce the Scots to extend the existing truce beyond the 19th of June, while at the same time they took no active measures of defence. The result was that shortly after coming into power their government experienced at Otterburn the worst disaster of the reign. Already by the end of June the Scots were raiding England heavily by both the eastern and the western routes; they had taken much booty and four hundred prisoners.[2] Early in August they returned in greater force and it was then that they scored their great triumph in defeating and capturing the best and strongest of the English borderers, Henry Percy (Hotspur), son and heir of the earl of Northumberland, at Otterburn on the Jedburgh-Newcastle road.[3] Hotspur seems to have planned a surprise attack on the Scottish camp by an English detachment under Sir Matthew Redmayne and this succeeded, but meanwhile he was himself taken in flank by the Scots' main body and lost five hundred and fifty men apart from prisoners. This disaster was little set off by his killing of the Douglas in single combat just before his own capture, or even by the exploits of Redmayne, who took James Lindsay of Crawford prisoner and, according to the Monk of Westminster,[4] forced the Scots to

[1] But see article 8—complaining that the wardens of the marches were unfit to hold their posts.
[2] Monk of Westminster, pp. 184–7; Walsingham, *Hist. Anglic.* ii, 176.
[3] See Ramsay, *Genesis*, ii, 259–61, for a clear account (with map) of the action, later known as the "hontynge off the Cheviot", or Chevy Chase.
[4] What he does not realise was that this success was over the camp-guard only. Walsingham on the other hand ignores Redmayne and his exploits entirely and gives all the credit of this local success to Hotspur, who had, it is true, planned that part of the operation, though he had not carried it out.

retreat before making good his own withdrawal. What is quite clear is that the whole action, which gravely jeopardised the Border for years to come and represented a loss of face such as the English had not experienced in the north for half a century, had been left almost entirely to local levies by the carelessness and incompetence of the appellants.[1] It is true that a council was hastily held at Northampton to consider reprisals, but by that time—it was now the end of August—it was thought to be too late in the year, with the result that Scots' raids on a smaller scale were renewed in October,[2] both on Berwick, where they were repulsed with loss, and on Carlisle, where they were more successful but provoked local reprisals by the English.[3]

All things considered, therefore, the appellants had little reason to be proud of their foreign policy by the end of the year; it had moreover cost the country one and a half subsidies and the continuance of the customs at the old level. But this was not all, for the domestic policy of the appellants during their twelve months of power was also marked by what Tout calls "the same conservative spirit".[4] That policy was almost entirely comprised in the vigorous but reactionary legislation of the one parliament which ever sat in Cambridge, where it occupied the priory of Barnwell from the 10th of September to the 17th of October 1388. Unfortunately its roll is lost and any authority for its proceedings is almost wholly confined to the Monk of Westminster,[5] eked out by the statute-book. The chronicler's account leads off with a significant dispute between the lords and commons on the subject of livery and maintenance leading ultimately to a statute, the precursor of much abortive legislation on this subject. Royal and baronial liveries were both attacked, but the main complaint was principally one of maintenance, that is the perversion of justice by retainers of

---

[1] Possibly jealousy of the Percies by the southern lords played some part, yet parliament eventually provided £3000 for Hotspur's ransom, Ramsay, *Genesis*, ii, 261.

[2] Monk of Westminster, p. 199.   [3] Knighton, ii, 308-9.

[4] *Chapters*, iii, 440.   [5] pp. 189-98.

the crown or of great lords.[1] The growth of such bands was in fact a general feature of the fourteenth century and may be closely connected with the substitution for the feudal host and Anglo-Saxon *fyrd* of troops raised under commissions of array, or royal conscription, and still more of men-at-arms and archers raised by individual lords and captains under contract with the king to serve in the French wars by what was known as the indenture system.[2] Private "companies" as a result had long been common, and personal loyalties of an almost Anglo-Saxon type were beginning to replace the old tenurial bond of feudalism; some of these companies, such as the famous White Company,[3] had taken to a roving mercenary life upon the continent of Europe, selling their services wherever there was need for them; others unfortunately had returned home. Men organised in this way had often seen long service in France under the lord or captain who had raised them and were ready enough to continue in his service on their return to England; it was obvious that they would not fit easily into civilian life and indeed in many cases brigandage or service in a free company abroad was perhaps the only alternative to livery.[4] The lord on his part, having usually made a fortune out of French loot and ransoms, was equally ready to support an armed force for the luxury of intimidating shire and hundred courts, sheriffs and even royal justices in the process of filching property from his neighbour. It was private armies of this sort that had fought the battle of Radcot Bridge, as they were to fight the Wars of the Roses, and it is interesting to find the commons so alive to the menace which they constituted towards the smaller country gentry—a menace vividly illustrated in the Paston Letters of a later age.

Royal livery, as distinct from baronial, though equally

[1] See the picture drawn by J. E. A. Jolliffe, *The Constitutional History of Medieval England*, pp. 414–15.
[2] See A. E. Prince in *Historical Essays in honour of James Tait*, pp. 283–98, for this system.
[3] Cf. Conan Doyle's well-known novel of that title.
[4] Cf. *Statutes of the Realm*, i, 364 ff. (1361).

attacked by the commons upon this occasion, was both later in date and the true cure of the disease. We hear little of it before 1387, when it was singularly ineffective, but Richard was forced to fall back on it in self-defence against the magnates in the next decade, when he introduced the famous badge of the white hart; then, as later, the weakness of the step lay in the difficulty of financing it as well as in the general suspicion and unpopularity it aroused. The Lancastrian dynasty, and to a less degree the Yorkist, could not afford it, since the dwindling crown revenues were burdened with state responsibilities from which the rising baronial revenues were free, and it was left to Henry VII in a more propitious time to make the numerous abortive acts of livery effective by monopolising military man-power, gunpowder and artillery for the crown. But even in Richard II's time the interests of crown and commons in the matter were obviously identical and it is therefore not necessary to see in his proposal to the Cambridge parliament that all liveries, royal and baronial alike, should be abolished, a mere attempt to sow discord between lords and commons. The offer to disband his own men in answer to the commons' petition, provided that the lords would do likewise, was perhaps as disingenuous as most offers of total and immediate disarma-ment, the more so since the merciless parliament can have left him few men to disband, but like most disarmament proposals it enshrined a valid principle. Eventually a compromise was reached by which all wearing of cognisances, royal or other-wise, more recent in origin than the accession of Edward III[1] was to be discontinued—this, Tout thinks,[2] was the original petition—but (and this perhaps was a royal compromise) only from the next parliament.

This was the main clause in the agreement, but there were others. Of these the most difficult to understand is a provision that all gilds and fraternities should be suppressed, saving chantries and ecclesiastical foundations; it is conceivable that parliament

---

[1] The date, so near the opening of the French and Scottish wars, is signi-ficant.

[2] *Chapters*, iii, 440.

had in mind the abuse of London gilds and their factions during
the past crisis in this very sweeping clause, but it cannot have
seriously intended to try to abolish craft gilds. It is true that
on the 1st of November the two sheriffs of London duly
received writs ordering a complete return of crafts and misteries,
fraternities and gilds and that similar writs were issued to all the
sheriffs in England,[1] but in fact those established by royal
licence were exempt from the beginning, while the further
exemption of those which increased the service of God could be
made to apply to most gilds and fraternities which did not
possess a royal charter, since practically all had their religious
side.[2] What was really aimed at in the first place is shown by the
concluding phrase, *sanz liverie, confederacie, meintenaunce ou
riotes en arrerissement du ley*,[3] that is, illegal associations with no
object other than the exercise of violence, and secondly it was
intended to prepare the way for the general extension of the
mortmain laws, alleviated by the usual licence system, to
the gilds[4]—an extension which duly took place by statute in
1391.

The second main activity of the Cambridge parliament took
the form of a renewed statute of labourers.[5] It was a drastic piece
of social legislation which shows how deeply the revolt of 1381
had eaten into upper-class consciousness and how little even
knights and burgesses were concerned with the interests of the
poor. It marked the beginning, in principle, of the bitter provisions of the sixteenth-century poor law and even of the act of
settlement and removal of 1661/2, but once again, more fortunately than in the case of liveries, social, economic and political
forces were too much for parliament. The statute begins with
an attempt to restrict and control the growing mobility of

[1] *Cal. of Letter-Book H*, pp. xlviii–ix.
[2] Cf. G. Unwin, *Gilds and Companies of London, passim.*
[3] Monk of Westminster, p. 191.
[4] For this system see K. Wood-Legh, *Church Life under Edward III*,
pp. 60–88.
[5] Monk of Westminster, pp. 192–6. For the original statutes cf.
B. Putnam, *Enforcement of the Statutes of Labourers*, 1348–59.

labour by an "internal passport"[1] system. Thus labourers were not to move about without letters patent issued by the justices of the peace under a seal provided by each hundred and borough and to be kept by a person appointed by the justices.[2] Anyone forging or being without such letters on his travels was to be imprisoned for forty days. If no one claimed him he might then be taken into service by the person who arrested him or else returned to his place of origin under fresh letters patent, in the course of which journey no one was to harbour him more than one day. Sturdy beggars, and even pilgrims unless *bona fide*, that is non-mendicant, were to be classed as runaway labourers and to suffer the same penalties, while impotent beggars were strictly enjoined to stay where they were born. Nobody, on pain of amercement, was to harbour any but mendicant religious, blind men, lepers and those who could not walk. Children of labourers were not to be put to learn a trade if they were wanted on the land—a provision which points to a continuing shortage of agricultural labour. Labourers were expected to have bows, but might carry no cutting or thrusting weapons, on pain of arrest; this perhaps was another echo of the revolt. The justices of the peace in quarter sessions were to enquire especially into the observance of these regulations, receiving four shillings a day from the fines and amercements and two shillings for their clerk, while in sharp contrast to these rates of pay the maximum[3] wages for various types of labourer and craftsman were fixed at between six and ten shillings a year, "or less in districts where they are accustomed to get less"—all under penalty of a rising scale of amercements for first, second and third offences, or alternatively forty days' imprisonment.

The remaining activities of the Cambridge parliament were unexceptionable; they included minor trade regulations and the so-called statute of Barnwell, which draws a vigorous picture of

[1] *Chapters*, iii, 440.
[2] Tout notes record evidence (*loc. cit.*) in the shape of sheriff's administrative accounts of the cost of making such seals for twenty-one shires in 1390–1.
[3] *Not* minimum, as Tout says, *Chapters*, iii, 440.

fourteenth-century sanitation.[1] More interesting is an order against the export of gold and silver, which refers to Rome and is accompanied by a reassertion of the statute of provisors.[2] The latter is remarkable in view of the recent wholesale translation of bishops by papal provision at the new government's own request, and Tout notes[3] the extent to which men like bishops Arundel and Wykeham, the orthodox enemies of Lollards and all anti-clericals, would be embarrassed by such action. M. Perroy, however, provides the explanation[4]—fresh financial demands by Urban on the English clergy had been allowed by the appellants only on condition that the translations were first carried out. No sooner had this been done than the consent to papal taxation was withdrawn and a rupture naturally occurred —this in turn led to the renewed insistence on the statutes of provisors. Urban died in the middle of the controversy (October 1389), but his successor continued the struggle, which reached its peak in 1390 and was not settled until 1393.

The appellants were evidently still in power when a great council was held at Westminster on the 20th of January 1389 and one or two measures of importance taken on that occasion[5] seem to have been due to them. In the first place the Border defences were strengthened by the appointment of the earl marshal (Nottingham) as warden of the east march and of Northumberland and two others as wardens of the west. They were to have 600 lances and 2000 archers at the king's expense until he should

---

[1] It begins: "For that so much dung and filth of the garbage and intrails, as well of beasts killed as of other corruptions, be cast and put in ditches, rivers and other waters; and also within many other places, within, about and nigh unto divers cities, boroughs and towns of the realm and the suburbs of them, that the air there is greatly corrupt and infect...": *Statutes of the Realm*, ii, 59. In the same year the chancellor of Cambridge university was called on by writ "to remove from the streets and lanes of the town all swine, and all dirt, dung filth and trunks and branches of trees, and to cause the streets and lanes to be kept clear for the future": B. W. Downs, *Cambridge Past and Present*, p. 30.

[2] Monk of Westminster, pp. 196–7.

[3] *Chapters*, iii, 441 n.   [4] *Schisme*, pp. 305 ff.

[5] Monk of Westminster, pp. 202–3.

arrive in person, which in fact he never did; the precaution was wise, if overdue. Secondly, the actual duchy, as distinct from the king's lieutenancy, of Aquitaine was now conferred on Gaunt, probably in a desperate attempt to keep him abroad still longer, while Ireland was entrusted to the keepership of Gloucester.[1] There was some doubt about the alienability of the regalia in these countries in view of the protest which had been made against the grant of Ireland to de Vere, but Gaunt's grant was certainly allowed to stand and was confirmed and elaborated in 1390. Gloucester on the other hand seems to have been simply named king's lieutenant in Ireland and was never formally duke of Ireland as de Vere had been.

With the year 1389, however, it is clear that in spite of these new appointments the sands, as far as the appellants were concerned, were running out. They had achieved little in the way of either peace or war with France; they had permitted a disaster in the north; they had quarrelled with the pope, made some reactionary statutes and spent a good deal of money. It is difficult to find evidence for any widespread disillusionment with their government; yet in view of this record such disillusionment there must have been, and the supposition is borne out, in part at least, by the ease with which in May 1389 the appellants were at last displaced. There were, however, many other and more potent factors in their removal and first among these stands the change in mentality which had overtaken the king. The ascendancy of the appellants once established Richard had been let alone. In spite of the autumn hunting, in which he took refuge after the Cambridge parliament, and of the usual Christmas festivities at Eltham,[2] it may be conjectured that he was still more or less numb from what had happened and was desperately trying to distract himself; this at least is a more charitable and a psychologically sounder explanation of his activities than the callous frivolity with which he is credited by his enemies. His personal losses had been extraordinarily heavy. Isolated enough even before the merciless parliament

[1] Walsingham, *Hist. Anglic.* ii, 196.
[2] Monk of Westminster, pp. 183, 201–2.

he had been deprived since the end of 1387 of his one close contemporary friend, de Vere, the extent of his attachment to whom may be gauged by the care he took to bring back his body to England for honourable burial in 1395, three years after he had died in exile.[1] There was no one else in de Vere's category for Richard, nor could there be until the new generation of the younger nobles grew up round him in the next decade; Thomas Mowbray, the one rival to de Vere, had betrayed him hopelessly in 1387-8, and that he could not forgive.

Apart from de Vere, all Richard's most intimate, if rather older, guardians and advisers had been put to death or exiled, from de la Pole and Burley, whom he had been used to rely on since his childhood, to the younger chamber knights and clerks and chaplains; all the best had gone. The release of the badly frightened Medford, Slake and others was little compensation, nor did the appellants' grudging conference of pensions upon exiled justices and bishops or on widows and heirs of the chief victims do anything to fill their place. In short, of Richard's immediate circle only his wife, on whom he does not seem to have depended greatly before 1388, was left to him, and she herself had been grossly insulted, both directly in pleading for Burley and indirectly in the attacks made on her Bohemians. It is therefore not surprising to find Richard turning more and more towards her and her influence was probably decisive with him from this time to her death in 1394.

Besides all this, allowance must be made for the great series of shocks to Richard's theory of the regality, the one fixed point in his life to which he clung to the end, represented by the threats of 1386, the probable "deposition" at the end of 1387, and the insults and fresh threats of 1388. These alone, even apart from his peculiar and solitary childhood and the violent disturbance of his adolescent life in 1381, would be more than enough to cause the growth of a neurosis, checked at first by the support and sympathy of Anne but much more rapid in its development after her death. In any case a schizoid mind of Richard's type

[1] *Annales Ricardi,* pp. 184-5. The scene has been reconstructed by Newbolt in his novel, *The New June.*

suffers in times of mental stress from a feeling that the outer world has less and less reality; it will become a mirror which reflects only what the subject wants to see—in Richard's case, the sacred mystery and unfettered nature of the royal power. By 1394 Anne was probably the only feature of the outside world which was altogether real to Richard, and could therefore, intermittently at least, make other features real to him, that is, give to reality a life deserving some consideration apart from his own fantasy. Anne's function was therefore not to keep Richard morally "good" or constitutionally orthodox but to keep him sane. After her death the neurosis deepened rapidly and the outer world came to reflect for him more and more a mere mechanical extension of his own favourite dream—the *plenitudo potestatis* of Boniface VIII translated into the English royal house; he even came to use some of Boniface's phrases. This of course was perfectly compatible with another favourite image of himself as the most Christian king and hammer of the heretic—they were simply different sides of the same psychological *persona*. This religious orthodoxy of Richard's, which may have gone back to his cradle and the uncertainty of his mother's marriage to his father, powerfully fortified in fact his mystic theory of the kingship; its best known practical expression was his dislike of Lollardry, which caused him to hurry home from Ireland in 1395 as soon as an outbreak was reported to him, though he had set his heart upon his Irish work and had left much of it undone.

Richard's real depression, in spite of any forced distractions, as the result of 1388 probably lasted into February 1389—otherwise he would hardly have sided with Gloucester, bishop Arundel and the canons of St Stephen's in a prolonged dispute with his friends the monks of Westminster, even though St Stephen's was intimately connected with the palace, in which the chapel lay.[1] Later in the same month, however, Richard showed his first sign of independence in trying to secure the provision of his ex-secretary Medford to the see of St David's from the pope.[2] But Urban, who had just protested against the

[1] Monk of Westminster, pp. 203–5.   [2] *Ibid.* p. 205.

re-enactment of the statute of provisors by the Cambridge parliament, promptly quashed the election and provided the treasurer, Gilbert, to the see, thus neatly registering a protest against the statute, while at the same time stopping the mouth of the appellant government by translating one of their own instruments. This then was a false step on Richard's part and he did not move again before the early summer, by which time Thomas Arundel had been formally installed in Neville's place as archbishop of York.

It was in fact the council held at Westminster on the 3rd of May 1389 which marked the traditional end of the appellants' period of power and the transition from Richard's "frustrated youth" to what has been rather prematurely called "subtle autocracy". Tout argues plausibly[1] that this was not, as used to be thought, a small but a great council; he adds that the small council, that is virtually the appellants' own commission, would have been certain to oppose the formal act of self-assertion which Richard now planned, while again the dramatic effect of the scene, which is in keeping with Richard's character and on which all historians insist, needed the presence of the moderate lords as a wider and friendlier audience. "To this body", writes Tout,[2] "Richard declared that, as he was now in his twenty-second year, he was entitled to the rights which the meanest heir in his kingdom acquired on attaining his majority. The magnates assured him that it was both his right and his duty to take upon himself the responsibilities of sovereignty. 'You know well', replied Richard, 'that for the twelve years of my reign, I and my realm have been ruled by others, and my

[1] *Chapters*, iii, 454 and nn., quoting Walsingham, *Hist. Anglic.* ii, 181 (*not* 184, which is an error) and Monk of Westminster, p. 210, in combination with the wording of letters close, issued to the sheriffs on the 8th of May and ordering them to proclaim the change of government. These letters refer to the assent of the prelates, lords, etc. *C.C.R.* 1385–9, p. 671.

[2] *Chapters*, iii, 454. The short speech which Tout puts into Richard's mouth is a reconstruction based upon the accounts of the incident to be found in the Monk of Westminster and Walsingham, with a leaning towards the former, where they differ, as the less prejudiced chronicler of the two.

people oppressed year by year with grievous taxes. Henceforth, with God's help, I shall labour assiduously to bring my
realm to greater peace and prosperity. Up to now I have been
allowed to do nothing without my protectors. Now I will
remove all of these men from my council, summon to advise
me whomsoever I will, and transact my own business myself.
I, therefore, order as a first step that the chancellor shall
surrender to me the seal....' This was enough for the day. It
showed in dramatic fashion that Richard had come into his
own." What Richard actually said is probably well represented
by Tout's combination in this passage of the accounts to be
found in the chronicles, in particular his ingenious repudiation
of all responsibility for what was past; thus in this council he
not only complained of appellant control but claimed that he had
never yet at any time been allowed a free hand and demanded
that he should be allowed to rule personally for the first time in
his reign. This half-truth, which Tout with some inconsistency
appears to take at face value, was perhaps the only way to get
rid of the appellants and represents another great advance in
Richard's political sense; it smoothed over past crises by denying
his responsibility for good and bad alike and made possible a
fresh start. This in view of the king's age could hardly be
denied to him, nor, being before a full council, could his
making of the claim be suppressed.

The appellants in short were cornered and had to give way,
so that in the circumstances it is not necessary to stress unduly
the impending return of Gaunt—he actually arrived in October,
though the chroniclers say November, and he was expected
earlier—or the example which Richard had just received from
France, where Charles VI had similarly thrown off his own
uncles' control.[1] Both these considerations, together with the
rather hypothetical disillusionment of the country with
appellant government, may have played their part, but the
circumstances of the moment and Richard's natural ingenuity

[1] Wallon, *op. cit.* ii, 17–19, works out the parallel between the history of
the two governments, which is certainly striking. Cf. Tait, *D.N.B.*
"Richard II".

in taking advantage of them really explain themselves.[1] From this point, cautiously enough—he had learnt caution in a hard school—Richard slowly began to tighten the reins of government.

Postscript to Chapter VI, pp. 150–3

The legal difficulty which I have outlined in beginning parliamentary proceedings against the king's friends in 1388 is essential to my argument. But after it was written Dr Helen M. Cam sent me an alternative explanation of such interest that I felt it would be of great value to print it here, and she was good enough to give her consent to my doing so. Dr Cam writes:

The opposition lords were not lawyers, and therefore there were probably some gaps in the theory which, I suggest, ran as follows:

If any supremacy is asserted, it is judicial-*cum*-legislative—not by any means purely legislative or generally political.

(1) Parliament is the highest *court of justice*. That seems valid from the time of Henry III, when two appeals from the court *coram rege* are being heard there (Bracton's *Notebook*).

(2) The lords constitute the highest *feudal court*. The crisis of 1341 had established the right of magnates to trial by their peers.

(3) Four of the five appellees might be considered peers who could claim trial by their peers in the lords.

As I see it Richard's action forces them to make the claim, and while Tout is being anachronistic as you say, I do think that it is a

---

[1] The impending return of John of Gaunt with the complete Lancastrian retinue meant of course the rebuilding of the moderate middle party to a strength which nobody could challenge. Gaunt had satisfied his own ambitions and until his death in February 1399 appeared to hold a moderate impartial attitude which was the mainstay of the crown.

There is also the fact, which seems to have been neglected, that the appellant régime, resting as it did upon a continuation and remodelling of the commission of November 1386, was illegal. The commission had officially expired on the 19th of November 1387 and nothing had been done to renew its powers, yet its personnel had been arbitrarily altered and its powers kept in being.

claim for Parliament *qua* Parliament. But its tone is definitely aristocratic and designed to put the civil servant—the judicial—element in its place.

The claim is twofold:

(1) We are the highest court of law.

(2) The judges must interpret the statutes as part of the body of law they administer.

The hit at civil law *may* have reference to the bias of Roman law in favour of autocracy—*quod principi placet legis habet vigorem*—as against common law (precedent) and statute law (legislation).

Parliament as the highest court of law had two aspects:

(1) The equitable discretionary judicial function of the crown—this would have been exercised by the judges originally, but was coming to be under the control of the magnates as it is to-day in the House of Lords.

(2) The feudal court, i.e. the court for the highest level of the population.

The petitioning function of the commons (or the general public) developed under (1), but note that as early as Edward I (parliament of Lincoln 1301), the lords were apparently co-operating, or claiming to co-operate, in hearing petitions. Impeachment also put the lords in the position of sharing the royal function of doing justice outside the ordinary courts of law.

Therefore I think that this statement is primarily concerned with the *judicial* supremacy of Parliament, and the mistake is to make it into a claim to political sovereignty in the Stuart sense.

It suggests an analogy with the later claim by the House of Commons of the privilege of regulating its own procedure, which also raised the issue of sovereignty (cf. Stockdale *v*. Hansard).

The attempt to bind the future is comparable with the laying down of judicial precedent.[1]

See Holdsworth, *History of English Law*, i, 359 ff., and note that as late as 1595 Coke, as Speaker of the House of Commons, can say "The nature of this House must be considered, for this Court is not a Court alone" (Holdsworth, iv, 184).

---

[1] Similarly Floyd's case raised the issue whether the House of Commons was a Court of Record.

CHAPTER VII

The Policy of Appeasement

AS far as action went Richard was content on this first occasion in May 1389 to relieve archbishop Arundel[1] of the great seal, but when the council reassembled on the 4th there was a wholesale change of ministers.[2] The veteran civil servants, Wykeham and Brantingham, both carefully neutral through the previous troubles, were brought out and forced against their wills to become chancellor and treasurer respectively, while the privy seal was given to a new man of royalist inclinations, Master Edmund Stafford. Gloucester and Warwick were temporarily dismissed from the council while the earl of Arundel, in spite of his partial success in 1388 and considerable success in 1387, was replaced, both as admiral and as captain of Brest, by the new earl of Huntingdon, whereupon, according to the Monk of Westminster,[3] he obtained leave to go to Palestine. The king then proceeded to appoint five new justices.[4] The appellant nominees, including the two chief justices, Clopton of the king's bench and Charlton, were retained, as well as Thirning of the common bench, who was to play a leading part in the revolution of 1399, but two more were added to the king's bench and three to the common bench, of whom William Rickhill, known for his connexion with the duke of Gloucester's death in 1397, is worth mention. In the exchequer only the appellant chief baron who had succeeded Cary was removed, though the Irish exchequer, on the other hand, was almost entirely reconstituted and in August a new chancellor of Ireland was appointed, while Sir John Stanley, formerly de Vere's deputy, was made justice of Ireland

---

[1] *Not* of course Neville, as Tout says—the slip is obvious.
[2] *Chapters*, iii, 456–7.   [3] p. 211.
[4] Walsingham, *Historia Anglicana*, ii, 182.

and nothing more was heard of Gloucester's keepership or lieutenancy.

On the whole these changes do not justify the sweeping statements of the Monk of Westminster,[1] who says that Richard now removed "all officers, both greater and less, even those beyond the sea", especially if they had been appointed by the appellants, and again that he "ejected from his household about four hundred persons, especially those brought into it by the barons". He adds later[2] that in the autumn of the same year Richard took into the hands of himself and of his "private council" the election of all the sheriffs in England—a charge which may very well be true of November 1397 and 1398 but for which there is no evidence in 1389. These exaggerations by this rather simple-minded chronicler may in fact reflect a successful piece of propaganda by the curialists themselves; the amount of peaceful change had to be stressed and made as spectacular as possible in order to emphasise the completeness of the king's recovery of power and also to annex for him the maximum credit for the minor successes which were now achieved; Richard was improving in technique from day to day. These successes were, firstly, the postponement of part of the last subsidy voted, that is in effect a remission of taxation, which had been clamoured for since 1377, and secondly, the negotiation of a three-year truce with France, in which Scotland was shortly afterwards included, though in the latter case the failure to extract any indemnity from the Scots for the raids of 1388 caused some criticism.[3]

But in spite of this show of activity the foundations of appellant policy were undisturbed; it is significant that Richard even paid off the balance of the £20,000 voted by the merciless parliament. Again, in the proclamation issued to the sheriffs

[1] p. 211.   [2] p. 217.
[3] Monk of Westminster, pp. 216–17. Cf. Walsingham, *Hist. Anglic.* ii, 182–3, who says that the Scots had prepared another invasion on a large scale and were only induced to accept the truce by considerable French pressure. Tout, *Chapters*, iii, 459, is right in saying that the truce was negotiated by an appellant commission, but the policy is pre-appellant.

on the 8th of May it was plainly stated that all graces and pardons made in that parliament were confirmed and no one was to be impeached for what had then been done. Richard did not dare to recall from exile de Vere, Neville, Michael de la Pole, Rushook or the justices of 1387; as late as 1392 he failed to recall the first two. Moreover, Gloucester and the earl of Arundel—perhaps also Warwick—were soon restored to the council, and Gloucester, if no longer keeper of Ireland, was allowed to act as justice of Chester and north Wales, which in view of Richard's special interests in those regions is significant and must to some extent discount Walsingham's story[1] of a violent quarrel and the permanent poisoning of Richard's mind against him. Nottingham too, in addition to his captaincy of Berwick and wardenship of the east march, which were confirmed to him, was soon admitted to the council, while Richard even went so far as to quarrel with that body about a large grant which he now wished to make to him. In fact from this time on until his fall in 1398 Nottingham seemed to recapture a considerable share of Richard's personal favour, though the king's suspicions were never fully quietened and his actions in 1387-8 were never fully forgiven him. When it is added that Derby, whom the king had never liked, was also readmitted to the council in the course of the year—a fact which Tout plausibly connects[2] with the return of Gaunt in the autumn—it becomes clear that the ministerial changes of May 1389 were not all they seemed to be and need a little reconsideration.

The appointments of Wykeham and Brantingham, the aged bishop of Exeter, were probably mere eyewash; in choosing these veteran administrators Richard wanted to impress political circles with a gravity and discretion which would give all the less excuse for opposing his dramatic resumption of personal power. He had probably little intention of keeping them long and though Wykeham, once he was in, characteristically clung to office until September 1391, Richard seems to have done what he could, short of actual dismissal, to get rid of him, and he did get rid of Brantingham, whose health was failing, within

[1] *Hist. Anglic.* ii, 182.   [2] *Chapters*, iii, 458-9.

three months. But the significant point is that he replaced neither of them by royalists but by the appellant chancellor and treasurer themselves, bishop Gilbert returning to the exchequer in August 1389 and Thomas Arundel to the chancery in 1391, where he remained until 1396 when he was translated, with Richard's full approval and consent, to Canterbury and took the opportunity to surrender the great seal. All this suggests, either that Richard was much weaker than he seems to have been or, more probably, that a real measure of appeasement was the order of the day. The king seems to have made his gesture of freedom with the initial appointments and after that to have reconciled himself to the prospect of his ex-enemies, who could hardly be very dangerous once Gaunt was home again, playing very much that part in the state to which their high position and, in some cases, talent entitled them. The one exception was the office of the privy seal.

Here Stafford became, as he was clearly meant to be, something of a permanency, remaining keeper until 1396 and then chancellor until the revolution. Quite apart from this *prima facie* evidence of his efficiency, which is further illustrated by the fact that like so many of Richard's most loyal officials he remained in high crown employment under Henry IV, the choice was a clever one. Stafford was a junior magnate in his own right,[1] being the son of a banneret lord of parliament to whose estates he had succeeded in 1380 and nephew to the first earl of Stafford. Through entering the church and devoting himself to the study of civil law he had hitherto avoided taking any part at all in politics. He had, however, been chancellor of Oxford university and dean of York since 1385, while his entry into Richard's service brought him the bishopric of Exeter ten years later and enabled him to become practically the second founder of Exeter college, Oxford.[2] If we ask why the privy seal in particular was reserved for such a man we have to remember the growing closeness of the

---

[1] Tout, *Chapters*, iii, 462–3, for the details which follow.

[2] It was first founded by an earlier bishop of Exeter, the famous exchequer reformer Stapledon.

connexion between the privy seal office and the small council
in these years and the continually increasing emphasis which
Richard was to place on its composition and activities. Again,
a knowledge of Roman law was not out of place in a man who
would have to sit regularly on a body which in its judicial
activities was coming to follow more and more the forms and
the procedure of that law; Tout has warned us that the connexion must not be over-emphasised,[1] but he himself has been
among the first to point out that it undoubtedly existed.

The first-fruits of the new régime were seen in the parliament of January 1390. This began with what Tout calls the
"curious comedy"[2] of chancellor, treasurer and lords of the
council[3] resigning in a body and submitting themselves to
what might almost be called a vote of confidence from lords
and commons. Thereupon they were all reappointed, with the
addition of Gaunt and Gloucester. The staging of this episode
may safely be attributed to the king himself, whose fit of statesmanship was not yet quite exhausted. Parliament meanwhile
requested and obtained the appointment of two special
treasurers of war on the precedent of 1377, to collect and
account for the subsidy which it granted. But two controllers
were appointed with these parliamentary treasurers and they
were both men, if not of royalist past, at least of royalist intention. The first was John Waltham, now bishop of Salisbury,
who though not yet a minister (Tout[4] appears to be mistaken
on that point) was already creeping back into the confidence of
the king; he succeeded Gilbert at the exchequer in May 1391
after the special treasurers and controllers had been discharged.
The other was John, lord Cobham, who had always been of a
moderate, if not of an actively curialist, complexion. Finally,
with regard to the "vote of confidence" itself Richard was
careful to preserve a loophole for future action by stating that
it was not to form a precedent and that he considered himself

[1] *Chapters*, v, ch. 16, *passim*; cf. iii, 468.   [2] *Ibid.* iii, 460 ff.
[3] But not the keeper of the privy seal, who held what was still regarded
as a household office.
[4] *Chapters*, iii, 455.

free to remove and appoint ministers at will in future, nor did parliament protest at this reservation.

The other acts of this parliament were also of some importance and there were several new appointments. Thus the earl of Huntingdon, Richard's half-brother, was made chamberlain of the household in place of Peter Courtenay and later in the year received a patent confirming him in office for life.[1] At the same time Sir Thomas Percy, brother of the earl of Northumberland, whose interests had been curiously neglected by the appellants, became vice-chamberlain and held the office until January 1393, when he was succeeded by William Scrope for the rest of the reign.[2] Gaunt's status in Aquitaine was redefined; he was appointed governor for life with full palatine powers, though at his own charges, and was given the new title of duke of Guienne. The change was unpopular in Gascony, though not in England; Gaunt's agents were systematically obstructed and he himself achieved little more when finally obliged to make a personal visit of fifteen months' duration while Richard was in Ireland in 1394–5.[3] Lastly Edward, eldest son of the duke of York and Richard's first cousin, was created earl of Rutland, thereby joining the circle of smart young men which was beginning to form round the king. He was to be the Judas among Richard's new disciples.

Any suspicions which may have been aroused by these appointments were perhaps set at rest by the fact that in certain other important respects this parliament of January 1390 deliberately continued the policy of the Cambridge parliament. Thus in the matter of provisors the Cambridge parliament had declared all benefices conferred in this way, *par licence ou sanz licence*, to be void, but the crown had freely gone on granting such licences in virtue of the now ancient collusion between successive English governments and the pope. Hence in January 1390 the statute was tightened up in order to defeat

[1] Monk of Westminster, p. 222; *C.P.R.* 1388–92, p. 252.
[2] *Chapters*, iii, 463. Percy became steward of the household for the same period.   [3] Armitage-Smith, *John of Gaunt*, ch. xv.

such licences, which for two or three days previously had been issued at the rate of twenty a day. This provoked a special mission of protest from the papacy, which, as M. Perroy has shown,[1] was itself largely responsible for the statute through its renewed demands upon the English clergy. The death of Urban in October 1389 had left the whole complex problem of papal taxation and provision in the air, but his successor, Boniface IX, while no less anxious to retain his limited obedience, was faced with the same difficulty (common to all popes of the Schism) of financing from only one half of Europe an institution which had come to depend on revenues drawn from the whole of Christendom. Urban had been cheated by the appellants when he had tried, by accepting some limitation of his right to provide to English benefices, to obtain freer access to the purses of the English clergy, and although he had recovered ground to some extent by exploiting royal licences the position when Boniface became pope was far from satisfactory. The English laity, though not the English church, were determined to restrict the licence system; this in turn led to counter-measures by the pope, notably a bull of February 1391. Even then there was never any question of a breach with Rome, though feelings ran high on both sides and were to run higher; parliament in November 1391 merely ignored the bull and reaffirmed its principles, though as a concession to archbishop Arundel it allowed without prejudice a strictly limited number of exemptions.

Another point in which the policy, or attempted policy, of the autumn of 1388 was continued in January 1390 was the limitation of livery,[2] which in theory was to have begun with this parliament but again met with small success. However, we should probably connect with this campaign a restriction placed by Richard on this occasion on grants of pardon for criminal offences, hitherto made too easily by the crown but hence-

---

[1] *L'Angleterre et le grand schisme d'Occident*, ch. viii, *passim*. Cf. Monk of Westminster, pp. 225–33, for the new statute. On the whole question of merit see G. Barraclough, *Papal Provisions*, *passim*.

[2] Walsingham, *Hist. Anglic.* ii, 196.

forward to be granted only after due enquiry and then under the privy seal.[1] Here again the influence of the commons, or rather their identity of interest with the crown, may be detected in restraining illegalities and self-help. The same cannot be said of another instance of continuity with the Cambridge parliament, when at the commons' request the drastic labour legislation of that parliament was reaffirmed with the very slight improvement of substituting for the fixed rates of wages a sliding scale, to be determined by the justices of the peace according to local conditions.[2] Here again Richard's easy acquiescence in demands of this sort shows what little interest he really took now or at any time in the continuing unrest among his poorer subjects, evidence for which is to be found among the chancery enrolments for this period.[3]

Finally, there is one more instance of the compromising spirit of this parliament, as far as the late troubles among the governing classes were concerned, in the attitude adopted towards certain of the new and unpopular prerogative jurisdictions. The Monk of Westminster in particular[4] mentions statutes in restraint of the activities not only of the constable's and marshal's court, the *curia militaris*, which the appellants had probably tried to use against Richard's friends, but also of the *curia mareschallie*, or marshalsea. This was the court of the steward of the household, so active under Sir John Montague in the years before the first "tyranny", when it had actually condemned John of Northampton to death, though the sentence was not executed, in 1383. In future it was to be confined to household disputes *infra virgam* just as the *curia militaris* was to restrict itself to those causes *quae ad arma pertinent*. Both courts were in fact abused again by Richard before long, especially the *curia militaris*, which enjoyed a certain popularity of its own

---

[1] Monk of Westminster, pp. 223–4.   [2] H. Wallon, *Richard II*, ii, 27.
[3] E.g. *C.P.R.* 1388–92, p. 217—withdrawal of services from the abbot of Thorney, February 1390—special commission appointed; *C.C.R.* 1392–6, p. 380 and *C.P.R.* 1391–6, p. 444—trouble with villeins shifting boundary marks in Lincolnshire, 1394. There was also some sort of obscure rising by the poorer classes in Kent in 1393.   [4] p. 222.

in feudal circles, but for the moment the surface compromise may have served its purpose.

The other parliament of the year, held in November 1390, did little more in the vital field of foreign policy than survey, somewhat anxiously, the long-drawn-out peace negotiations with France and Scotland, to the progress of which we must now turn.

Negotiations with these two countries had for some time been linked together by the insistence of the French. There was now in any case a special need for peace between France and England, for in 1389 the victory of the Ottoman Turks at Kossovo had been followed by the accession of one of their greatest rulers, Bajazet, and not only Constantinople but Hungary were desperately appealing for western help.[1] There was in fact a chance for a real crusade, in contrast to the futile expeditions of the duke of Bourbon to Tunis and the earl of Derby to Prussia[2] in this year, and M. Perroy makes much[3] of the wild scheme of Charles VI, framed as early as April 1390, for an Italian crusade on the part of the French feudal host, which was now out of action owing to the truce with England. They were to pick up pope Clement at Avignon on the way and restore him to Rome by force of arms, after which they might or might not have proceeded to the support of Hungary against the Turks. News of this plan caused some alarm in England and an appeal was sent to Wenzel to protect Boniface in Italy, but in spite of the fact that Clement is said to have promised Charles VI the empire if he would go through with it, the whole scheme broke down owing to the active renewal of Anglo-French peace negotiations in 1391.

This *rapprochement* is not surprising in view of the stalemate in the war and the general weariness of the Schism. Both Froissart and Walsingham note the natural friendliness between Frenchmen and Englishmen at this time; a friendliness

[1] Wallon, *op. cit.* ii, 36, 407.
[2] Whither Gloucester, though somewhat easily deterred by a bad storm, attempted to follow him in 1391.
[3] *Schisme*, pp. 355–7.

which extended from the higher to the lower classes. Thus, according to Froissart,[1] the fishermen of both countries had long since ceased to take the war seriously and lived at peace with each other, while the fellow-feeling between the French and English chivalry, as against Spaniards and Germans for example, is still better attested, and showed itself at this time in frequent jousts which were the medieval equivalent of the Test match. Thus the tournament at St Inglevert in March 1389[2] was attended by Huntingdon and other English noblemen and the return match at Smithfield the next year by several Frenchmen, including the count of St Pol. All through 1391 French and English drew slowly together in spite of the efforts of the two popes,[3] seconded by a few professional soldiers such as Gloucester, to keep them apart. Still Richard seems to have hesitated to take any decided step towards peace and in fact it was the French who were making all the running. But the coincidence between the warm welcome given to a French embassy which arrived just too late for a September council at Canterbury[4] and the departure of Gloucester on his would-be crusade clearly shows the trend of events.

The parliament which followed Gloucester's departure in the autumn of 1391 did something to dispose of Richard's hesitation by showing that it might be safe for him after all not to limit the policy of appeasement to the home front. The question was becoming a simple one, namely peace with France, the ending of the papal schism by the adoption of a strong line towards both popes, and perhaps a joint crusade, or the continuance both of the French and Scottish wars and of the Schism. Early in the year Boniface had gone so far as to annul the existing English statutes on papal provision,[5] while at the same time continuing to make his incompatible demands for more money and the prosecution of the war with Clementist

[1] Ap. Wallon, op. cit. ii, 40.
[2] See Newbolt, The New June.
[3] Monk of Westminster, pp. 251–4.
[4] Ibid. pp. 260–1; cf. Walsingham, Hist. Anglic. ii, 198–9.
[5] Those of 1307, 1351 and 1390.

France.[1] Parliament, relieved of Gloucester's presence, took up the papal challenge by refusing to repeal provisors[2] and by adding Gaunt to the negotiators with the French, "because he is the most sufficient person in the realm". It also went out of its way to express its confidence in Richard by the famous declaration, made at the petition of the commons, that "our lord the king should be as free in his royal dignity as any of his predecessors, despite any statute to the contrary, notably those in the days of Edward II, and that if any such statute had that effect under Edward II it should be annulled".[3] It would seem that Richard had once again squared the oracle, but squared or not he could have had no better answer from it; yet it is probable that his previous hesitations had been genuine. He had already had bitter experience of the dangers of outrunning parliamentary opinion in his foreign policy—dangers which were now greater owing to the confusion of the French war with English relations to Boniface IX. This again involved the statutes of provisors on which the English church and laity did not see eye to eye. According to Walsingham,[4] both Richard and Gaunt had originally been in favour of giving way to Rome, at any rate in part, over provisors, which might also have meant giving way on the question of peace with France; it is plausible to see in this the influence of archbishop Arundel. However, the decided line taken by parliament put an end to any thoughts of surrender. From this time on, even though Gloucester's crusade proved a fiasco and he was back in England before the end of the year, only one line of policy was possible, and there was no need to summon parliament at all in 1392.

In the spring of that year the duke of Lancaster opened fresh

[1] Perroy, *Schisme*, pp. 319–22.

[2] Walsingham, *Hist. Anglic.* ii, 203, says that the entire operation of provisors was none the less postponed to the next parliament (January 1393), but Walsingham cannot be trusted on this subject.

[3] Tout, *Chapters*, iii, 474. There were also other measures of some importance in this parliament, concerning e.g. the staple and the submission of the gilds to the mortmain laws.

[4] *Hist. Anglic.* ii, 203.

and serious peace negotiations in great state at Amiens, and all went well until proceedings began to be interrupted by the fits of madness to which from August onwards the French king became liable. During 1393 the extremely unwise addition of Gloucester to the negotiators made further progress difficult;[1] Gaunt was also hampered by the mysterious Cheshire rising of that year, of which more will be said later. On the other hand the honouring of a fifteen years' old undertaking by the English in relation to the fortress of Cherbourg during the winter of 1393–4 made things rather easier. By the treaty of 1378 Cherbourg had been pawned to England by its lord, Charles III of Navarre, on the understanding that after three years' interval[2] it could at any time be redeemed for the same amount. Charles, who had turned Clementist in February 1390, had for some time been anxious to redeem the place, since the Urbanist captains of Cherbourg had been worrying, among others, the Clementist bishop of Coutances, but he had had difficulty in raising the money on his side while Richard had cautiously professed religious scruples connected with the Schism.[3] Now, however, the French lent the money to the king of Navarre and on the 21st of January 1394 Richard acknowledged receipt of it and surrendered the fortress. The immediate effect of this step was to forward the new peace policy of Richard, Gaunt and parliament, but it outraged the die-hards led by Gloucester, who three years later made this unavoidable surrender into a charge against Richard.

Meanwhile the January parliament of 1394, meeting six days after the event, took little or no notice of it, but merely continued to debate the peace proposals. These went so far as to authorise the concession of homage, short of liege homage, to the French king for Guienne and, most noticeably, substituted York for Gloucester on the peace commission. The trend of

[1] Ramsay, *Genesis*, ii, 291–2, for these negotiations generally.

[2] Not fifteen years, as is usually said: Perroy, *Diplomatic Correspondence*, no. 124, p. 83.

[3] Perroy, *Schisme*, pp. 83–5, 222; *Diplomatic Correspondence*, no. 124, p. 84.

these developments is unmistakable, but as English readiness
to treat grew, feeling stiffened on the French side and a demand
was now made for the surrender, not only of Cherbourg, but
of Calais,[1] which was out of the question. As a result the
negotiations ended in May 1394 with a simple prolongation of
the existing truce, but this time for four years instead of three
(that is, to Michaelmas 1398). Not one of the real issues between the two countries, such as homage for Guienne, the
Schism, the crusade, the English claim to the French throne,
had been settled. The truce was none the less destined to be
prolonged again, this time for the considerable term of twenty-
eight years from 1398, on the occasion of Richard's second
marriage.

The space which has so far been given to parliament in this
chapter may suggest that it was more important as an institution
in these years than was the case. In fact, the growing identity of
policy and interest between king, lords and commons in the
thirteen-nineties in face of the disunion and jealousies of the
opposition magnates, of which there will be more to say soon,
resulted in a positive dwindling, rather than in an increase, of
parliamentary time and importance and a renewed emphasis
on the council, particularly the small council. Tout notes[2] that
between 1380 and 1388 there were thirteen parliaments, with
an average duration of forty-one days, while between 1389 and
1397 there were only seven, with an average duration of
twenty-one days. It is, however, important to realise that this
change took place for the very reason that Richard had
broadened the basis of his royalism and found allies, not tools.
Again, there were so few parliaments very largely because this
free allied element, being primarily aristocratic, as all medieval
political parties were, found expression as easily in councils,
small and great, as in the more cumbrous machinery of parliament. Richard did not dominate these councils of the early
'nineties any more than he dominated the parliaments, though

[1] Cf. the well-known ballade of Eustace Deschamps, composed at this
date and printed in Wright's *Political Poems* (R.S.), i, 300, with its refrain,
"paix n'arez jà s'ilz ne rendent Calays".   [2] *Chapters*, iii, 473.

he has been too easily credited with dominating both by those historians who see in him a luxurious weakling, magically metamorphosed at this point into a crafty tyrant. Once his claims had been formally admitted by both bodies, he did little but maintain the outward show of kingship for four or five years more, as he had done in 1384–6, and he seems only to have exercised a fitful and occasional control over policy, which was left mainly in the council's hands—less perhaps because he could not rule than because he was in the main too indolent and too satisfied to try. There is little doubt, however, that his mentality was slowly changing and maturing all the time along lines that have already been suggested; there was no chance of his forgetting the commission and the events of 1386–8, and if he was not consciously planning revenge, which seems doubtful, he was at least fully determined never to submit to anything which looked like an attempted repetition of the events of those years.

The conciliar government of the period of appeasement none the less sprang out of the initial fit of energy, compromise and statesmanship of 1389–90. It is therefore, as we should expect, in March 1390, immediately after the parliament in which the new régime was "registered", that we get the first extant ordinance for the government of the king's council.[1] This ordinance was, as a whole, a singularly conservative, not to say platitudinous document; the most interesting and significant features of it were certain well-marked restraints upon the crown. Thus in the first place the king was not to make gifts or grants without the advice of the council, the three dukes his uncles, and the chancellor, or any two of them. This, however, was not so formidable for Richard as it sounds; he could always count on the complaisant duke of York, and had then only to win over Lancaster—a fact which may help to account for his assiduous cultivation of Gaunt during these years. Secondly, no ministerial office was to be granted in future without the

---

[1] For this ordinance see the analysis in Tout, *Chapters*, iii, 465–6, and also the chapter on Richard's reign in Baldwin, *The King's Council*, pp. 115–46, to which Tout pays tribute, while making certain criticisms and corrections.

advice of the council and ministers, and no steward or justice was to be appointed for life. It is doubtful how seriously this clause should be taken. Small councils could always be forced to adopt the views of great councils, as in 1389, and reappointment, which was not forbidden, was a good substitute for life appointment; on the other hand, even great councils could not always be managed, as Richard found in 1392.

Another clause in the ordinance is worth record, though it did not directly affect the king; it is that which laid down that bills of small importance or touching persons of limited means might be examined and determined by the keeper of the privy seal and other councillors. This is interesting in that it provides for the automatic functioning of the routine administration of the council without royal intervention, and there is no doubt that Richard soon grew tired of attending even the more important meetings. Secondly, if Tout is right,[1] we may see here the distant ancestor of the Tudor court of requests—the practice of the council sitting in chancery and developing into a court of equity under the chancellor was being mimicked for poor men's causes by a less formal session under the chairmanship, if we may call it that, of the keeper of the privy seal.

Something has already been said, apropos of the keeper of these years, Edmund Stafford, about the growing closeness of this connexion between the small council and the privy seal. It undoubtedly existed and even grew more close in process of time, but it is important not to over-emphasise it as Baldwin and some others have done. While it is true to say that the privy seal now bore much the same relation to councils, small and great, as the great seal did to parliament, it is not correct to regard the privy seal office as in any sense the servant of the council or under its unique control; it remained what it had been in Edward II's time, in theory a household but in fact a national department. None the less about 1390 a particularly able and energetic secondary of the privy seal, John Prophet, did undoubtedly become clerk of the council[2] and probably did a great deal towards its organisation and development, especially

[1] *Chapters*, iii, 468.   [2] *Ibid.* v, 102; cf. Perroy, *Schisme*, pp. 105, 218.

upon the record side. His minutes for 1392–3 survive and have been printed as a journal by Baldwin.[1]

The extent to which councils organised on these lines were able to modify the king's policy from time to time, even against his will, can easily be illustrated. As early as October 1389— perhaps because Richard was not yet fully sure of his position— the small council was able to oppose him with some effect in support of Wykeham, then chancellor,´on the question of the lavish grants already mentioned which he proposed making to the earl of Nottingham. This led to a scene, including an ominous retreat on Richard's part to Kennington, but the council stood firm and at any rate secured a compromise. Great councils were in a still stronger position; thus Prophet's journal and the Monk of Westminster[2] give a mutually consistent account of an important council held in February 1392. Although at any one session this council never exceeded twenty-five persons in all, not counting the king, Tout is probably right in holding[3] against Baldwin that it ought to be regarded as a great council owing to the proportion of specially summoned magnates present and the importance of its business. This included an attempt by Richard, if we are to believe the Monk of Westminster, to recall Alexander Neville and de Vere; the council, however, stood firm and the king was forced to declare that he did not wish to recall any person condemned by parliament, the magnates promising for their part to stand by him against all his enemies and to guarantee him full power to rule within this limitation, which remained a real one. The same council also dealt with Gloucester's abortive appointment as king's lieutenant in Ireland, which had been superseded before he sailed, with questions of the staple and of relations with France; it is noteworthy however that its conclusions were not only accepted but amended by a smaller council.

A much larger great council, actually attended not only by magnates and officials but by knights from every shire, met at

[1] *Op. cit.* Cf. Lodge and Thornton, *English Constitutional Documents*, p. 67, where the minutes are misdated 1390.

[2] pp. 264–5; Baldwin, *op. cit.* pp. 489–507.   [3] *Chapters*, iii, 471.

Stamford on the 25th of May 1392 and listened to a debate between the duke of Gelderland, who wanted to prolong the French war, and the duke of Lancaster, deciding in the end for peace, as had become usual. A similar great council was held at Nottingham on the 25th of June and was followed by another on the 22nd of July [1] to hear the king's reasons for his famous quarrel with London, and to witness the condemnation of the mayor and aldermen; and there may even have been another in September of this year at Canterbury, though the Monk of Westminster [2] assigns this to 1391. Tout notes [3] that in 1392 these frequent great councils took the place of parliament, and shows that their presence or absence did not affect the steady working of the ordinary council, which can be traced in Prophet's journal again from December 1392 to February 1393 and in the regular warranting of chancery writs "by king and council" right up to the end of the reign. That as late as 1393, just after the king's remarkable assertion of his power over London, even the small council could oppose him effectively is shown by a random extract from the close rolls, [4] which reveals it quashing a royal nomination by signet letter to the mayoralty of Northampton and ordering a free election.

Professor Baldwin thinks [5] that Richard soon came to forestall such opposition by swamping the council with chamber knights like Stury, Clifford and Dalyngrigge—a policy which was rendered easier for him by the alleged failure of the magnate members to attend with any regularity, except for really important discussions, such as those concerning peace with France (1392) or the government of Gascony (1395). From this he deduces the growth of a royal bureaucracy plotted against by the ex-appellants in 1397, when however Richard got wind of their intentions and made the first move. This theory is over-simplified and over-stated, though there may be something in it as applied to the last two or three years of the reign when, as Baldwin points out, a bitter resentment was

[1] Tout, *Chapters*, iii, 473; cf. Monk of Westminster, p. 272.
[2] p. 260.   [3] *Loc. cit.*   [4] *Ap.* Tout, *Chapters*, iii, 469.
[5] *The King's Council*, ch. vi.

very widely felt against the king's knights on the council. He assumes, however, at all times far too much unity among the lords against the king and in effect denies Richard what he certainly possessed, namely the support of a substantial section of the aristocracy. It was upon these moderate lords, fortified by the new generation of *duketti*, that Richard came more and more to rely; if there was one thing which he had learned from 1386-8 it was to have his own party among the magnates. The swamping theory, moreover, ignores the fact that archbishop Arundel as chancellor must have been the most important member of the council up to 1396 and that at this date decisions were not necessarily taken by counting heads; *maioritas* and *sanitas* had not yet been finally identified. It also tends to suggest that there was something new in relying on king's knights as a secondary source of strength for the routine work of the council, whereas this policy was at least as old as the minority, and indeed much older. Nor is there anything very remarkable in Baldwin's discovery that the first step in the elaboration of the second "tyranny" was a change in the king's councillors; it would have been much more strange if this had not been so. He also tends to exaggerate both the amount of resentment caused in these last years by the gradual extension of conciliar jurisdiction and the degree of parliamentary and common-law reaction under Henry IV.

None the less Baldwin's chapter on the council under Richard II, which broke entirely new ground at the time when it was written, remains of very great value. He is right in stressing the fact that the curialists of whom he speaks, the men in the second rank, were not, as their enemies represented them to be, *novi homines*, adventurers or personal favourites, but men of experience, ability and, not infrequently, good birth. He is also right in saying that their attendance at the council was much more regular than that of irreconcilable malcontents like the duke of Gloucester, even if he still, in the last analysis, does not attach enough weight to the numerous magnate members of the council well disposed towards the king.

The years 1392-4 were marked by certain events of importance outside the fields of foreign policy and of purely conciliar or parliamentary history. There was Richard's famous quarrel with London in the summer of 1392, the story of which has so often been told that there is little point in repeating it in any detail.[1] It is in any case rather an obscure story, but the gist of it appears to be a failure on Richard's part to raise a voluntary loan from the city, with the result that its mayor and other officials were arrested and its liberties wholly suspended from May to September, when in return for a fine of £3000 and a gift of £10,000, and as a result of personal mediation by the queen, the city was taken back into favour again. If that were all, the episode would be discreditable to Richard, but it is noteworthy that not only Lancaster and Huntingdon but also John Waltham and even archbishop Arundel and the council in general appear to have been in sympathy with him, so that the extremely one-sided account in the chronicles,[2] which is all we have, may be due, as Tout suggests, to bias of one kind or another,[3] since the other side of the story is not known. What is certain is that the incident gravely prejudiced Richard's relations with the Londoners and may account for the fact that in the crisis of 1397–9, unlike that of 1386–8, he had no party whatever in the city on his side; it was therefore perhaps one of the most serious, as it was certainly the first in time, of the many grave mistakes he was to make during his concluding years.

January 1393 was for centuries held to be a date of some importance in Richard's reign for a totally different reason; it was the month in which a parliament held at Winchester made the "great" statute of *praemunire*. Both this parliament and the famous statute connected with it made curiously little im-

[1] There is a good summary in Tout, *Chapters*, iii, 479–81.
[2] Walsingham, *Hist. Anglic.* ii, 207–11, 213; Monk of Westminster, pp. 267–70, 272–8.
[3] His idea that the bias in the chronicles is south-country bias as against the supposed north-countrymen, Arundel and Waltham, who for that reason made no objection to Richard's penal removal of government departments to the north for the time being, seems however rather thin.

THE POLICY OF APPEASEMENT 199

pression on contemporaries—thus the *Annales Ricardi* [1] merely
record a money grant, made in connexion with the mission of
Lancaster and Gloucester to the French, while the Monk of
Westminster [2] simply notes that Sir Aubrey de Vere was now
permitted to succeed to his dead nephew's title of earl of
Oxford, that the statute of provisors (*sic*) was once more pro-
mulgated and that the remaining activities of this parliament,
though numerous, were of such little interest that he has omitted
them entirely! This indifference on the part of two reasonably
intelligent contemporary monks to important ecclesiastical
legislation can only be explained by the assumption that
perhaps that legislation was not so important after all, and that
is very largely what W. T. Waugh has proved.[3]

There was of course a statute, and a new one, aimed broadly
at anyone who should connive at a papal bull translating a
bishop, passing sentence of excommunication or infringing the
royal prerogative. The precise meaning of this threat is more
difficult to determine—did it, for example, forbid the introduction of all papal documents into England or merely the
introduction of those which were prejudicial to the interests of
the crown? The preamble to the statute [4] makes it clear that
even the second interpretation is too wide, for the statute
referred only to papal documents passing sentence on an English
bishop for obeying the mandates of the royal courts or those
arranging for the arbitrary translation of prelates from see to
see, and it must be admitted that even this limited objective
could not have been achieved if the papacy had chosen to press
the point against it; this perhaps accounts for the indifference
of the chroniclers. The true explanation of the move is to be
found in Boniface IX's continued attempts to modify or abolish
the statutes of provisors; in pursuit of this object he had recently
threatened to excommunicate all clerks presented to benefices

---

[1] p. 155.   [2] p. 279.

[3] *E.H.R.* xxxviii, 173–205 and *History*, viii, 289–92. Cf. Perroy, *Schisme*,
pp. 332 ff., who in general accepts Waugh's findings and confirms them.

[4] *Statutes of the Realm*, ii, 84; Adams and Stephens, *Select Documents*,
pp. 156–9.

by laymen, together with any ecclesiastical authority who should consent to institute or induct them, and he had added that he would throw the English government out of gear, if necessary, by moving the Caesarian bishops from see to see and even ordering them abroad.

To this intention of Boniface the preamble of 1393 was the real rejoinder; it amounted to a threat of transfer of allegiance, which would be powerfully reinforced by the existing peace negotiations with the French, and as such it soon brought Boniface to heel. Once its purpose had been served in this way it became a dead letter; it was simply a move in the current political game and it is arguable that the chroniclers were justified in ignoring it or treating it, as the Monk of Westminster does, as a mere restatement of provisors. The truth of this view can be proved by several considerations, of which two will suffice: Boniface himself did not agitate for the repeal of this statute, though he continued to plead, more diplomatically, against provisors; and secondly, it was not only ignored in a letter from Richard to the pope, written on the 20th of June 1393,[1] but never invoked in any English official record of any kind for nearly forty years to come. The reasons for the undue importance subsequently attached to it belong to later history; it was rediscovered in or about 1431 in the course of Humphrey duke of Gloucester's struggle with cardinal Beaufort and was perhaps invoked as a result in 1434 and certainly in 1439, after which it was fairly frequently mentioned during the later fifteenth century, and it eventually became famous through the use made of it in procuring the fall of Wolsey in 1529. In all these instances, however, the originally vital preamble was ignored.

More immediately important than the "great" statute of *praemunire*, and much more difficult to explain, was the mysterious Cheshire rising, which also took place in 1393.[2] There seems to be little doubt that there had been constant disturbances and border forays in Cheshire since the appoint-

[1] Perroy, *Schisme*, pp. 139–40, 243.
[2] Tout, *Chapters*, iii, 482–4, puts together the existing references, but does not profess to explain them.

THE POLICY OF APPEASEMENT

ment of Gloucester as justice of Chester and north Wales in
June 1388 and the conversion of this appointment into a life
grant, as far as Chester was concerned, in the autumn of 1389.
The king no doubt had not been altogether displeased at this
development, but he had at least attempted to fine the men of
Cheshire 3000 marks in 1390 in return for confirming their
liberties; of this fine, however, only 1000 marks had been collected, the payment of the rest being resisted by force through
1391. In the spring of 1393, while Gloucester and Gaunt were
abroad negotiating with the French, the men of Cheshire
found a leader in a certain Sir Thomas Talbot and broke into
open revolt on the pretext that Gloucester and Gaunt were
plotting both the surrender of the king's claims in France and
the destruction of the Cheshire franchises. This revolt was further
associated with a still more mysterious rising on Gaunt's
estates in Yorkshire led by one William Beckwith, whose death
is erroneously recorded by the Monk of Westminster[1] under
the year 1392. He seems, however, to have been still very
much alive in 1393 when he complained of dismissal from a post
in Gaunt's forest of Knaresborough three years previously,[2]
since when he had been an outlaw. Furthermore, the earl of
Arundel was known to be awaiting developments with a large
force in his castle at Holt on Dee, and the *Annales'* strong
assertion of his innocence[3] must be read in the light of two
known facts, first, that he made no attempt to repress the
rising, and secondly, that he was notoriously on bad terms with
Gaunt, though not of course with Gloucester.

On the 6th of May 1393 Richard, in a significant phrase,
proclaimed his own innocence of any attempt "to destroy the
magnates of the realm", which looks as if he himself was being
suspected, as in that particular district he very well might be,
of fostering the rising; he directed this proclamation not only
to the dukes of Gloucester and Lancaster but to the sheriffs
of Shropshire, Staffordshire, Derbyshire, Leicestershire and
Warwickshire, which shows the wide area affected by the

[1] p. 265; cf. *Annales Ricardi*, pp. 160–1.
[2] Monk of Westminster, pp. 239–40.   [3] p. 162.

disturbance. According to the *Annales*[1] Richard and his council did not want Gaunt and Gloucester to return to England lest the French negotiations should be hindered, but they insisted on coming home to clear themselves and, once arrived, Gaunt easily repressed the rising, earning praise from the *Annales*[2] for his leniency and tact. Gloucester, though he had also collected an armed force, does not appear to have done anything at all— a fact which, taken in conjunction with the similar inactivity of Arundel, suggests that they may have hoped that Lancaster would fail and that they might then come to the rescue themselves and, if necessary, blame the king. If so, their plans miscarried owing to Gaunt's loyalty and energy; it is significant that in spite of his life grant Gloucester was removed from his office of justice of Chester and north Wales in favour of the earl of Nottingham—a very skilful choice—in March 1394.

The spring parliament of that year is notable as the occasion on which the obvious ill-feeling between Gaunt and Arundel at last came to a head. The *Annales Ricardi*, which up to this point and later is marked by an undercurrent of hostility to Gaunt overlaid by surface compliments, perhaps inserted later, blames the duke exclusively[3] and says that he made unworthy accusations concerning Arundel's inactivity at Holt the previous year. But the rolls of parliament show clearly that Arundel took the initiative by accusing Gaunt of overfamiliarity with the king[4] and excessive arrogance to his peers; he also accused him of having dissipated the resources of the crown in Castile and alleged that Richard had remitted all his debts of 1386, incurred when his great expedition had been fitted out, in return for his services in Aquitaine and elsewhere.[5] Arundel's case, however, broke down badly; he had to apologise to the duke in full parliament and temporarily left the court, taking a cheap revenge on Richard through his rudeness at Anne's funeral later in the year.

The other main activities of this parliament related to the

---

[1] p. 160.   [2] p. 161.   [3] p. 166.
[4] Wallon, *op. cit.* ii, 72 notes the incongruity of Arundel's anxiety for the dignity of the crown.   [5] Perroy, *Schisme*, p. 259.

proposed peace with France, certain slight modifications in the constitution of London, and the raising of minor mercantile restrictions. As regards supply, the *Annales* suggests[1] that this parliament, in ordering payment of the conditionally granted second half of a subsidy and continuing tunnage and poundage at the full rate, already had before it Richard's proposals for an Irish expedition on a lavish scale. This is not certain, but it is quite clear from the order of subsequent events in 1394 that Richard had in fact formed this scheme before Anne's death to deal with a real and urgent problem as a matter of serious interest and an important part of his general policy of appeasement; it cannot therefore have been, as many have said, a mere distraction carried out as a direct result of the queen's death.

The year 1394 was remarkable for many deaths of importance; it is a watershed in the later history of the reign. That of Anne, which took place at Sheen on the 7th of June,[2] was perhaps the most serious in its immediate effects. In spite of the earlier unpopularity attaching to her, or to her Bohemians, it was deplored by all the chroniclers[3] and there is no doubt that Richard, who was so violently moved that he ordered at least the partial destruction of the manor-house in which she died,[4] became progressively more unbalanced, reckless and impatient after her death than he had ever been before it; his neurosis rapidly took hold. It may be seen at work not only in the destruction of the manor but, more pardonably, in the famous scene at Anne's funeral to which the heartless and deliberate discourtesy of the earl of Arundel gave rise.[5] From this moment the tempo of the reign quickens; the policy of appeasement was not extinct, indeed it only reached its climax two years later with Richard's formal re-marriage with the child princess Isabelle, in the interests of peace with France, but the nearer it was brought to a successful conclusion the less

[1] p. 166.   [2] Not July, as Tout says (*Chapters*, iii, 486).
[3] E.g. Monk of Westminster, p. 283; *Ann. Ric.* p. 168.
[4] This detail is added by Adam of Usk (ed. E. M. Thompson), p. 8.
[5] He arrived late and was personally assaulted by Richard. Cf. *Ann. Ric.* pp. 168–9, 424.

certain it became that Richard would content himself with it. Before long the slightest hint of opposition would be enough to arouse tortured memories of the appellant régime and pathological suspicions of a plot; not only the preservation but an extreme, almost an insane, interpretation of the regality became his main obsession and in 1399 it was accompanied, after his long run of successes, by an equally unbalanced and unreasonable sense of false security, which was his downfall in the end. Much of this might have been averted had Anne lived, and the comparatively moderate policy of 1389–94 might have been continued until the course of nature had removed most of the appellants and perhaps healed Richard's wounds, but even so the failure of Anne to bear children must have caused grave difficulties over the succession. All this, however, is anticipation, for although the course of Richard's mental disease was certainly accelerated from 1394 it cannot be said that it took an active or dangerous form before the early months of 1397.

Two more obits of 1394 were almost equally important in the history of the Lancastrian dynasty. The first of these was the death, which occurred in March, of Gaunt's Spanish wife, Costanza of Castile; this made possible the legitimation two years later of the Beauforts, the children of his mistress, Catherine Swynford, and that in turn tended to alienate both Gaunt himself and Richard, who had granted the legitimation, from Derby, Gaunt's true heir, who had hitherto been completely disassociated, as far as can be judged, from the gradually reviving opposition. The death of Derby's own wife, Mary Bohun, the younger co-heiress of the great Bohun inheritance, which followed at the beginning of July, may perhaps have had an opposite though temporary effect. She was the sister of Eleanor, duchess of Gloucester, and it is possible, though by no means proved, that her disappearance did something to weaken the perhaps never very powerful ties which connected Derby with his uncle and brother-in-law. This, however, is extremely hypothetical; all we can say is that Derby was not involved in, at any rate, the early part of the long crisis which began in 1397.

Meanwhile Richard, after burying his queen, passionately flung himself into the execution of the plans he had already been maturing for an Irish expedition.[1] The significance of this expedition is twofold: first and foremost it represented an honest, though not particularly successful, attempt to grapple with the Irish question as no previous king of England had grappled with it since John's visit to the country in 1210, and secondly, it undoubtedly revealed to Richard something of his own potential strength; as Tout says,[2] from this time his "autocracy began to clothe itself in military garb". Ireland at this date was in theory governed by a complete duplicate of English institutions, as were other palatinates; it had its own exchequer, chancery, justices and law courts, even its own parliament. But these purely Anglo-Norman institutions were effective, if at all, only in the dwindling area of the Pale, and the *Annales* puts the case in a nutshell,[3] though its figures are not to be trusted, when it says that whereas in the time of Edward III £30,000 *per annum* had flowed into the Irish exchequer the revenue was now nil and the costs of administration to the English 30,000 marks a year. This financial problem was perhaps at the back of Richard's intervention, though it may be noted that only forty years later the author of the *Libel of English Policy*[4] was to point out the economic value of Ireland as a market and a source of supply as well as the potential danger it represented as a possible *point d'appui* for England's continental enemies, and it is not altogether impossible that some inkling of these enlightened considerations may have crossed the mind of Richard or his advisers. M. Perroy, on the other hand,[5] having shown so clearly the decisive part played by the Great Schism at this time in all questions of foreign policy, cannot altogether resist the suggestion that it was this cause more than

[1] For the expedition in general see especially E. Curtis, *History of Medieval Ireland* (1938 ed.), pp. 265–75. Tout barely does it justice.

[2] *Chapters*, iii, 487.   [3] p. 172.

[4] A poem on the use of sea-power dating from *c.* 1436. The anonymous author may have been Adam Moleyns, clerk of the council. See Sir George Warner's edition, Oxford, 1926.   [5] *Schisme*, pp. 97 ff.

any other which took Richard to Ireland in 1394. The wild Irish were Clementist, and that was enough; all the trouble they were causing could be cured in Richard's view by persuading them to speak English and recognise Rome. Something of this may have been present in Richard's mind, but he was not so close a friend of Boniface IX as to make the treatment of his expedition as another anti-Clementist crusade completely plausible, and in a later passage M. Perroy himself somewhat reluctantly admits that the Irish may have been Clementist[1] less from conviction than because they hated the English and the English were on the other side. M. Perroy does not venture to bring forward the same argument to explain the Scottish wars and on the whole the theory of a crusade must be rejected.

There was one obvious reason for the unprofitable state of Ireland, namely the virtual disappearance of the Anglo-Norman settlers in the Pale; the island was rapidly going native, which at that date meant relapsing into comparative barbarism. Thus only two great families of the original Anglo-Norman conquest still survived, the Geraldines of Kildare and Desmond and the Butler earls of Ormonde.[2] Several minor families, such as the de Burghs of Connaught, had intermarried regularly with the native Irish and even taken Irish names; the statute of Kilkenny (1367) had been vainly meant to check this process. Many other settlers had returned to England in despair and everywhere the chiefs were recovering their tribal lands.[3] The only effective king's lieutenant of the reign hitherto (1379–81) had been Edmund earl of March, husband of Philippa of Clarence, and the western limits of even his authority had been the river Bann in Ulster and in Connaught the castle of Athlone, while his administration, so far from yielding any profit, had cost the English exchequer 20,000 marks in three years. By 1392–3 the outer limits within which the writ of the justiciar (then the earl of Ormonde) ran were represented by the semicircle Drogheda, Trim, Kilkenny, Waterford; in short,

[1] *Schisme*, p. 128. The main Clementist centre was the province of Tuam, roughly modern Connaught.　　　　[2] Ramsay, *Genesis*, ii, 297–8.

[3] Details in E. Curtis, *History of Medieval Ireland*, p. 254.

"outside Leinster little except the seaport and corporate towns could be said to acknowledge English rule".

Richard's first step,[1] taken in June 1394 but modified for Oxford, Bristol, Hereford and Gloucester in August, was to order all Anglo-Irish living in England back to their own country. The number affected may be gauged by the twelve pages of exemptions from this order in the calendar of the patent rolls; clerks in particular seem to have been generally excused.[2] Then in August he himself and his entire household began to move westward, reaching Haverfordwest by the middle of September and waiting there until the beginning of October for ships, which had been sent for from the original rendezvous at Bristol. Meanwhile, throughout the whole summer active preparations had been in progress all over England; writs had been addressed to all the sheriffs, calling up crown reservists for the 3rd of August; fresh yeomen and archers had been widely enlisted for wages at the crown's expense; ships with their crews from the Cinque ports and from the western ports had been impressed in the usual fourteenth-century manner, and concentrated first at Bristol and then in Milford Haven. On the 20th of July Baldwin Raddington, Sir John Stanley and the bishop of Meath had crossed the Irish channel with a large advance-guard consisting of squires and archers. It is clear from this description that the bulk of Richard's force on this occasion was made up of a great household expansion or mobilisation,[3] led by the ordinary household officers and financed through the wardrobe[4] in the manner of Edward III's earlier campaigns in Flanders.

But there was also a large contingent of magnates with imposing retinues, nearly all friendly to the king and mostly of the younger generation now growing into manhood. Friendly or

---

[1] *Ann. Ric.* pp. 171–2.
[2] Tout, *Chapters*, iii, 485–6.   [3] *Ibid.* pp. 488–9.
[4] Wages of war were paid for the last time through paymasters, in this case officials of the household, who held great "prests" or balances for the purpose from the exchequer. Cf. A. Steel, "English Government Finance, 1377–1413", *E.H.R.* li, 41–2.

not, all alike were paid the king's wages both for themselves and for their men. The most senior was the duke of Gloucester, who led three bannerets, twenty knights bachelor, seventy-seven squires, two hundred horse-archers and a hundred foot-archers; of his brothers, Gaunt was in Aquitaine and York had been left behind as keeper of England. Next perhaps in importance came the young earl of March, destined to succeed his father at this long interval of time as king's lieutenant, and perhaps for that reason and as a great Irish landowner the leader of the largest retinue, including only two bannerets and eight knights, it is true, but no fewer than ninety-nine squires and two hundred horse-archers and four hundred foot-archers. Thomas, earl of Nottingham, whose Irish properties were second in value only to the earl of March's; Edward, earl of Rutland and now made earl of Cork;[1] Thomas Holland the younger, the king's nephew, and son and heir to the earl of Kent; and Sir Thomas Despenser, banneret, each with about two hundred men, made up the train, which was also joined by the earl of Ormonde and the scanty loyalists among the Irish baronage. There were a number of bishops and minor clerics, each with a military retinue, such as the archbishop of Dublin, bishop Medford of Chichester and the bishop of Llandaff; they were aped upon a smaller scale by household clerks such as the secretary, Roger Walden, formerly treasurer of Calais, John Carp, treasurer of the wardrobe, Nicholas Slake, Thomas Merke, a Westminster monk of some importance and future bishop of Carlisle, and many others.

There was, however, little actual fighting.[2] From Waterford, where he landed on the 2nd of October, Richard marched with some difficulty, caused mainly by the nature of the country, through Leinster into Dublin. One Art MacMurrough, the self-styled "king" of Leinster and claimant to the barony of Norragh in Kildare, was his chief opponent, but he and other

---

[1] E. Curtis, *Richard II in Ireland*, p. 27.

[2] This is perhaps an under-statement—there was a great deal of harrying ("journeys") and cattle-lifting ("preys"). See E. Curtis, *Proc. Roy. Irish Academy*, xxxvii, section C, pp. 276–303, for the details.

Irish chiefs soon promised submission, surrendered their lands within the Pale in return for compensation promised elsewhere, and even followed Richard quietly into Dublin, where they attended his courts and parliaments, accepted knighthood (in four cases), set their marks to certain notarial instruments of surrender and took his money.[1] Tout, who at this stage is a hostile critic, admits[2] that Richard and his magnates showed intelligence in dealing with these chiefs; their mistake was that they were too easily satisfied with words and bonds from men who were in effect little better than illiterate savages and to whom in consequence such things, once Richard and his army had disappeared, would mean little or nothing at all. Richard, however, can hardly be blamed for experimenting in the first instance with peaceful measures; he took a more cynical, and what might have been in the end a more effective, line during his second expedition but was recalled at a relatively early stage by the invasion of England.

Meanwhile an Irish parliament had been called for the 1st of December 1394, but it is doubtful whether Richard arrived in time to hold it on that date, though the *Annales*[3] says that he kept Christmas in Dublin. About this time, however, funds began to give out, which was understandable, for according to the issue rolls[4] Richard had to spend £12,000 all told in the half-year ending Easter 1395, of which by far the larger part had been absorbed by the Irish expedition. Gloucester was accordingly sent back to England to ask for supplies from a parliament which had been summoned to meet at Westminster in January. The parliament was opened under the duke of York by the chancellor, archbishop Arundel, who may, Tout thinks,[5] have gone to Ireland with Richard in October, but if so

[1] E. Curtis, *Richard II in Ireland*, *passim*, for the instruments of surrender. For the romantic story of the captive English knight "Christede", now liberated, see Froissart, *Œuvres*, xv, 168–81—it is summarised in E. Curtis, *History of Medieval Ireland*, pp. 273–4.

[2] *Chapters*, iii, 491.   [3] p. 173.

[4] F. Devon, *Issues of the Exchequer*, p. 258. The payments on account of the expedition are unfortunately not isolated from the rest.

[5] *Chapters*, iii, 493 n., criticising Curtis's contrary view.

had almost immediately returned again. It is noteworthy that the archbishop's speech was wholly friendly to Richard and complimentary on his activities,[1] and that Gloucester's request for a money grant was immediately complied with; Richard's Irish policy in short was endorsed in the most practical way by all parties. Moreover, although parliament showed a certain nervousness in other directions, which ultimately resulted in Richard's premature return, practically the whole session was devoted to the Irish question.

Several letters which passed between Richard and the council in England have survived; two of these, which may well be a message and a reply both received while parliament was still sitting, are worth mention.[2] The first of these is a signet letter from Richard, dated at Dublin on the 1st of February 1395 and warranted "Lincolne", apparently an assistant to the new secretary, Walden, and very probably the John Lincoln who had been arrested in 1388. This letter ably formulated Richard's policy of conciliation and the reasons for it, explained to the council the very real differences between the "wild Irish, our enemies, rebel Irish (i.e. lapsed Anglo-Irish) and obedient English (i.e. loyal Anglo-Irish)", stated their grievances and argued that leniency was the best policy. We also have a letter from the council, written probably in reply, of which separate copies were sent to the prelates and secular magnates for approval, which was freely given under seal or signature, even by the earl of Arundel; it was no doubt intended to represent the views of parliament as a whole, including the commons.[3] The prelates' copy was dated the 13th of February 1395, two days before the break-up of the parliament, which in Curtis's view [4] just gives time for the council to have considered Richard's letter dated the 1st of February. It politely but firmly asked Richard to return to England, while in no way deprecating the importance of his success.

[1] Tout, *Chapters*, iii, 494.
[2] H. Nicolas, *Acts of the Privy Council*, i, 55–7. Cf. E. Curtis, *Proc. Roy. Irish Academy*, loc. cit., for several other letters.
[3] Tout, *loc. cit.*   [4] *Richard II in Ireland*, pp. 137–40.

This Richard was, not unnaturally, very reluctant to do; he had been voted more money and seems to have been aware that his resettlement of Ireland was far from complete. Eventually it took a special visit by archbishop Arundel and bishop Braybrooke of London—perhaps after earlier appeals by Gloucester and Huntingdon had failed—to make him move, and even then he did not leave Waterford before the 1st of May, by which time he had held another Irish parliament and appointed the earl of March king's lieutenant, to remain behind him. The reasons for this parliamentary pressure are evidently not to be found in any contemporary criticism of Richard's activities in Ireland which indeed, as has been shown, afford an excellent example of the policy of appeasement at work in both countries, but rather in anxiety about the relations of the realm with France and Scotland, which were not yet sufficiently secure to permit the diversion of almost its entire resources elsewhere. This argument of the first or lay mission of recall was not, however, sufficient in itself to move the king, who was already developing that strange sense of security and over-confidence which marked his last years. What really moved him seems to have been the sudden outbreak of Lollard activity in Westminster, which may well have been reported to him in detail by the bishops; it appears that heretical placards had been fixed during the parliamentary session to the doors of the abbey and St Paul's, and some of Richard's own chamber knights who had not accompanied him to Ireland were said to be involved.[1] There was of course a considerable interval, for which allowance is too seldom made, between this outrage and the king's return, but it looks as if it may have tipped the scales in favour of return and it is certain that even if there were no condign punishments, so that in the words of the *Annales*[2] the Lollards "merely retired into their shells like tortoises", at least a number of recantations were extorted by the king. Moreover, orders were issued for expelling one Robert Lechlade and other Lollards from Oxford[3] and the chancellor of the university

[1] *Fasciculi Zizaniorum* (R.S.), pp. 360–9; *Ann. Ric.* pp. 174–82; Ramsay, *Genesis*, ii, 302. [2] p. 183. [3] Rymer, *Foedera*, vii, 805–6.

was required to examine and report on Wyclif's *Trialogus*, to which one of the "conclusions"[1] in the placards had referred as an authority. But once again there was no violence and, within a month or two of Richard's return from Ireland, the policy of appeasement reached its climax in the negotiations for his second marriage, which was intended to set the seal on peace with France and to lead on towards the ending of the Schism.

The traditional view of the French marriage is to regard it as the beginning of a deep-laid plan to establish Richard's complete autocracy—the last phase of his reign. Thus Tout suggests[2] that on his return from Ireland in May 1395 he immediately set himself to establish peace, sealed by a dynastic alliance, with France not merely as an end in itself but with the ulterior object of obtaining help against his domestic enemies, and that he already meant to build up a new party of royalist magnates, again not only for its own sake, but so that with its help he might liquidate the ex-appellants and unmask himself in the full force of the regality to which he had always laid claim. The only evidence in support of this view is to be found in a single phrase of the final mandate of January 1396, addressed to the earls of Rutland and Nottingham and William Scrope and ordering them to bring to a conclusion the French negotiations which a rather larger commission had been carrying on since the previous July. This mandate begins by reducing the preposterous English money demands[3] which were preventing any progress, in return for the conclusion of a twenty-eight years' truce, which was the most to which the French would consent without the surrender of Calais. It ends with a definite promise on the part of the French king, his uncles and his brother "to aid and sustain [Richard] with all their power against any of his subjects".[4]

This clause may at first sight seem decisive, but it is at least as plausibly explained by Richard's fears as it is by his intentions.

---

[1] No. 4 in *Ann. Ric. loc. cit.*   [2] *Chapters*, iv, 1.

[3] 500,000 marks, the balance of John's ransom. See Ramsay, *Genesis*, ii, 305 and D. Broome, "The Ransom of John I, King of France, 1360–1370", *Camden Miscellany*, vol. xiv.   [4] Rymer, *Foedera*, vii, 811.

It is even conceivable that what was contemplated was a class alliance directed against the danger of another peasants' revolt—there was perpetual unrest among the villeins, as we have seen above[1]—though it is more likely that it was Gloucester and the earl of Arundel whom Richard had in view, for the recent conduct of these noblemen, at any rate in 1393-4, had not done much to allay his natural fears. Richard was by this date probably neurotic, and his disease may well have led him to exaggerate his precautions against a renewal of the commission of 1386 and of the merciless parliament. But it does not follow that he was already planning the *coup d'état* of 1397, in which year incidentally there was no more question than in 1398-9 of appealing for French help.

Apart from the existence of this clause Tout's case is weak. Perhaps the best argument against it is the general inconsistency of so far-reaching a scheme with Tout's own view of Richard's fitful, idle and vacillating character, but in any case Richard's actions are susceptible of a more innocent interpretation. It must be remembered that all parties, with the exception of Gloucester, Arundel and their immediate followers, were by now converted to the wisdom of peace with France, and yet this could not be obtained without the surrender of Calais, which all parties were agreed to refuse. Richard's solution of a long truce fortified by a marriage was therefore very probably the best obtainable and required no ulterior motive; in fact there was no real alternative. Moreover, if this policy was to be pursued at all it obviously had to be pursued wholeheartedly, and it was in Richard's character that, once it had been decided on, he flung himself impulsively into it with all the energy with which he usually began, but seldom completed, his good resolves; the alleged dislike felt by the English on the other hand for "the effusive friendship now professed between the two courts"[2] is really quite illogical.

A more serious ground of objection to the marriage was the fact that the French princess Isabelle was not yet eight years old and there could be no prospect of an heir for years to come.

---

[1] Cf. Monk of Westminster, p. 220.   [2] Tout, *Chapters*, iv, 2.

But it must be remembered that in 1396 Richard was still only twenty-nine himself, so that there was still plenty of time as far as the husband was concerned, while in view of the violence of his attachment to Anne it would have been unreasonable to expect him to enter on negotiations for a real marriage with an adult within a year or two of her death. No one disputes the fact that he became very fond of the French child, and the most obvious explanation of this lies precisely in her childishness; nor is there any reason to doubt that the marriage would have turned out well in time and might have solved the problem of the succession. Meanwhile, as a stop-gap heir during the next few years, there was an adult with a good claim to the throne through his mother, Philippa of Clarence, namely Roger Mortimer, earl of March, now king's lieutenant in Ireland, whom indeed Richard may have formally recognised as such— and if so without recorded opposition—as long before as the autumn parliament of 1385.[1]

There was one alternative to the plan, but it was not a very good one. This took the form of an uncongenial royal marriage to the grown-up heiress of Aragon,[2] to be followed, it must be assumed, by the adoption of the Aragonese plan to end the Schism through a general council of the church, which however would have involved continued bickering with France; moreover, quite apart from Richard's personal views, the Spaniards were at this date already more unpopular in England than the French.[3] The French marriage, on the other hand, apparently involved adoption of the slightly less popular plan of Charles VI, known as the "way of cession", that is, to end the Schism by withdrawing obedience simultaneously from both popes; but even if this were so—and it did not prove to be the case[4]—it had at least the positive and undoubted merit of

[1] Ramsay, *Genesis*, ii, 229—but Miss Clarke, *Fourteenth Century Studies*, p. 107, dismisses the story as a later Yorkist fabrication.

[2] Adam of Usk, p. 9.   [3] See p. 189 above.

[4] Perroy, *Schisme*, pp. 383-7, shows that Charles VI did withdraw his allegiance in July 1397 but that Richard failed to follow suit, and that the only effect of a French protest in August 1398 was to draw tighter the

ending a particularly futile war already nearly sixty years old and of creating a united front against the Turks, so that on the whole it needed no "subtle autocracy" on Richard's part to commend it to him and his advisers.

Tout's other allegation, namely that from this time on Richard was building up a party of royalist magnates, is perfectly true—the process had begun even earlier—but again it is difficult to see why there can only be a sinister interpretation. Richard had been isolated all his life and was now at last finding friends, or at any rate sympathisers, among his own contemporaries; the promotion of the younger generation among the nobility was therefore the most natural thing in the world. Was it possible for him, in view of the events as well as of the years which lay between them, to make friends of, or even give further state employment to, men like Gloucester and the earl of Arundel, whom indeed no power on earth could have brought into good relations with the king? Richard did his best with the older men; he remained on good terms with Lancaster, accepted Thomas Arundel as chancellor for five years and did not oppose his translation to Canterbury on archbishop Courtenay's death in 1396 and, as regards his younger enemies, he had apparently forgiven Derby for his father's sake and Nottingham for his own; what more could have been expected of him?

The detailed history of the long negotiations leading up to the French marriage is of slighter interest than the policy behind it. The treaty was eventually sealed upon the 9th of March 1396

English alliance with Boniface. In this Richard had the support not only of a rather nondescript body of prominent clerks and laymen assembled at Oxford early in 1399 but also of the university of Oxford itself and of English opinion generally, which was glad to see the French mend the error of their ways, but was not prepared to admit that it had ever been in error itself. Cf. *ibid.* p. 390: it was really a physical impossibility for Richard to ally himself wholeheartedly both with France and Boniface, and as a matter of fact in the last resort it was Boniface whom he chose. Yet his enemies subsequently accused him of betraying England to the French as well as of betraying the English church to the papacy, which was impossible—a fact that M. Perroy does not make perfectly clear.

and a marriage by proxy took place in Paris on the 12th. Even after this, however, there was an extraordinary delay upon the French side in handing over the bride, which involved a special mission in June by William Scrope and two visits to Calais by Richard in person at the extreme end of the summer. In October came at last the final festivities,[1] in the form of a meeting between the two kings, leading up to the handing over of Isabelle (early in November) together with about £50,000 in English money as an instalment of her dowry. Before the end of the month Richard and his new queen were back in England; she made her first state entry into London on the 23rd of November 1396 but was not crowned until the 7th of January 1397.[2] The expense of the whole delayed process was enormous and far outweighed the dowry; for apart from the £200,000 (£7000 in presents alone) which Richard is believed to have spent on the ceremonies in France, and in England on the coronation, the new queen brought a large retinue from the most luxurious court in Europe. There was, however, little contemporary criticism of Richard's heavy expenditure on this occasion; to the fourteenth-century mind it was incumbent on him to maintain the reputation of the English monarchy by rivalling or surpassing the magnificence of the French; it was an earlier Field of the Cloth of Gold. But it is easy to understand that after it was all over Richard was as pressed for money as he had ever been, and though this was very far from being the whole cause it is at least a partial explanation of the acute neurosis and suspicion which now finally overtook him and dominated his last three years.

[1] See the long account in *Ann. Ric.* pp. 188–94.
[2] Tout, *Chapters*, iv, 9.

CHAPTER VIII

The Second "Tyranny"

BY the end of 1396 the new curialist party, which was to make Richard indisputably master of the realm, was more or less complete.[1] Its most important component was an aristocratic clique, which may be analysed into three or four groups. There was the Lancastrian interest, represented above all by Gaunt but still to some extent by Derby; there were Richard's half-brothers, the earl of Huntingdon and the earl of Kent, who however died and was succeeded by his son, another Thomas Holland, in 1397; there was the duke of York and his son Edward, earl of Rutland; there were a few "converts" from the magnates, such as Nottingham, and tried royalists such as Salisbury (John Montague the younger), the earl of March, who however remained in Ireland, Thomas Despenser and William Scrope. The proportion of young men does not seem high in view of the chroniclers' insistence on the youth of Richard's advisers; it accounts for barely half the list. The strength of the group contrasts markedly with Richard's isolation ten years earlier; he had clearly learned that in the last resort it was on the support of magnates that he must rely. Perhaps the most important omission was the Northumberland interest from the Border, but even this was represented to some extent by the presence of Sir Thomas Percy in the household. There were in addition several moderate lords, such as Cobham, who could be described as friendly neutrals at the worst.

The support of magnates would be required in emergencies; meanwhile the routine administration of the kingdom was in safe hands. The treasurer, John Waltham, bishop of Salisbury, had died in the odour of royalism on the 17th of September

[1] Tout, *Chapters*, iv, 6 ff., for this and a few succeeding paragraphs.

1395 and in spite of a somewhat doubtful past had become the first person not of royal blood to be buried in Westminster abbey,[1] to the great scandal and annoyance of the opposition lords. This timely death released a great office of state for a new man and enabled Richard to reward Medford with the richer see of Salisbury. Meanwhile the treasurership was given to Roger Walden, a king's clerk of some years' standing who had filled the important post of treasurer of Calais from 1387 to 1392 and had recently commended himself to Richard as keeper of the signet on the Irish expedition.[2] Adam of Usk,[3] unlike the *Annales*, does Walden full justice; though a steady adherent of Richard's to the end, one moreover who did not hesitate to take the dangerous responsibility of filling Arundel's place as archbishop of Canterbury after his disgrace and translation in 1397, Walden survived the deposition and became bishop of London under Henry IV; he represents the best type of clerical civil servant. He is also worth remembering for his reorganisation of the signet office in what proved to be a lasting form.

It may be remembered that Thomas Arundel's stand as chancellor against the signet in 1386 had been approved by the merciless parliament, which forced the crown to embody in a statute the petition that no letter of signet or secret seal be sent out to the disturbance of the law and damage of the realm,[4] and though signet letters reappear from 1392 no true secretary can be traced, except perhaps John Macclesfield in that one year,[5] until Walden's definite emergence in that office in 1393.[6] For a further four years it is only during the Irish expedition that much signet activity can be discerned, and that activity is purely utilitarian, not political, while even after

---

[1] Perroy, *L'Angleterre et le grand schisme d'Occident*, p. 340.
[2] J. Otway-Ruthven, *The King's Secretary and the Signet Office*, pp. 8, 106.
[3] p. 38. Cf. *Annales Ricardi*, p. 213.
[4] Tout, *Chapters*, v, 209. Cf. B. Wilkinson, *Chancery under Edward III*, appendix VI, on the chancery ordinances of 1388-9, pp. 214-23.
[5] Otway-Ruthven, *op. cit.* p. 153.
[6] He was succeeded by John Lincoln, 1395-9.

the *coup* of 1397 its political importance does not revive immediately; indeed it was hardly necessary in view of Richard's complete control of the great and privy seals. On the other hand in the last year or two of the reign the signet was admittedly used from time to time to seal patents "in the absence of the great seal",[1] while in 1399 the sheriffs were instructed to obey it equally with the other seals; again it was under it that Richard scattered pardons and releases on his way to Flint,[2] and it was the signet itself which he handed over to Henry in the Tower as the most intimate symbol of personal sovereignty. These considerations help to account for the fact that the signet was not discredited by the revolution, as it had been ten years earlier, but on the contrary went from strength to strength during the fifteenth century;[3] it had been a subsidiary, but not a major, agent in Richard's second "tyranny" and had become too useful to be dropped.

In February 1396 another king's clerk, Guy Mone, receiver of the chamber since 1391, took the privy seal in place of the new bishop of Exeter, Edmund Stafford, who was destined for higher office. Compared with Walden, Mone is a somewhat colourless figure who does not seem to have attracted the attention of the chroniclers, though in 1398 he rose as high as the treasurership of the exchequer and the bishopric of St David's and was always a loyal partisan of the king. Of the principal offices of state this leaves only the chancery, in which Richard. was obliged to make a change after the death of archbishop Courtenay in July 1396, since he could not well oppose the claims of Thomas Arundel, which were supported by the monastic chapter,[4] to be Courtenay's successor, while it was not until the fifteenth century that it was thought fitting for the offices of chancellor and archbishop of Canterbury to be combined in one man. It is therefore unnecessary to see in this change any deep-laid design on Richard's part to get rid of Arundel in favour of a more pliable chancellor, in view of the fact that Arundel had held the great seal for five years and

[1] Tout, *Chapters*, iv, 41.   [2] *Ibid.* v, 210.
[3] Otway-Ruthven, *op. cit.*   [4] *Ann. Ric.* p. 194.

seems to have been on good terms with Richard in 1396 and during the earlier part of 1397; moreover, according to the hostile *Annales*,[1] he himself had suggested Stafford as his successor, while it is well known that he saw eye to eye with Richard about Lollardry.[2]

These new "courtier bishops", who form one of the points of complaint in Haxey's famous petition, included the faithful Medford at Salisbury, together with Tydeman of Worcester, a former Cistercian monk of Winchcombe and ex-physician to the king, who had been with him in Ireland and had recently been translated from Llandaff, the Dominican John Burghill, Richard's confessor and successively bishop of Llandaff and Lichfield, the ex-Westminster monk Thomas Merke, another veteran of the Irish expedition and now bishop of Carlisle, and another former royal physician, Robert Waldby, archbishop of Dublin, who succeeded Arundel at York but died a few months later. According to M. Perroy[3] all new bishops at this date were compelled to take a special oath of loyalty to the régime; we should perhaps add to them Henry Beaufort, the future cardinal, one of Gaunt's sons by Catherine Swynford who received the see of Lincoln a little later but was still no more than a boy. Most of these prelates appear to have been habitually non-resident in their dioceses and, together with the great ladies who swarmed at court in the last years of the reign, they certainly help to account for Richard's high household expenditure and to some extent justify the criticism voiced by Haxey. Tout's "strange recruits" however[4] is perhaps an unfortunate phrase; for this episcopal clique must have performed the useful function, as Tout himself says in a later passage,[5] of reducing opposition among the higher clergy.

More important than the bishops at court, however, were the professional leaders of the household. These were headed by Sir Thomas Percy, an experienced soldier of long standing and brother to the earl of Northumberland; the veteran Baldwin Raddington, a survivor from 1386, and William Scrope,

---

[1] *Loc. cit.*   [2] Perroy, *Schisme*, p. 344.   [3] *Ibid.* pp. 345–6.
[4] Tout, *Chapters*, iv, 10.   [5] *Ibid.* p. 23.

the vice-chamberlain, who as negotiator of the king's second marriage and nephew of the dead de Vere had inherited some of the influence of Burley. These men controlled not only the knights of the chamber, men-at-arms and yeomen of the household, but also the numerous reservists dotted all over the shires, but especially strong in Cheshire, wearing the white hart, in receipt as a rule of small retaining fees, pensions or even lands, and ready to be mobilised through the sheriffs as soon as the king should have sheriffs he could trust. Their numbers were steadily increasing and the expense of this royal livery mounted with them, representing as they did not the nucleus or shock troops but the mainguard of a royal army, which was to do what parliamentary statutes had failed to do, that is crush any revival of livery and maintenance with forces identical in kind but at the service of the crown.

Also under the household as king's knights, though not as chamber knights, should be reckoned the three special links now imported for the first time into Richard's system in order to co-ordinate council, parliament and court with these minor gentry of the countryside, namely the somewhat sinister trio formed by Sir John Bushy, Sir William Bagot and Sir Henry Green. All three were distinguished by having shown great local activity in the past as sheriffs, justices of the peace, escheators and commissioners, e.g. of array—a fact which specially commended them to Richard as representatives of the dominant groups in the county courts, and far outweighed the other curious feature they have in common in all having been active in their districts on the appellant side in 1386–8; Richard seems in fact, irrespective of past records, to have bought the best political agents he could buy.[1] Sir John Bushy was a Lincolnshire knight, who sat in every parliament from 1386 to 1398 except the merciless parliament, but in spite of that exception was then appellant in sympathy, as the formal pardon granted to him in May 1398 attests.[2] He first appears as a king's knight, "retained", in the usual formula, "to stay with him for

[1] Tout, *Chapters*, iv, 11-13, for the details which follow.
[2] *C.P.R.* 1396-9, p. 331.

life" at a salary of forty marks *per annum*, which was afterwards increased, in 1391. From that year he served Richard steadily in at least two capacities, as the chancery enrolments show; first in securing the royal cause at Lincoln[1] and secondly in acting as speaker of the commons, certainly in 1394 and 1397 and probably also in 1395. Sir Henry Green, who probably came from Drayton near Thrapston in Northamptonshire, took out a pardon for his appellant sympathies at the same time as Bushy; he was, however, much less important in his earlier phase, though he rose with great rapidity at the end and shared Bushy's fate in 1399. Less conspicuous in local politics than the other two, he cannot even be traced in parliament before 1390 at the earliest, and not for certain before 1394, and seems to have entered Richard's service by way of the Lancastrian interest; thus he was retained by Gaunt for life at fifty marks *per annum* in 1391 and only became a king's knight at an additional[2] forty marks on the 1st of March 1397. But by August of that year both he and Bushy were receiving no less than £100 *per annum*, being "charged to attend the kings' council during his pleasure", and this large salary[3] was subsequently increased. There is no doubt that from this time on both he and Bushy, with Bushy in the lead, played a highly responsible part, as the popular lampoons against them show,[4] and if Richard's policy deserved condemnation it was right that they should suffer for it.

Sir William Bagot was a Warwickshire knight, who had acquired the castle of Baginton[5] near Coventry, in 1382; he was sheriff of that county and of Leicestershire as early as 1382–4 and represented it continuously in parliament from the beginning of 1388 to the end of the reign. In early life he had been a squire of Gaunt's (1379), but as a knight was associated

[1] *C.P.R.* 1388–92, pp. 220, 270–1; 1391–6, p. 240; and *C.C.R.* 1392–6, pp. 133–4, for the whole history of this very interesting trouble.

[2] His Lancastrian grant was confirmed on Gaunt's death in 1399.

[3] By the standards of the day, e.g. more than a judge's nominal salary.

[4] See T. Wright, *Political Poems* (R.S.), vol. i, pp. 363 ff.

[5] It has recently been excavated—see *The Times* of 23rd January 1934 for a full account.

with the earl of Nottingham and in 1388 played a prominent part in that capacity on the appellant side, not only in parliament but in his own county. It might therefore be supposed that it was Nottingham who, in changing sides, brought Bagot over to the king; but it was not until August 1397 that he became a king's knight, when, however, he quickly distinguished himself in Richard's service. He soon seems to have been admitted to the council, but never quite achieved the importance of either Bushy or Green, though he figures almost to the same extent in the lampoons against them; alone of the three, he escaped with nothing worse than imprisonment in the Tower and temporary forfeiture after the revolution, possibly by good luck in the actual fighting and possibly because he had lodged Henry Bolingbroke in Baginton castle on the eve of the famous duel between Henry and his old lord, Thomas Mowbray, at Coventry in September 1398.

In January 1397, however, when Richard's last parliament but one met at Westminster, neither Bagot nor Green was as yet in the king's service. The first parliament for two years, it had been necessitated by Richard's recent heavy expenses in connexion with his re-marriage and with the development of his household, both on the social and the military side. Beyond this he had rashly promised Charles VI to send the earls of Nottingham and Rutland with an army to support the duke of Burgundy against Gian Galeazzo Visconti; this was really a private venture, on the analogy of Gaunt's in Spain, and Richard had had no right to pledge it national support. In actual fact the project did not at all commend itself to the few lords who were present at the beginning of this parliament, while the commons politely but firmly refused any financial backing for it whatsoever and urged the king to summon more magnates, apparently in the knowledge that they would find further support for their views in that quarter. The incident shows that even though Bushy was speaker the commons were by no means subservient to the crown, and the point is further illustrated by the presentation of the famous petition to which Thomas Haxey gave his name, upon the 1st of February.

This petition demanded in the first place that no sheriff or escheator should be continued in office in the same shire for more than one year, implying that the opposite practice had been the rule. It was countered by Richard with what Stubbs[1] seems to consider a sensible plea for continuity, namely that the sheriffs needed more than one year of office in order to gain experience and consolidate their power against the great men of the neighbourhood. The request may be read as suggesting that Richard's choice of sheriffs had already been systematically royalist, and in view of the charges of this nature made in 1388 and 1399 has usually been so interpreted; there is, however, absolutely no evidence for such a view before the late autumn of 1397 and that of 1398. As regards reappointment an analysis of the Public Record Office lists of sheriffs and escheators has shown[2] that while the reappointment of a man to serve as sheriff in two or more successive years in the same shire is not by any means unknown at any point in the reign, including the minority, the average number of reappointments is quite low and remains fairly constant until 1398, when no less than seventeen out of twenty-eight sheriffs, many of them admittedly "special" sheriffs, were reappointed instead of the usual three or four (excluding hereditary and other abnormal shrievalties). On the other hand, the complaint about continuance of the same man in office is much more true of escheatorships, for which a four-year tenure is not uncommon, and it is still more usual to find the same man alternately holding the office of sheriff and escheator in the same county over a short period of years. Historians have hitherto overlooked the insistence on escheators as well as on sheriffs in the petition, and in the absence of any proved political appointments the objection was probably not to political bias for what one might call national or Westminster reasons, but to the purely local abuse of the same man, whoever he might be, continuing to hold these powerful local offices, with all the control they gave over property, and defeating the statute enjoining annual shrieval-

[1] *Constitutional History*, ii, 491–2.
[2] See my article in *C.A.S. Proc. loc. cit.*

ties[1] by a simple system of rotation. What was being alleged was in short an administrative and not a political abuse, as might be expected from what was still the period of appeasement. Richard replied that the practice was not an abuse of any kind but a necessity, in view of the fact that the statute against the wearing of cognisances by retainers not actually of a lord's household was being openly disregarded.

The second clause, to the effect that the marches were being insufficiently guarded so that the Scots were always violating the truce, was unexceptionable and Richard promised to attend to it, but the fourth and last clause, complaining of the excessive cost of the king's household on account of the presence of so many bishops and ladies and their retinues, was a very different matter and therein lies the sole real importance of the episode in the history of the reign; it may in fact be taken as the trigger which set off the second "tyranny". It at once recalled to Richard the inquisitorial days of the minority and the commission of 1386–7; his most deep-seated neurosis was galvanised at once into activity, and his fear and fury[2] were redoubled when he learned by enquiry through the duke of Lancaster that the complaint originated in a bill handed in to the commons and "coloured" by them on behalf of a certain Thomas Haxey, who was an obvious man of straw set up by some sinister but unknown power in the background and not even a member of the commons.

Haxey was in fact a prosperous king's clerk of some fifteen years' standing[3] who held the office of keeper of the writs and rolls of the common bench, and was furthermore a dependent of the earl of Nottingham[4] for whom, together with Bagot, he had acted as a proxy when the earl was in France in the

---

[1] 14 Ed. III, s. 1, c. 7; Lodge and Thornton, *English Constitutional Documents*, p. 346.

[2] See Richard's reply in Lodge and Thornton, *op. cit.* p. 69.

[3] Tout, *Chapters*, iv, 17–19, especially the long note on pp. 18–19.

[4] Although Nottingham was probably not involved on this occasion, it may have started the suspicions which led to his self-denunciation and ruin in 1398.

previous October. The fact that he is now known not to have been a member of parliament has disposed of the old view that the incident has any constitutional significance, but that is not to say that it has not got very great legal and political significance, for Richard's anger once more led him rashly to invoke the loose interpretation of the law of treason, as he had in 1387, and with the same disastrous consequences. The commons themselves soon made their peace with him by specifically surrendering any claim to criticise the conduct of his household which might have been implied by the petition; there was no harm in this, since any right to enquire into the cost of the social side of the household rested only on the dubious precedents of Richard's own minority, while the king on his part, in return for the surrender, abandoned his unpopular proposal for an expedition against Milan and did not press for a money grant. The damage in short was done not in the commons but in the lords, where Richard's friends not only condemned the commons' action in colouring the petition but under royal pressure went so far as to stir up the dangerous waters of the treason laws by creating *ex post facto* an offence for which Haxey could be punished.

This they did upon the 5th of February by declaring it treason for any man to excite the commons in parliament to reform anything affecting the person, government or regality of the king, and on the 7th Haxey was duly condemned to a traitor's death for having broken the terms of this declaration at a time when it did not exist. The fact that he had already been handed over to the archbishop of Canterbury as a clerk and in any case received a full pardon three months later[1] is irrelevant; the decisive point is that to have extracted this decision from the lords at all was once more to go behind the statute of 1352 and to reopen all the doubts and cruelties of 1386–8. Richard should have known better than this and might well have been content to relieve Haxey, at any rate for a time, of all his benefices,

---

[1] He was restored to crown employment and became still more prosperous over a long period of years during the fifteenth century, when his name constantly crops up, e.g. in the receipt rolls.

pensions and royal employment; this would have been not only feasible and well within his competence, especially if, as was probable, Nottingham co-operated, but also reasonably well deserved. However, his sudden and impulsive temper, or perhaps the progress of his disease, prevented him from being satisfied with anything short of extreme measures, and he was therefore unwise enough to reopen an old wound in what on the mildest interpretation is perhaps his first real act of tyranny.[1] He was of course himself no lawyer and it is just possible that, ignoring the essentially *ex post facto* character of the judgment, his mind was harking back to the wide definition of treason given at Nottingham in 1387 in the genuine belief that it was good law; it is at any rate significant that during this parliament he went on to secure the recall of the exiled justices from Ireland, which might doubtfully be held to restore force to their rulings. Yet the fact that Richard was conscious that he had gone too far is shown in the words accompanying the recall, which asserted the continued validity of all other acts of the merciless parliament.

Certain other parliamentary activities in January and February 1397 were less dramatic but almost equally important. One of these was the legitimation of the Beauforts, which has already been mentioned, coupled with the creation of the eldest boy, John Beaufort, earl of Somerset. Another honour pointed to the belief on Richard's part that whoever was behind Haxey his nominal patron, Nottingham, was not; otherwise he would hardly have taken this particular opportunity to make the marshalship of England hereditary in the family of Mowbray. Another ex-appellant, on the other hand, the earl of Warwick, of whom little is known in these years, was in disgrace; he was fined on this occasion for contempt of royal judgment against him in a long-standing dispute with Nottingham over property in Gower. Finally there was a significant ruling, which swept away the last shred of the early Norman theory of the *curia regis*, to the effect that magnates might not in future sit as

---

[1] Cf. H. Wallon, *Richard II*, ii, 193: "procès inoffensif pour la personne, mais mortel déjà pour la constitution".

assessors of royal justices of assize; this, according to Tout,[1] partly met the repeated complaints by the commons against maintenance and the perversion of justice.

Gloucester, Richard earl of Arundel, and Warwick in particular must have been alarmed and irritated by the events of this parliament. It is not impossible that they were at the back of Haxey's attack upon the household,[2] which in that case was clearly a kind of *ballon d'essai* and no doubt gave them the information they needed. Their general uneasiness must have been considerably increased by Richard's concentration of maritime offices at this time in the hands of his young friend and cousin, the earl of Rutland, as well as by the extraordinary jurisdiction, both in England and Italy, conferred about this date by pope Boniface upon that "violent and mediocre baron",[3] Huntingdon, who was to be "captain and counsellor of the Roman church" and apparently end the Schism once and for all by a crusade like that of Lancaster or the bishop of Norwich, but with even wider powers.[4] It is also the period at which Richard's attempts, incessant since 1395, to get Edward II canonised on account of the miracles wrought at his tomb, reached a climax, while about midsummer he actually received through the medium of the provost of Cologne certain offers of election as king of the Romans, for which he may have been angling as early as 1394.[5] It is perhaps doubtful whether he ever really had serious designs upon the empire, which would have involved displacing Wenzel, his former brother-in-law—not that there were sentimental objections, for Anne was dead and Richard cared nothing for Wenzel— but because the whole wild scheme reads more like Urbanist diplomacy than English megalomania, and if the proposals did

[1] *Chapters*, iv, 20.
[2] Cf. K. H. Vickers, *England in the Later Middle Ages* (3rd ed.), p. 289. Tout, *Chapters*, iv, 18–19, disagrees, but his own explanation, viz. that Haxey was trying independently to do what Geoffrey Martin (who did not act independently) had done in the merciless parliament, is unconvincing.
[3] Perroy, *Schisme*, p. 343.   [4] *Ibid.* pp. 341–2; cf. *Ann. Ric.* pp. 200–1.
[5] Perroy, *Schisme*, p. 342.

originate with Richard they may have been only bargaining counters. Boniface was certainly trying by every means in his power to detach him from the French plan of ending the schism by a joint withdrawal of obedience from both popes and he may be held to have scored an important success when Richard granted pensions of £1000 a year to two of the Electors, namely the count palatine and the archbishop of Cologne, and sent Rutland and Nottingham to the Rhineland.[1] Negotiations about the empire went on well into 1397.[2]

Yet Richard seems to have been fully as interested this year, and to have spent as much money, in the rebuilding of Westminster Hall, which we owe in its present form substantially to him. It was probably the expenditure under this head, as well as on the household and the foreign pensions, which led him to raise a large number of loans, commonly described as "forced loans",[3] late in the summer; long lists of them are to be found in the receipt rolls, and also, rather significantly, in the patent rolls, which record the issue of letters under the great seal as security for the lenders. If they were forced there was good precedent for the forcing—"persuasion" is perhaps a better term—during the minority in the great loans of 1379, while it is certain from the receipt rolls that the loans of 1397 were not only meant to be but were actually repaid; moreover, the *Annales* itself admits[4] that in the summer of 1397 the country was very prosperous and the credit of the government was good.

None the less the January parliament of 1397 left a very real feeling of tension in the air. According to one rather indifferent authority[5] Gloucester and the earl of Arundel gave Richard grounds for suspicion in February by absenting themselves from an otherwise unknown great council held at Westminster in that month, though the crisis was not to come to a head before July. Richard indeed had some reason for anxiety.

[1] *Ann. Ric.* p. 199; Tout, *Chapters*, iv, 20, for a rather different view.
[2] Perroy, *loc. cit.* [3] *Ann. Ric.* p. 200, but see A. Steel, *E.H.R.* li, 29–51.
[4] *Ann. Ric.* p. 201.
[5] The Monk of Evesham, *ap.* Tout, *Chapters*, iv, 21.

Except that he was now far better prepared to meet it the situation was superficially not unlike that of the autumn of 1386, when complaints about the household and discontent among a section of the magnates had led to the commission of reform. His determination not to be caught that way again must have been increased by Gloucester's open criticism of his foreign policy, made at a royal banquet held in Westminster in late June or early July[1]—a criticism which was aimed particularly at the surrender of Brest to the French, which had taken place in April; some of the former garrison were present on the occasion. Actually there was little real force in Gloucester's criticism; Brest, like Cherbourg, had only been pledged to the English in April 1378 for the duration of the war in return for the equivalent of about £20,000 in English money and certain grants in England to its lord, the duke of Brittany. It had now been redeemed and there was no case for retaining the fortress, especially in view of the new twenty-eight years' truce with France, yet Gloucester took the opportunity to use the surrender of both Brest and Cherbourg in his indictment of the king and his advisers. Richard replied with some heat, and though they parted politely and with civil words there was enough bad blood between them over the incident for the French chronicle of Richard's last years[2] to insist that this was the real beginning of the crisis which now rapidly developed.

There seems to be no reason to reject this story, whatever may be thought of the circumstantial account, to which the *Traïson et Mort* proceeds, of a plot laid at St Albans in the next few days between Gloucester, John Moot, the new abbot of St Albans, who was Gloucester's godfather, and the prior of Westminster; the two Arundels and the earls of Derby, Nottingham and Warwick are said to have been involved at a later stage. Froissart[3] even adds the earl of March, who at least cannot have been present in person, and says that though he refused to join in the first instance he did not denounce the conspirators, as he should have done, to the king.

[1] *Traïson et Mort de Richard II*, ed. B. Williams, pp. 2, 119.
[2] The *Traïson et Mort*, pp. 3, 121.   [3] *Ap.* Wallon, *op. cit.* ii, 151.

This, however, is almost certainly either calumny or confusion; Froissart is not a good authority for English history. The story in the better informed *Traïson* goes on to say that Nottingham, the most likely person to do so, betrayed the whole affair to Richard and that then, after consultation with Huntingdon in London and with the council, Richard ordered the famous arrest of Gloucester at Pleshy, followed by that of Warwick and the earl of Arundel.

Tout, it is true, rejects the whole story of this conspiracy as a later fabrication intended to excuse Richard's action,[1] on the ground that if he had known of it he would certainly have included it in his formal accusations. This is a strong argument, and it is certainly true that the story in the *Traïson* contains obvious improbabilities. Thus if Nottingham had really been involved and had confessed, Richard's later embarrassment in finding concrete charges to bring against his victims could hardly have occurred, and it is in fact very unlikely that either Nottingham, Derby or even archbishop Arundel were ever taken into the confidence of any possible conspirators. On the other hand Tout does not seem to allow enough weight to the partial admissions extorted from Gloucester at Calais and from Warwick at his trial, and though there is a suspicious lack of detail about these "confessions", Adam of Usk at least makes Warwick say[2] that he was lured on by Gloucester, "by the then abbot of St Albans and by a monk recluse of Westminster". It is not surprising in the circumstances that our main narrative sources, the Westminster and St Albans chronicles, are silent, and there is always the possibility that more evidence came to light after the trials and was later embodied in the *Traïson*, though not known specifically to Richard as early as 1397. The supposed implication of Nottingham and Derby suggests a date after their disgrace in 1398 for the writing-up of the affair in the French version, while their mysterious mutual accusations in that year may themselves be explained if either of them had really been involved in a plot in 1397. Finally it may be noted that the *Traïson*, like the allied French chronicle of Creton who begins

[1] *Chapters*, iv, 21.   [2] p. 16.

his eyewitness account a little later, is not given to wholesale
and circumstantial fabrication, and the tendency of most recent
critics of these French authorities is in general to uphold their
evidence.

None the less the point must be left open, but even without
assuming a plot there were sufficient grounds for suspicion and
mistrust on both sides to explain, though not necessarily to
justify,[1] Richard's actions. Following the arrests further steps
were immediately taken, beginning with the issue of a proclamation justifying them on the ground of certain new offences,
to be explained in the next parliament and carefully distinguished from anything that had been done in 1386–8; this
effort at general reassurance was followed by a warning against
any attempt to criticise the government either directly or indirectly, for instance by offering prayers on behalf of the
accused.[2] Next, eight picked magnates of the king's party,
namely Nottingham himself, Rutland, Kent, Huntingdon,
Somerset, Salisbury, Thomas Despenser and William Scrope,
publicly accepted joint responsibility for these measures and at
a council held at Nottingham prepared an appeal of treason
against the accused on the exact model of the appeal of 1388.[3]
Writs were then issued in the ordinary form for the necessary
parliament to meet at Westminster on the 17th of September,
the last parliament, as it turned out, of Richard's reign. The
Annales states categorically [4] that it was packed and this seems at
first sight to be confirmed by Arundel's famous cry to speaker
Bushy during his trial,—"The true commons of England are not
here!" [5] Mr H. G. Richardson however has recently suggested [6]
that these words may equally well be a personal taunt directed
at Bushy, Bagot, Green and others for having changed sides

---

[1] The *Annales*, pp. 201–6, far from justifying, gives lurid details of
Richard's "treachery". Newbolt's reconstruction in *The New June* is
picturesque and friendlier to the king.

[2] Tout, *Chapters*, iv, 22, and *Ann. Ric.* pp. 206–7.

[3] This in itself was perhaps the order of a not entirely sane man.

[4] p. 209.   [5] Adam of Usk, p. 14.

[6] *Bull. John Rylands Library*, vol. xxii (April, 1938).

since 1388; he can find no evidence for the alleged packing of the commons, whether by magnates or sheriffs, while Tout's suggestion[1] that many of them may have been returned by "special" sheriffs loses sight of the fact that the shrieval appointments were made in October or November and that few if any such sheriffs had in fact been appointed in 1396, as can be seen from the rarity of reappointment, which is quite normal, in 1397; it was the 1397-8 and the 1398-9 appointments which were abnormal, and they took place too late to affect this parliament.[2] Finally, if it was packed, it is difficult to see why it was thought advisable by Richard to menace it with his Cheshire archers, yet the story that he did so menace it seems well established.

What seems to have happened is that certain crown reservists of the humbler type, especially from Cheshire, were ordered to meet at Kingston-on-Thames on the 15th of September, and were then formed into the special bodyguard, known as the "Cheshire archers", which aroused the peculiar maledictions of the *Annales* and other hostile chronicles. The connexion with Cheshire is an old one and may go back to the days when the palatinate had first fallen into royal hands; the Black Prince had drawn extensively from Wales and his Chester palatinate for man-power during the Crécy-Calais campaign;[3] Richard's mother had possessed the manor of Macclesfield, with which his bodyguard is said to have been specially associated;[4] and it is perhaps not too fanciful to see some connexion between his choice of the white hart as a badge and the deer of Macclesfield forest, a neighbourhood where numerous *White Hart* inns still attest a local tradition. However that may be, there is no doubt that the men were raised in Cheshire on this occasion, embodied in a corps of archers, probably four hundred strong,[5]

[1] *Chapters*, iv, 23 n.   [2] See my article in *C.A.S. Proc. loc. cit.*
[3] P. Shaw, "The Black Prince", *History*, xxiv, 5.
[4] *Times Lit. Supp.* 19th January 1933, p. 35—no authority quoted. But cf. M. V. Clarke, *Fourteenth Century Studies*, pp. 97-8.
[5] Adam of Usk, p. 11, who was an eyewitness, says 4000, but only 400 accompanied Richard on his travels in 1398-9 and from the point of view of expense alone it is a much more probable number.

and brought to Westminster in time to be present at the opening of the parliament. In addition certain selected magnates,
notably Lancaster, York and Derby, and of course the new
appellants, especially Huntingdon, were allowed to carry arms
and bring their own retinues to Westminster, while the peace
of the countryside was assured by the appointment of specially
royalist and aristocratic commissions of the peace and of *oyer
et terminer*, beginning in July 1397 and continuing for a full
year.[1]

Lastly, a special building open at the sides was put up somewhere in the precincts of Westminster palace to accommodate
the parliament. This gave the king an opportunity to over-
awe those present in it; according to Usk[2] he surrounded it
with his archers, who were not only placed ready to shoot but
on one occasion drew their bows to the ear. Tout believes,
however,[3] that these arrangements were due in the first instance
to the rebuilding of Westminster Hall and, although Richard
may have taken advantage of them, were not part of his
original plan.

Intimidated or not, parliament was opened in the usual form
by the chancellor, Edmund Stafford, who called on it to
punish the offenders and to take precautions to prevent a
repetition of their offence. This invitation was specially directed
to the commons, of whom as has been mentioned Bushy again
became speaker, while Usk[4] and the *Annales* agree[5] in insisting
that from the first Green and Bagot and he domineered over
the assembly. Proceedings seem to have begun with an annul-
ment of the acts of 1386,[6] though not of those of 1388, and a
general revocation of all pardons issued to members of the 1386
commission, including one freely granted to the earl of Arundel
by Richard at a time when he was his own master (1394).
According to the *Annales*[7] the revocation of the pardons took
place after a discussion by the bishops in which only archbishop
Arundel dared to oppose the king; Richard however immediately excepted from the revocation all members of the

[1] *C.P.R.* 1396-9, pp. 227-40.   [2] p. 11.   [3] *Chapters*, iv, 24 n.
[4] pp. 10-12, 14.   [5] p. 209.   [6] Usk, p. 10   [7] pp. 211-13.

commission other than Gloucester, Warwick and both Arundels, an occasion on which the duke of York and Wykeham are said[1] to have both burst into tears. The addition of the archbishop for the first time to the accused was perhaps due less to his opposition to the revocation than to the fact that Bushy had already added his name to those of the three chief victims and Richard had forbidden him to defend himself.[2] On the 20th of September he was impeached, not appealed like the others, of treason,[3] and that only for his conduct in the years 1386–8, which was in flagrant contempt of the king's own proclamation. On the 25th he was sentenced to forfeiture and exile and his place was later filled by complaisant papal provision of the treasurer, Roger Walden.[4] It is impossible to defend this treatment of Thomas Arundel on any grounds other than those of pure expediency, and it was expedient only on a very short view; it is however true, as is shown by a letter written by Richard to Ghent,[5] that this deprivation and exile were considered a sufficient punishment for the past and precaution for the future; there was never any question of proceeding further against him. On the other hand this was very far from being the case with the other victims of this parliament.

To begin with, the appeal of Gloucester, Warwick and the earl of Arundel seems to have been held up by the canonical difficulty of securing the concurrence of the bishops in the expected judgment of blood.[6] It was at first agreed that criminal charges could in fact be heard in their absence, but two days later it was felt that this might leave a loophole for subsequently questioning the authority of this parliament, and on the 20th of September they were therefore forced to nominate the steward, Sir Thomas Percy, as a general proxy to act for them in this matter with full powers. This curious precedent does not seem to have been followed on subsequent occasions with the result that, by the end of the fifteenth century, the higher clergy

[1] Usk, pp. 12–13.
[2] Tout, *Chapters*, iv, 26.
[3] Usk, *loc. cit.*
[4] *Ann. Ric.* p. 213.
[5] Perroy, *Schisme*, pp. 172–3, 255.
[6] Usk, p. 11; *Ann. Ric.* p. 213.

entirely lost their peerage through inability to take part in the increasingly frequent judgments of blood occasioned by the wars of the roses, and became mere "spiritual lords of parliament".

Meanwhile, this preliminary difficulty having been overcome, the appeal of the three lords began on the 21st of September,[1] strictly following the procedure and the "law" of treason[2] practised in the merciless parliament. There was the same offer of battle in Arundel's case as in Brembre's, and it was ignored in the same way, but it is noteworthy that in spite of Richard's proclamation to the contrary no new charges could in fact be brought against any of the three and it was necessary to have recourse after all to the events of 1386-8, coupled with nothing more than vague and abusive generalities. These met with a flat, but unreasoned, denial from the hot-tempered Arundel, who had never lacked personal courage; Gloucester, whose absence had not yet been explained, was not present; while Warwick, "like a wretched old woman",[3] broke down completely, incriminated Gloucester, John Moot and the prior of Westminster, though not in any detail, and so succeeded in saving his own life. The extravagance of Richard's delight[4] at this "confession" is, however, almost inexplicable as it stands and lends some colour to the theory that a more detailed admission of recent treachery, whether hatched at St Albans or elsewhere, was in fact extracted from Warwick but ignored by the unfriendly chronicles and subsequently excised from the parliament roll.[5] This would justify the extremely unpopular

[1] *Ann. Ric.* pp. 213-15 and 214-20.

[2] As a matter of fact four points of treason were defined on the 20th of September 1397, namely to compass and design to slay the king, to depose him, to withdraw homage from him, to raise his subjects and ride against him in war. *Rot. Parl.* iii, 351; Clarke, *op. cit.* p. 106. Usk, p. 16, shows that the precedent of the merciless parliament was also followed in not permitting the statute of 1352 to protect entailed estates.

[3] Usk, p. 16.   [4] Recorded by *Ann. Ric.* p. 220.

[5] Tout, *Chapters*, iv, 25 n., freely admits the hostility of all the English chronicles and himself adds the possibility of the parliament roll having been tampered with at a later date, but he does not seem to realise that this may equally well have been done, not in Richard's interests, but against them, i.e. by the Lancastrians after Richard's fall.

THE SECOND "TYRANNY" 237

execution of the earl of Arundel and would explain the comparatively small resentment aroused by the palpable murder of
Gloucester in his Calais gaol, of which more will be said very
shortly; it would also fit in with the terms of the proclamation
made after the original arrests, which suggest that Richard then
had good grounds for suspecting new treasons but no positive
proof of them. This had not deterred him from taking immediate action, but his hand would have been greatly strengthened in taking his final measures if such proof had at last been
forthcoming; moreover, it must have been something of real
value to have saved Warwick's life. It could easily be slurred
over at the time by the hostile English chronicles, two of them
at least proceeding from incriminated houses, and excised in
Henry IV's time from the official record;[1] Richard himself set
the precedent before his fall, as will be seen later, by tampering
with another part of the roll of his last parliament. The inconsistency of such extravagant expressions of pleasure on the
king's part with his own account of Warwick's alleged confession might well be overlooked by a tendentious chronicler,
while the total absence of the confession from the friendly
French authorities can be explained by the fact that they only
report the proceedings of this parliament very briefly or not
at all, while the *Traïson et Mort* has in any case already dealt at
great length with the alleged plot at St Albans.

But this is guesswork—all that is certain is that, however
much or little he may have said, Warwick alone escaped comparatively lightly with a sentence of forfeiture and banishment
to the Isle of Man under the guard of William Scrope; he was
even promised a handsome allowance in his exile, though the
Annales says[2] that this was never paid and it is necessary to add
that he was soon brought back for close imprisonment in the
Tower, from which he was only freed by Henry IV. Usk
adds[3] another victim of the appeal in the person of Sir Thomas
Mortimer, an illegitimate son of the second earl of March, who
was accused on this occasion and condemned in absence

---

[1] It must, however, be admitted that the existing roll bears no visible
signs of this hypothetical operation.   [2] p. 220.   [3] p. 15.

after the parliament had been adjourned to Shrewsbury. The reasons for his inclusion are not clear unless it was intended as a hint to his nephew the fourth earl, then in Ireland, who was in fact summoned to Shrewsbury in January 1398 in order to take a special oath of loyalty and appears to have been suspected at least of harbouring his uncle and perhaps of more than that.[1] Usk is careful to record[2] a law-suit over the lordship of Denbigh between him and a courtier in high favour at this time, the new earl of Salisbury, and a little later he says outright that the earl of March was not in sympathy with the king and that though he successfully dissimulated on the Shrewsbury visit he was in fact in some danger; it may well have been some confused impression of this coolness between March and Richard which led Froissart to make the fantastic ascription to the earl, already mentioned, of some share in the supposed St Albans plot.

Meanwhile when the duke of Gloucester's turn came for trial it was announced that he was already dead, and a "confession" of his was produced, which had been obtained at Calais by that William Rickhill who had been made a justice of the common bench on the occasion of Richard's reassertion of his regality in May 1389. It was alleged that Gloucester had died a natural death but it has long been generally agreed, as was suspected at the time, that he had in fact been murdered in prison in order to avoid such scenes of popular protest as had taken place at Arundel's execution.[3] There is little difficulty in making a plausible reconstruction of the true story out of the chroniclers' very natural suspicions but a considerable controversy has sprung up of late concerning the record evidence. Professor Tait has argued[4] that Gloucester was alive not long before his condemnation and that Richard had to falsify the dates of his murder and confession in order not to make the

---

[1] Tout, *Chapters*, iv, 30.   [2] pp. 17–19.

[3] *Ann. Ric.* p. 221; Usk, p. 15. Wallon, *op. cit.* ii, 179, curiously suggests that it may have been to save Gloucester the pain and shame of a traitor's death that he was murdered in prison! Cf. *ibid.* pp. 181–2.

[4] *Manchester University Historical Essays* (1907), pp. 193–216.

murder appear too obvious. He thinks that Richard first spread a rumour that Gloucester was dead when he was not, then secretly extorted a "confession" from him through Rickhill, then ante-dated the confession and that then, and not till then, the actual murder was committed. The late A. E. Stamp on the other hand brought fresh evidence to prove [1] that Richard made no such Machiavellian plans as those with which Professor Tait was obliged to credit him, but that he sent out Rickhill some three weeks before Gloucester's death, which took place on the official date for it, namely the 15th of September. This slightly weakens the case for murder but by no means destroys it; the whole question is really one of method and of the degree of premeditation rather than of guilt or innocence on Richard's part, and though Stamp professed to retain an open mind upon the whole matter the murder itself, if not proven, is most probable. The question who carried it out is even more obscure; Usk [2] and the *Annales* [3] blame the earl of Nottingham, who was then captain of Calais, while at least one attempt has been made [4] to associate Gloucester's successor as constable of England, the earl of Rutland, with the crime, but it is impossible to prove either of these ascriptions. The actual agent is supposed to have been either a man called Serle, who was tried and executed for treason under Henry IV, or a certain Halle, who put in a "confession", which had a high market value at that date, in Henry IV's first parliament, but Stamp is inclined to reject both candidates [5] and there is no decisive answer to the question.

Meanwhile the September parliament of 1397 had already turned from the proscription of Richard's enemies to witnessing the rewarding of his friends and the celebration of his triumph. Richard created no less than five dukes: Nottingham becoming

---

[1] *E.H.R.* xxxviii, 249–51. The controversy has been carried further by R. L. Atkinson, *ibid.* pp. 563-4, by H. G. Wright, *ibid.* xlvii, 276–80, and by Stamp again (answering Wright), *ibid.* p. 453, but the later articles add little to the main issue.

[2] p. 15.   [3] p. 221.   [4] By Atkinson, *loc. cit.*

[5] Adam of Usk, p. 86, under the year 1404 attributes it to Serle, but he was certainly executed for a different offence.

duke of Norfolk, Derby duke of Hereford, Huntingdon of Exeter, Kent of Surrey and Rutland of Albemarle; this cheapening of the title caused them to be nicknamed the *duketti*.[1] In addition John Beaufort, earl of Somerset, became marquis of Dorset; Thomas Despenser earl of Gloucester, Ralph Neville, one of Richard's lesser-known northern supporters, earl of Westmorland; Thomas Percy, of the rival house, earl of Worcéster, and William Scrope earl of Wiltshire. They were mostly endowed in their new honours with the forfeited lands of Warwick and the duke of Gloucester; those of Arundel Richard kept for himself, annexing them to the royal principality of Cheshire, while he also took in hand Warwick's hereditary shrievalty of Worcestershire, leaving the chattels of the fallen lords to be sold—the proceeds are recorded in the receipt rolls. On the other hand Richard's assumption of the arms of Edward the Confessor, which Tout rather hesitatingly[2] attributes to this occasion, more probably took place at Dublin during the first Irish expedition and is to be explained in part by the special reverence which the Irish were believed to have for the Confessor;[3] it is however true that Richard, like Henry III, was specially attached to Westminster and the Confessor's shrine, and it was before that shrine and after high mass in the abbey that the last act of the session took place on the 30th of September. On that day certain selected lords spiritual and temporal individually, together with Thomas Percy in his capacity as proxy for all the clergy in the realm, and all the knights of the shire in a body, "holding up their right hands as a sign of consent",[4] took a solemn oath to uphold all the acts of this parliament in perpetuity; it was then adjourned to Shrewsbury for the 27th of January 1398. The *Traïson et Mort* adds[5] that these proceedings were followed by a review of the Londoners, conducted by Richard and Lancaster, and that in turn by a great feast, in which "my lady of Exeter received the prize as the best dancer (and the best singer)".

---

[1] *Ann. Ric.* p. 223.   [2] "Now…if not…earlier"; *Chapters*, iv, 28.
[3] E. Curtis, *History of Medieval Ireland*, p. 267.
[4] M. V. Clarke, *Fourteenth Century Studies*, p. 103.   [5] pp. 11, 140.

Up to this point Richard's actions at least bear comparison with those of the merciless parliament and, plot or no plot at St Albans, are politically though not morally defensible. Only two persons had been put to death and three exiled, as against the much more numerous deaths and exiles of 1388; nor had there as yet been any equivalent of the original appellants' £20,000, while on the whole Richard had had better excuse for his violence than his enemies had had ten years before. If he had been content to stop there it is possible that the revolution would never have occurred, but unfortunately he seems to have regarded his work as only half done—hence the mere adjournment, instead of the dissolution, of his last parliament, and that to the Cheshire border. The *Traïson* says[1] that Shrewsbury was chosen in order to punish the pride of the Londoners, but at the moment Richard's relations with London, on the surface at any rate, seem to have been sound enough, and it is more probable that this time Richard decided to bring parliament to the Cheshire guard in place of bringing the guard to parliament. It is at Shrewsbury that he really began to overreach himself, although the crowning act of folly did not occur until over a year later, and it was important to him that parliament, having recovered from the first shock, should not venture to impede his plans.

The programme for Shrewsbury included not only certain arrangements made to complete Richard's revenge and the reconstruction of his government but also the financing of it, and it was got through in only four days, that is, even more quickly than the first session, which had already been in striking contrast to the length of the merciless parliament. Passus IV of *Richard the Redeless*, a poem which Skeat wrongly attributed to Langland,[2] the author of *Piers Plowman*, contains a reference to

---

[1] *Loc. cit.*

[2] T. Wright, *Political Poems* (R.S.), i, 368, does not accept Langland's authorship, and I am informed that modern scholarship supports him on the point. Its composition may perhaps be dated from internal evidence to the first half of September 1399, when Richard was a prisoner but not yet formally deposed.

what is almost certainly the Shrewsbury session of this parliament; it stresses the preoccupation of the commons with their money grants together with their fear of dukes—"some dradde dukis"—which can only be a reference to the new *duketti*.

To begin with, the judgments and acts of the merciless parliament were at last repealed in addition to those of the parliament of 1386; this, incidentally, did specifically involve the rehabilitation of the rulings of the justices at Nottingham in 1387, as was stated in so many words by the justices of 1398. There followed the already mentioned condemnation of Thomas Mortimer, to which was unexpectedly added a similar condemnation of that friendly moderate, lord Cobham, for his share in the commission of 1386; Cobham was, however, let off comparatively lightly with banishment to Guernsey and the promise of an allowance, even if the *Annales* is right in saying,[1] that as in Warwick's case the allowance was left unpaid. The *Annales* goes on to insert at this stage[2] the promulgation of a general pardon but adds that at the same time all previous pardons had to be renewed at a heavy price,[3] while both this chronicle and that of Adam of Usk[4] agree that fifty unnamed exceptions from the general pardon were reserved for future use by the king. Usk alone adds that even Bushy protested against this dangerous and disturbing reservation, which could only make everyone feel insecure, but that Richard held to it saying that the immediate publication of the names would cause the guilty to escape before they could be arrested and thus alarm their innocent associates! Tout notes further[5] that the general pardon itself was to be voided as a whole if any future parliament raised difficulties about the life-grant of the customs which now followed.

This strengthening of Richard's financial position was in fact one of the main objects of the adjournment from Westminster; Usk complains[6] that though the townspeople of Shrewsbury

[1] p. 224.
[2] Adam of Usk, p. 11, wrongly puts this in the September session.
[3] See also no. 7 of the articles of accusation, 1399, *Ann. Ric.* p. 263.
[4] Usk, *loc. cit.*   [5] *Chapters*, iv, 31.   [6] p. 18.

were distressed by the king's failure to pay anything for the maintenance of his household during the session, parliament none the less granted him one and a half subsidies, to be raised at intervals of six months,[1] as well as the unprecedented addition of the wool and leather duties for life, together with an extra impost of 6s. 8d. on the sack for aliens,[2] and this although the existing duties would in any case have run until November 1401. Finally, the lords and bishops renewed their Westminster oaths of loyalty, "this time on the cross of Canterbury; the commons, clerical proctors, and knights standing round the king swore with their right hands raised";[3] and the treason law was once more stretched to include any attempt to reverse the acts of this parliament.[4] Tout also quotes Gregory's *Chronicle*[5] to the effect that Richard looked to the pope for yet another sanction for what he had done, by obtaining letters apostolic, which were subsequently published at St Paul's Cross in London; he is inclined to doubt the truth of this statement, but fails to note that it is also to be found in the *Annales*[6] and in no. 10 of the *gravamina* of 1399,[7] so that it deserves better credence. It is also confirmed by M. Perroy, who says[8] that Richard had in fact by November 1398 reached a complete concordat with the pope; this provided for habitual collusion on episcopal appointments, to the great advantage of the crown, while surrendering to the pope one presentation in three to offices of middle rank and one in two in the case of humbler benefices. In effect the arrangement abrogated the statute of provisors, for which Boniface had been working for so long, in exchange for royal control over the bishoprics, but M. Perroy admits a little later[9] that Richard was only following English secular tradition in this respect.

In short the king's triumph had been so complete, and his reservations for complete liberty of future action so threatening,

---

[1] Ramsay, *Revenues*, ii, 405, for these financial details generally.
[2] Lodge and Thornton, *op. cit.* pp. 158–9.
[3] Clarke, *op. cit.* p. 103.   [4] Tout, *Chapters*, iv, 30.
[5] A fifteenth-century London chronicle.   [6] p. 225.
[7] *Ann. Ric.* p. 264.   [8] *Schisme*, pp. 348–50.   [9] *Ibid.* p. 352.

that even before this parliament ended mutual jealousies and suspicions had arisen among the magnates of his own party. We have in the first place Usk's story[1] of an intrigue led by Surrey against the young earl of March who, as we have already seen, had in any case been disputing the lordship of Denbigh with another courtier, the earl of Salisbury. The attack on March's kinsman Mortimer, to whom, according to Usk, he had lent money, suggests that he may have incurred Richard's suspicions and that that was the reason why he was specially summoned from Ireland to take the oath of loyalty, but it is also possible, as Miss Clarke suggests,[2] that he was summoned merely because he had not been present at Westminster. In any case his prudent bearing at Shrewsbury seems to have warded off these suspicions, if they existed, and he was allowed to return to Ireland, where his murder by the wild Irish in July[3] helped to provoke the second Irish expedition. Much more serious than this incident, however, was the fatal quarrel between Hereford and Norfolk, which came to a head before the parliament broke up and is given considerable space by all the leading chronicles;[4] their accounts are, however, confused and contradictory and it is not easy to determine exactly what happened.

According to Usk, Norfolk had for reasons unstated plotted to waylay the old duke of Lancaster on his way to Shrewsbury, but the duke was forewarned and escaped. There is no other evidence for this story and it is most improbable in itself, quite apart from the fact that, if the *Traïson* is to be believed, Norfolk's treachery was reported to Richard and his arrest at once ordered, together with that of Hereford, before the court left Westminster. Usk's editor, Maunde Thompson, however, suggests[5] on the authority of the Monk of Evesham[6] that his story may represent a confused recollection of a similar incident which

---

[1] p. 19.   [2] *Loc. cit.*

[3] Tout, *Chapters*, iv, 37, wrongly says August.

[4] See especially the *Traïson et Mort*, pp. 12, 141 ff., and Usk, p. 23; there is a brief account in *Ann. Ric.* p. 225.   [5] p. 109 n.

[6] Who, however, does not mention the name of the conspirator.

was said to have taken place as long before as 1384. This probability is strengthened by the *Traïson's* statement that Norfolk,
when accused of treachery by Hereford, made the solitary
admission of having taken part in an old plot against Lancaster
many years before, for which he had long been forgiven.
Dismissing Usk's opening words then, as we are entitled to do,
the fact remains that for one reason or another Norfolk dared
not attend the Shrewsbury parliament; indeed the *Traïson et
Mort* goes so far as to say that his head would have been forfeit
if he had gone there and that he was well aware of the fact.
What actually happened seems to have been something like
this.[1]

In the first place Hereford is known to have attended the
parliament, although Norfolk did not; the *Traïson* is wrong in
saying that he too was absent and in the same danger as
Norfolk, though less conscious of it.[2] Then on the 30th of
January Richard asked Hereford to repeat in full parliament a
story of which rumours had been circulating for some time; in
fact even before parliament met Hereford is said at Richard's
request to have put it in writing. The story was that in the
previous month Norfolk had confided to Hereford his belief
that the king had not forgiven them any more than he had
forgiven the other three appellants for their share in the events
of 1386–8, and that he had reason to believe that the duke of
Surrey and the earls of Wiltshire, Salisbury and Gloucester
were plotting their destruction. The implication was that the

---

[1] The reconstruction is broadly that of Tout, *Chapters*, iv, 30–1.
[2] Both Usk (p. 23) and the *Traïson (loc. cit.)* say that on the original
arrest of both men Hereford found bail, but Norfolk could not and was
imprisoned at Windsor: this may have been why Hereford, but not Norfolk,
was present at Shrewsbury. The *Traïson* adds that Hereford's pledges were
not only his father, Lancaster, but also York, Albemarle and Surrey, which
looks as if Norfolk's recent honours had excited the jealousy of other
magnates and may lend some colour to the rumours of a plot against him.
It is noteworthy that, according to Usk (pp. 23–4), Surrey at once received
Norfolk's marshalship and Exeter his captaincy of Calais, and that this
caused much ill-feeling. These two no doubt worked against Norfolk upon
the mind of the king.

two dukes should save themselves by flight or counter-plot while there was still time, but Hereford after reflection had preferred to repeat the conversation to the king. Richard, however, apparently did not wish the scandal to develop publicly at Shrewsbury, and Tout thinks that this is the main reason why parliament was abruptly dissolved upon the 31st of January and the famous parliamentary committee of 1398 created in its stead. The later history of the dispute is bound up with the constitution and powers of this notorious committee to such an extent that it becomes necessary at this point to turn aside and explain its real nature.

The facts are simple. As the result of an inspired petition by the commons a committee of eighteen persons was set up on the last day of the Shrewsbury parliament for two specific purposes; it was to deal with all outstanding petitions with full parliamentary authority and was to settle the controversy between Hereford and Norfolk.[1] The personnel consisted of eleven magnates, namely seven new appellants, Lancaster, York and the earls of March and Northumberland; six knights of the shire, all actually king's knights or esquires and including Bushy and Green, but not Bagot; the earls of Worcester and Wiltshire acted as proctors of the clergy. For settling petitions a quorum of six lords and three knights was stipulated, while for settling the Norfolk-Hereford dispute at least one of the two proctors of the clergy was to be present as well. The chroniclers[2] and many modern historians, such as Stubbs, exaggerate both the novelty of this appointment and the powers given to the committee. Actually there were plenty of precedents for it, not only from the remoter history of parliament but also from 1371 and 1388, that is from the merciless parliament itself;[3] moreover, the business of the committee was strictly limited to the subjects already mentioned. Hence the old view that the

---

[1] Lodge and Thornton, *op. cit.* p. 158; Tout, *Chapters,* iv, 31 and 35–41.

[2] E.g. *Ann. Ric.* p. 222 and Usk, p. 24.

[3] Jolliffe, *The Constitutional History of Medieval England,* p. 433, points out that in 1437 a much greater voluntary derogation of powers took place from parliament to council.

Shrewsbury parliament was a "suicidal parliament", which ended by granting away all its powers to a permanent committee of Richard's personal supporters, is now known to be incorrect.

On the other hand, Professor Tait has pointed out[1] that there is real force in article 8 of the *gravamina* of 1399,[2] which Stubbs quotes but hesitates to accept,[3] namely that about a year later Richard falsified the parliament roll with the deliberate object of extending the committee's terms of reference to anything he chose to bring before it. None the less it is improbable that Richard ever meant to abolish parliament entirely, for Mr J. G. Edwards has shown[4] that the forgery did not take place until early in 1399 and that there are other powerful considerations to be taken into account. In fact the whole purpose of the committee and the forgery alike can best be explained by a brief summary of the committee's history and actual activities.

It met first in March 1398 at Bristol,[5] where it dealt with five outstanding petitions of small importance, as it was empowered to do, and decided that unless Hereford could bring proof of his charges against Norfolk, which now or later included the murder of the duke of Gloucester and the misappropriation of pay due to the garrison of Calais,[6] trial should be by battle, that is before the *curia militaris*.[7] It is perhaps worth noting that on this occasion the committee is referred to as a council by later rolls of parliament. It met again at Windsor in April 1398, where it finally decided that Hereford's proofs were insufficient and arranged for a judicial combat at Coventry upon the 16th of September. This time, again according to a later roll of parliament,[8] it was afforced by a large number of magnates "and a great multitude of the chivalry of England", and was practically a great council. It met for the third time at

---

[1] In *D.N.B.* "Richard II".   [2] *Ann. Ric.* p. 264.

[3] There are in fact three existing MSS. of the parliament roll of 1397–8, two of which express the committee's powers in narrower terms than the third, from which the printed version is taken, which is apparently the only version Stubbs read.

[4] *E.H.R.* xl, 321–33.   [5] Tout, *Chapters*, iv, 36.

[6] *Traïson et Mort*, pp. 15, 146–7.   [7] Tout, *loc. cit.*

[8] *Ap.* Tout, *loc. cit.*

Coventry on the actual occasion of the duel and approved the king's action in forbidding it at the last moment and then exiling both combatants. By this time the earl of March and one of the king's esquires on the committee were already dead, but their places were not filled, and the implication is that the committee had now fulfilled all its objects and was being allowed to expire. The reason why it was suddenly resurrected and with wider powers appears to have been something like this.

In October 1398 Richard had granted letters patent to the exiled Norfolk and Hereford authorising them to appoint attorneys to receive any inheritance that might fall to them during their banishment. On the 3rd of February 1399 the duke of Lancaster died and Richard had to decide whether he would really let his heir, Hereford, who was only exiled for ten years, add to his already large estates in England the gigantic Lancastrian inheritance, including an hereditary palatinate from which the crown was virtually excluded. When he decided to break his pledged word on this vital matter he seems to have fully realised the extreme seriousness of the decision and to have felt that he needed not only an excuse but some support for the intended revocation; hence at this stage he not only resurrected the parliamentary committee but added to its original authority in the roll "to terminate petitions" the further words "and all other matters and things moved in the presence of the king...in accordance with what seems best to them".[1] The first use made of this forged authority by the revived committee was to revoke the letters patent, the chancellor explaining that the authority "inadvertently" granted by them to receive any inheritance during exile had been found incompatible with the sentence at Coventry. Legally perhaps this ruling fell within the bounds of the new "law" of treason as stated in 1388 and 1397, since under that law it might well be argued that the "judgment" of Coventry had in effect declared both men traitors and a traitor clearly could not inherit what would *ipso facto* have been forfeit to the crown. But the dubious nature of the "judgment" in a case where the issue

[1] Edwards, *loc. cit.* and Tout, *Chapters*, iv, 38.

had been neither proved by witnesses nor settled by battle, coupled with the transparent subterfuge of the "inadvertent" grant, displays the hollowness of this pretence, whether sanctified by parliamentary authority, expressed through the committee, or not.[1] Even the original "inadvertence" may mean simply lack of courage; Richard did not dare to prohibit Hereford's succession while Gaunt was still alive, and even after his death he tried to break the blow by endeavouring to ensure that out of all the vast Lancastrian interest none but Hereford himself, whose term of exile was now extended to life, and the faithful few who had accompanied him into exile should suffer personally. This is shown by the long list of grants and pensions for Lancastrian dependents which Richard carefully confirmed,[2] though it is true, as Tout points out,[3] that many of the Lancastrian estates were bestowed on curialists and that at least thirty Lancastrian retainers were simply transferred to the royal service.

In any case the sequestration of the Lancastrian inheritance was a fatal blow to the credit of Richard's government in the minds of all men of property and is generally taken as marking the beginning of the final revolution. If this could happen to the great house of Lancaster it was felt that no man's lands or revenues anywhere were safe, and the revolution when it came was carried out by Henry as above all else the champion of property rights—a rôle in which he was so generally accepted that, when it came to the point of "challenging" the realm, chief justice Thirning in his own interest would not let him claim by undiluted right of conquest.

Meanwhile Richard found the revival of the parliamentary committee with its extended powers so convenient that he was reluctant to let it lapse again into oblivion immediately after it had achieved its object; his appetite grew by what it fed on. Accordingly the same meeting at Westminster on the 18th of March 1399 proceeded from the revocation of the letters patent to the posthumous condemnation of Sir Robert Pleasington,

[1] Cf. *Ann. Ric.* pp. 232–3.
[2] *C.P.R.* 1396–9, between pp. 534 and 571.　　　　[3] *Chapters*, iv, 53.

formerly chief baron of the exchequer, for his share as spokes-
man of the original appellants in the merciless parliament; he
had in fact died in 1393, but there were forfeitures to be
extracted from his heirs. The committee met only once more
—at Windsor on the 23rd of April 1399—when it repeated
this act of petty vindictiveness by similarly condemning as a
traitor a favourite clerk of Hereford's, Henry Bowet, who
however was still alive; he had been constable of Bordeaux
since July 1398 and was now in exile with his master. Oddly
enough Bowet had apparently started his career as a strong
royalist who had actually been excepted from the appellants'
pardon in 1388,[1] which may account for Richard's anger when
he subsequently attached himself to Hereford; but he had
chosen wisely, for he survived the committee's sentence to
become one of Henry's treasurers of the exchequer and later
archbishop of York.[2]

No further trace of the committee's activities can be found
in the remaining four months during which Richard was still
his own master, but in view of the shortness of this period the
question still remains whether Richard in fact meant it to
supersede parliament or not. In spite of Tout's reference[3] to a
clause in his will dated the 16th of April 1399, which revokes
his bequests to his successor if not only past but also future acts
done *auctoritate eiusdem parliamenti* are not upheld, it seems very
doubtful whether Richard really meant the committee to have
any permanent place in his constitution. We have already seen
that he did not make any attempt to fill the vacancies caused by
death[4] and Mr Edwards has pointed out[5] that Wallon[6] is wrong
in thinking that he ever took a quorum of the committee with
him to Ireland, where he was in fact accompanied by only one
of the committee's squires and not a single one of its knights,
though there was a full quota of magnates. Mr Edwards concludes that while the Shrewsbury grant of the wool and leather
duties for life may show that Richard intended to avoid calling
frequent parliaments the very fact that he took the trouble to

---

[1] Tout, *Chapters*, iv, 39.   [2] *D.N.B. sub nom.*   [3] Tout, *loc. cit.*
[4] No more in 1399 than in 1398.   [5] *Loc. cit.*   [6] *Op. cit.* ii, 237.

falsify the rolls of parliament at all proves that he had some respect for its records and can hardly have meant to dispense with it entirely, while it must be remembered that the general pardon of January 1398 was to be withdrawn if the customs grant was challenged by any future parliament, so that Richard cannot have hoped to make the abolition of parliament permanently effective, at any rate beyond his own reign. Dr Chrimes goes even further [1] in believing that the phrase, and he thinks the idea, "by authority of parliament", occurs for the first time in history in the 1398 delegation of parliamentary powers; Richard therefore, so far from derogating from the importance of parliament, was actually advancing its pretensions!

Whatever may be thought of Dr Chrimes's paradox it seems fairly safe to conclude that the parliamentary committee of 1398–9 was a purely temporary instrument whose life was prolonged for some six months, but not longer, in order to give weight to Richard's sequestration of the Lancastrian inheritance and to complete the process of weeding out his few remaining opponents. It was not a permanent substitute for anything, not even, as Tout suggests, [2] for the great council, and its importance has in general been unnecessarily exaggerated. As the chancellor's speech in September 1397 shows, Richard's plan was plainly not to deny his subjects the "reasonable"—that is, the traditional—use of their liberties and franchises, but simply to make sure that there should never be any reversion to the hated commission of 1386 or the conditions of the minority—"that there be not several rulers in the realm, but one".

Before turning to the final stages of the second "tyranny", which involved measures other and more sinister than parliamentary committees, rather more attention must be paid to the concluding phases of the Norfolk-Hereford dispute, especially the duel at Coventry. As there was really no evidence either way beyond the unsupported assertions of the two lords Richard's first impulse seems to have been to try to reconcile

[1] *English Constitutional Ideas in the Fifteenth Century*, p. 138.
[2] *Chapters*, iv, 41

them,[1] not as is commonly held, to aggravate the quarrel. This he endeavoured to do at Windsor in April 1398, at first through the mediation of the constable (Exeter) and marshal (Surrey), an office of which Norfolk had now been deprived in spite of his hereditary grant, and again later in person. When both these attempts failed he seems to have reluctantly accepted the view that there was something behind these mutual accusations and he accordingly allowed arrangements to be made for the trial by battle at Coventry. The occasion, as is evident from the long and picturesque eyewitness account in the *Traïson et Mort*, was the social event of the year and drew great crowds of knights and nobles and their womenfolk to Coventry, and when Hereford rode out from Baginton to Gosford Green, "mounted on a white courser, barded with green and blue velvet, embroidered sumptuously with swans and antelopes",[2] there is little doubt that he was the popular favourite. Moreover he was the more experienced knight, and Richard may have felt that in view of the excitement which had been aroused he could not afford to let this old rival and enemy of his, with whom he had never once been upon cordial terms, enjoy a victory which would have taken him at one bound from the position of a suspected traitor to that of the most popular man in the kingdom. Much too must be allowed for Richard's own thwarted ambitions towards prowess in the lists; it would have been a bitter pill for him, apart from personal and political considerations, to see any contemporary of his achieve so publicly a triumph in the field of chivalry such as his own father had more frequently achieved, but one which his own slight physique and lack of skill denied him. Probably he could not bear to see either of them win,[3] and in any case Bushy was there to whisper in his ear[4] the political advantages of distrusting

---

[1] *Traïson et Mort*, pp. 14, 145–6.   [2] Holinshed, *Chronicles*, ii, 87.

[3] Adam of Usk's story (p. 24) that Richard "had had it by divination" that Norfolk would win and only stopped the fight when he saw that Hereford was winning, must be rejected—all the other authorities are agreed that the fight never actually began.

[4] *Traïson et Mort*, pp. 19, 154 ff. for the prominence of Bushy.

judgment by battle, which after all must err if both were guilty, whereas if the fight were stopped God could not be held to have spoken and the king could rid himself of both men. The anticlimax must have been tremendous when Richard threw his staff into the lists and it must have been long before the chivalry of England were able to forgive him for depriving them of the spectacle they had come to see, but when he solemnly pronounced sentence of exile on Hereford for ten years and on Norfolk for life[1] he must have felt that he had cut the Gordian knot and that no price was too high to pay. The heavier sentence on Norfolk may reflect the fact that if both were to remain under suspicion Norfolk, owing to the recent favours he had enjoyed, was perhaps the worse offender or, more probably, that Hereford was the popular favourite and Richard dared not ignore it at the time; he prolonged his ten-year sentence to a sentence for life six months later, when the excitement had died down, at the time of the Lancastrian sequestration.

Before proceeding to the last and worst excesses of the second "tyranny" it may be convenient to mention the ministerial changes of the last two years of the reign, though they were not of outstanding importance.[2] In September 1398 Mone after a very short tenure of office was superseded at the exchequer by the new earl of Wiltshire, William Scrope, though he remained a salaried member of the council until the revolution. He had already been succeeded at the privy seal by Richard Clifford, one of the four king's clerks attacked, but eventually released, in 1388, who had been keeper of the wardrobe since 1390, belonged to the Westmorland family of Clifford and had a great future in the fifteenth century before him. Another rising man was Sir John Stanley, sometime king's lieutenant in Ireland, who in October 1397 replaced the time-expired

---

[1] He died at Venice, probably on the 22nd of September 1399. Adam of Usk's theory (p. 24) that his exile was really a blind and that Richard had meant to recall him as soon as a suitable opportunity presented itself is probably a gratuitous piece of malice.

[2] Tout, *Chapters*, iv, 49–52 in general.

veteran Raddington in the important confidential post of controller of the wardrobe and chief organiser of the military side
of the household for the remainder of the reign.[1] He was a
Cheshire man from the Wirral peninsula by origin and a
gentleman of some standing in his own county, where he was
a justice in 1394, besides being a soldier who had gained experience on the Scottish marches as well as in Ireland, notably
with Raddington in 1394-5. Early in life he had married a
Lancashire heiress, and this had brought him into conflict with
Gaunt, who complained of the claims he made through her as
long before as the parliament of 1385, which may account
for his subsequent attachment to the king. None the less he
deserted him for Hereford in the crisis of 1399 and like Clifford
had a great career in the fifteenth century; eventually his family
received the earldom of Derby itself, and he became the ancestor
of the present earl.

The abuse showered on these and other official ministers of
Richard by the chroniclers is recognised by Tout[2] to be mis-
placed; three at least, including chancellor Stafford, continued
in high and even higher royal office under the next dynasty
and none, not even archbishop Arundel's successor at Canterbury, were wholly disgraced by the events of 1399. Yet these
men were also for the most part good servants of Richard II
and their later successes should be attributed to merit rather
than to treachery or careerism. What Tout fails to do is to
draw the obvious corollary—that in that case Richard should
have full credit for having chosen and promoted them—without
qualifying this praise by suggesting that as honest men of
affairs they cannot have enjoyed his full confidence. Indeed if
Richard had shown as much judgment in all aspects of his
policy during his last three years as he did in choosing personnel
it is not too much to say that the revolution might never have
occurred; however, this was very far from being the case.

After the Shrewsbury parliament Richard avoided London
and the south as much as possible,[3] first making a long progress

---

[1] See especially on Stanley, Tout, *Chapters*, iv, 199–200.
[2] *Ibid.* iv, 50–1.   [3] *Ibid.* iv, 35, for his itinerary.

down the Severn valley to Bristol, where he held his March
meeting of the parliamentary committee, and then returning to
the Midlands in time for the September duel at Coventry by
way of Westminster and London. He spent Christmas 1398
at Lichfield with his old confessor, Burghill, who had recently
been translated to that see, and did not return to Westminster
until the late winter or early spring. During all this time he
was accompanied by his four hundred Cheshire archers[1] and
was still "retaining" knights and squires for money pensions;
for example, five knights were retained at twenty marks a year
and seventeen squires at ten marks at Bath alone in March 1398.[2]
Tout also notes that he was at times accompanied by chancery
officers and by justices of the king's bench, though this had been
regarded as a court sedentary at Westminster since the latter
part of Edward III's reign; in addition there was, as has been
seen, some revival of signet activity, especially when the great
seal was not with him.

Another feature of this period was the persistent attempt made
by Richard, based again on his disillusionment in 1387, to
capture local government. Tout points out[3] the "enormous
number of local authorities" in the form of "innumerable
temporary commissions, judicial and administrative, which the
crown was always calling into being"; such authorities, mostly
composed of minor gentry, had hitherto tended to represent
the interests of their own class or locality rather than those of
the crown, but Richard now tried to control them through the
medium of his "special" sheriffs, first appointed in 1397 but
mostly continued for a second year, and also by introducing
other known curialists, including royal serjeants-at-arms, into
vacancies on the commissions. Even the chroniclers, usually
not very observant of the subtler administrative expedients,
note these tendencies; the *Annales* adds[4] that any criticism was
visited with imprisonment, and the charges are repeated in
articles 13, 18, 19 and 20 of the *gravamina* of 1399.

The continued development of prerogative jurisdiction,

[1] Usk, p. 23 and *Ann. Ric.* p. 237.   [2] Tout, *Chapters*, iv, 33–4.
[3] *Ibid.* pp. 42–4.   [4] p. 236.

though it goes back further and had been employed by both
sides, should perhaps be included in the various aspects of the
second "tyranny".[1] In particular there was the increasing use
made through the 'nineties of the *curia militaris* and the stimulus
given to the royalist use of this court by the appointment of
the new duke of Albemarle to take Gloucester's place as constable in 1397 and of Surrey to replace Norfolk as marshal in
1398. If any evidence was submitted or witnesses called trial in
this court was supposed to be by civil, that is Roman, law—but
generally both evidence and witnesses were lacking for the
peculiar charges which were brought in it and in that case the
decision lay "by law of chivalry", that is, combat. The *Annales*
complains bitterly[2] that in this way the old and infirm were
often unjustly vanquished by the young and strong. Admiralty
courts again, where Roman law with its authoritarian implications was regularly practised, were accroaching more and more
business in spite of limiting statutes made in 1389 and 1391,[3]
and it is significant that Richard was careful to keep the office
of admiral in the hands of the earls of Huntingdon and Rutland
successively and later John Beaufort, marquis of Dorset.
Finally the period was marked by the rapid growth of the already
existing special council and chancery jurisdictions with their
Romanising procedures, and in 1397 there was even an attempt
to revive the office of justice of the forests, obsolete since 1311,
in favour of the earl of Rutland.[4]

But undoubtedly the most striking characteristic of the new
régime was, as Miss Clarke has pointed out,[5] the multiplication of
special oaths of loyalty which, though they may have been based
upon similar oaths enforced in towns and counties by the appellants in 1388, went beyond them. Thus in addition to the oaths
taken by parliament in September 1397 and January 1398 all

[1] Cf. Tout, *Chapters*, iv, 44–5.   [2] pp. 236–7.

[3] Tout, *Chapters*, iii, 468 and iv, 45.

[4] See in general Selden Society, *Select Pleas in Admiralty*, R. G. Marsden;
Select Cases before the Council, I. S. Leadam and J. F. Baldwin; *Select Cases in
Chancery*, W. P. Baildon, especially the introductions.

[5] *Fourteenth Century Studies*, pp. 103–4.

the acts of the parliamentary committee itself had to be sworn to twice over by the leading prelates, lords and commoners, once in March 1398 and again a year later. Besides this, writs were issued in Richard's last year demanding special pledges from many of his leading subjects; thus the bishop of Norwich was adjured [1] to assemble all the clergy of his diocese and make them swear to maintain the statutes and judgments of his last parliament and of its committee—an action specially objected to in the articles of deposition. Further, the "crooked pardon" of Shrewsbury was suddenly interpreted to exclude the whole of seventeen counties from Norfolk to Wiltshire, including London and the Midlands, all of which were said to have supported the appellants in 1387-8—that is, more than half the population of England as it was then distributed. The 21st article of deposition says that all the people of these counties had been forced to submit themselves to Richard *tanquam proditores*, and though he restored to them in due course their letters of submission and "servile petitions" for pardon,[2] perhaps in order to placate them before setting out for the second time to Ireland, he made them appoint proctors with full powers who were forced to buy back the king's pleasure[3] with sums ranging from a thousand marks to a thousand pounds for each shire. The legal basis for this proceeding was probably held to be assumed knowledge of treasonable intent ten years earlier, such knowledge being a recognised offence which could be purged by confession and fine, but at this date fines of this sort were too often negotiated not before the justices but before a small council consisting exclusively of the three chief ministers and the three knights, Bushy, Bagot and Green,[4] which did not add

[1] Writ printed by Clarke, *op. cit.* pp. 111–12.

[2] Clarke, *op. cit.* pp. 104–6; submission printed, *ibid.* pp. 112–14.

[3] This was the fine known as *le plesaunce*: *Ann. Ric.* p. 235; Tout, *Chapters*, iv, 48.

[4] Nicolas, *Acts of the Privy Council*, i, 76; Tout, *loc. cit.* notes that the complaints about these fines are not confirmed by the chancery calendars, but there are a number of small fines *coram consilio* at this date in the receipt rolls, though only Essex appears (for 1200 marks) out of the seventeen county fines.

to their popularity; refusal to pay was punished with imprisonment. Lastly, the proctors of the seventeen counties were forced to furnish Richard with blank charters under their seals which the king kept for a mysterious purpose of his own, until Henry IV's first parliament caused them to be declared invalid and then destroyed them.[1]

There were, therefore, in Miss Clarke's words, at least three "categories of bonds" exacted by Richard from his subjects in his last years, but in addition to these there was a fresh series of forced loans, totalling no less than £20,000 and raised during the seven or eight months beginning August 1397. Some of these may have been produced under the "letters obligatory" which, according to the *Annales*,[2] individuals of property were forced to give to Richard—letters, that is, obliging them to lend him various sums by a certain date or dates, perhaps, as Tout says, by instalments;[3] but the great bulk of them were certainly raised by the now traditional methods of "persuasion", which dated from 1379 at least, if not earlier, were improved on by the Lancastrians themselves, notably in 1417 and 1421, and were still being employed by Elizabeth and the early Stuarts.[4] Much has been made of Richard's failure to repay most of these loans, but although he was certainly in default from Easter 1398 he had once more definitely granted letters patent under the great seal as security and we cannot be certain that if the revolution had not taken place repayment would not ultimately have been effected.[5] Be that as it may, the £6570 of outstanding debt to the Londoners, the £5550 to seventy-one other towns, the £3180 to seventy-two individual clerks or religious houses and the £1220 owing to thirty-six influential commoners must all

[1] *Ann. Ric.* p. 236, though the reason there assigned for these blank charters (to facilitate the sale of Calais!) is improbable. Ramsay (*Genesis*, ii, 344) was clearly mistaken in thinking that bundles of them are still extant in the Public Record Office.

[2] p. 235.

[3] *Loc. cit.* There are five such payments, averaging rather over £100 each, in the receipt rolls. See my article, *E.H.R.* li, 43.

[4] Dietz, *English Public Finance*, 1588–1641.

[5] Wallon, *op. cit.* ii, 467–8, takes the same line. Cf. *ibid.* pp. 539–40.

have played their part, together with "the oaths, the crooked pardon, the forced confession, and the blank charters",[1] and the fears aroused by the Lancastrian sequestration, in bringing about the widespread acquiescence of the country in the revolution which broke out almost immediately after Richard's departure in the late spring of 1399 upon his second Irish expedition.

[1] Clarke, *op. cit.* p. 111.

CHAPTER IX

The Revolution

IT is of course possible, but it seems quite unnecessary, to argue as some have done that Richard's household and military extravagance, and especially his retaining fees and pensions and the livery of the white hart, had threatened to impoverish him to such an extent that the sequestration of the Lancastrian inheritance and the financial exactions which have just been described were unavoidable. The corollary to such an argument is that the wretched man then fled to Ireland, leaving the earl of Wiltshire, Bushy, Bagot and Green and others to bear the burden of the unrest he had created; alternatively, it is possible to take Tout's view and to regard the second Irish expedition as an act of almost meaningless megalomania on the part of "the fatuous king".[1]

Actually that expedition had been rendered necessary by the death of Richard's lieutenant, the earl of March, in an ambush laid by the wild Irish in July 1398 and the refusal of the Irish chiefs to honour their bonds of 1395; O'Neill and MacMurrough were virtually in open rebellion,[2] and it was necessary either to take drastic action of some kind or to abandon Ireland altogether; indeed by the spring of 1399 the expedition was long overdue. The difficulty of financing it may account in part for Richard's desperate efforts to raise money, culminating in the Lancastrian sequestration; after this, says Tout,[3] Richard ought not to have dreamed of leaving the country, but this argument ignores the probability that it was largely in order that he might leave the country that Richard had risked the sequestration. There is not much doubt about the unrest in England, a good example of which is to be found in a well-known libel on Richard's ministers, one of many such which were in

[1] *Chapters*, iv, 53.
[2] E. Curtis, *History of Medieval Ireland*, p. 275.   [3] *Loc. cit.*

circulation that year.[1] Expressed in the significant language of livery and cognisances the lampoon declares that the Bush, the Bag and the Green are running wild and must be placed under control; it contrasts with these miserable symbols the late lamented Swan (the duke of Gloucester) and the Horse (the earl of Arundel) and places its hope in the Bear (Warwick), the Eagle (Hereford), the Peacocks and the Geese who will join the Eagle at need (perhaps the Percies and the Nevilles).

Meanwhile preparations for the punitive expedition against Ireland were hurriedly completed. York was again appointed keeper of England, reinforced by the three great ministers of state and four trusted knights of the council, Bushy, Bagot, Green and John Russell,[2] and the yeomen of the crown were again called up, this time to London for April, through the medium of the sheriffs as before. The duke of Surrey, king's lieutenant and justice in Ireland in place of the dead earl of March, had been sent on ahead,[3] and the king himself was accompanied by the dukes of Exeter and Albemarle, the earls of Worcester, Gloucester and Salisbury, Sir John Stanley, the whole wardrobe staff, including even the privy wardrobe from the Tower, which was in effect an ordnance department, John Lincoln the secretary with his clerks, and a number of minstrels and miscellaneous artists and artificers. The *Annales* adds[4] that he took with him all the crown jewels and treasure, a fact which was afterwards brought up against him in no. 23 of the articles of accusation.[5]

Most of the courtier bishops, such as Merke of Carlisle, Medford of Salisbury, Burghill of Lichfield, Mone of St David's and Braybrooke of London also accompanied Richard; Tout, however, notes[6] that of these Medford was titular treasurer and Braybrooke chancellor of Ireland. Magnates on the other hand, apart from those mentioned, were discouraged from attending the expedition and only a few barons served.

---

[1] T. Wright, *Political Poems* (R.S.), vol. i, pp. 363–6.
[2] Tout, *Chapters*, iv, 53–6; *Ann. Ric.* p. 243.
[3] *Ann. Ric.* p. 239.   [4] p. 239.
[5] *Ibid.* p. 270.   [6] *Chapters*, iv, *loc. cit.*

Even these, according to the *Annales*,[1] were only allowed to bring small retinues in comparison with 1394, and this is attributed to jealousy on Richard's part by the chronicle and by Tout, but considerations of expense, whether his own or his subjects', are not altogether impossible. In any case it was a grave mistake to denude England of the military forces of the crown while leaving the private armies of the nobility practically intact, and this can only be attributed to Richard's pathological self-confidence. He was, however, careful to take hostages in the persons of Henry Beaufort (as security for his brother Dorset) and the sons both of Hereford and the dead duke of Gloucester. It had been his intention to take the son of the dead earl of Arundel as well, but the boy escaped from Exeter's custody and joined Hereford in France. The *Annales*[2] says that the children of many other nobles were also taken.

The course of events in Ireland is fully described by the French squire Creton, who was now in Richard's train. The army landed as before at Waterford on the 1st of June 1399, and after waiting six days for Albemarle marched to Kilkenny, where it had to wait a further fourteen days for Albemarle, who according to Creton now began to behave in "an evil and strange manner", foreboding his future treachery. From Kilkenny the army marched through Wicklow, suffering heavily from the mobile Irish and failing to bring their leader Art MacMurrough, "king" of Leinster, to action.[3] Richard therefore pushed on to Dublin, leaving the earl of Gloucester to negotiate with Art "in some unnamed glen".[4] Art, however, demanded an unconditional peace, and when this was reported to Richard in Dublin he as usual lost his temper, offered the rather modest reward of a hundred marks for MacMurrough dead or alive, and marched back to Waterford searching for him as fruitlessly as when he had come.

[1] pp. 238-9.   [2] p. 248.   [3] Curtis, *op. cit.* pp. 276-7.
[4] There is a well-known illumination of this scene in Creton, Harleian 1319 B.M., which has often been reproduced, e.g. in Green's *Short History of the English People*.

Meanwhile the invasion of the duke of Lancaster—to give Hereford his rightful title—had occurred, but bad weather had prevented the news getting through to Ireland.[1] It was known, however, after Richard's return to Waterford and his original idea was to set sail for England within two days, but at this point Albemarle, who was now definitely plotting against Richard, persuaded him against the advice of older men[2] to send Salisbury with a strong detachment on ahead in order to raise a second army in north Wales, while he himself remained to concentrate the whole of his scattered forces at Waterford before crossing. The Dieulacres chronicle,[3] though without mentioning Albemarle by name, confirms the story of this false advice, the real object of which was to gain time for Lancaster.

Creton himself sailed with Salisbury "for the sake of merriment and song", and therefore ceases to be an eyewitness or a first-hand independent authority of value until he meets Richard again some time later in Flint after his fatal surrender at Conway. Richard followed on the 27th of July, much earlier than Creton seems to have supposed; he cannot therefore, as Creton thinks, have heard before he sailed of the execution of the earl of Wiltshire, Bushy and Green at Bristol on the 29th of July;[4] on the other hand he was not in England, as Tout following Usk believes,[5] as early as the 22nd. This reconstruction at least fits in with the statement in the *Annales*[6] that Henry of Lancaster was still at Bristol when news arrived of Richard's landing in south Wales and attempted concentration at Haverfordwest. But at this point it becomes necessary to deal in greater detail with events in England while Richard was abroad.

Richard's departure to Ireland with all his men and money had released, as might have been expected, a swarm of angry rumours,[7] most of which probably had no foundation but which illustrate the unrest and disorder in the countryside; they

[1] Creton, pp. 45–6.　　　　　　　　　　　[2] Creton, pp. 55–8.
[3] For this chronicle see Galbraith and Clarke in *Fourteenth Century Studies*, pp. 53–98.　　　[4] *Ibid.*　　　[5] Adam of Usk, p. 27.　　　[6] pp. 246–7.
[7] Tout, *Chapters*, iv, 56–9.

are faithfully reported by the *Annales*,[1] not as rumours, but as fact. It was thought that Richard never meant to return but to rule England despotically as a military monarchy based on Cheshire, Wales and Ireland, and that no man's property was safe from him, or rather from his creature the earl of Wiltshire, treasurer of England. Tout adds that even the carefully selected sheriffs began to neglect summoning the shire courts and that the confusion was general; nor had matters been helped by the widespread proclamation of the council throughout the country of the validity of the statutes made in the last parliament and of the revocation of Henry's letters of attorney. The country was in short ripe for revolt even before Henry had appeared.

Henry had remained in Paris with the small retinue which Richard had allowed him, including the disinherited Bowet, and here he had been joined by archbishop Arundel and Arundel's young nephew. At the end of June they had set sail with a few ships and, after touching at Pevensey in the Arundel sphere of interest, had made for the north, where the stronger Lancastrian interest lay, and landed at Ravenspur in the Humber. According to the *Traïson*[2] Henry had circularised London and the boroughs, saying that Richard meant to abrogate all municipal privileges and extort unheard-of taxes with foreign aid; he had also approached the magnates, laying emphasis on Gloucester's old complaints about the surrender of Cherbourg and Brest. The result was that so many flocked to join him that a large number had to be sent home for lack of means of feeding them. From Ravenspur Henry and his friends advanced into Yorkshire, where they were at once joined not only by the Lancastrian tenants but also by the Percies, the Nevilles and all the great families of the north.[3] At this stage Henry swore not to usurp the throne but said that he had come merely to claim his rightful inheritance.[4] It is not impossible that he was telling the truth.

[1] pp. 239–40.   [2] pp. 35, 181.

[3] Adam of Usk, p. 25, not yet an eyewitness, but a good authority.

[4] Hardyng's *Chronicle*, p. 352, confirmed by Dieulacres, p. 57; *ap.* M. V. Clarke, *Fourteenth Century Studies*, p. 57.

Meanwhile, in view of the general sympathy felt with this intention of Henry's, the keeper of the realm (York), the chancellor and the keeper of the privy seal seem to have hesitated to take action. The treasurer, Wiltshire, however, and the four knights of the council soon persuaded them to move from the dangerous neighbourhood of London[1] to St Albans, which they reached on the 7th of July, and from there to try to raise men-at-arms and archers through the sheriffs by promising large rewards. Not only was this appeal generally ignored[2]— except by that old war-horse bishop Despenser of Norwich— but even the clerks themselves soon struck work and the necessary writs could not be issued any longer. When, on top of this, news arrived that Henry had struck across the north of England with the obvious idea of coming down the Severn valley to cut communications between Richard and his council, the latter broke and fled in a wild attempt to get through to the west in time. Wiltshire, Bushy and Green reached Bristol, where however they were trapped by Henry and surrendered by Sir Peter Courtenay, the constable of the castle, without fighting; "deserters swarmed...through doors and windows and down ropes from the walls",[3] and the unfortunate trio were immediately executed. York had already made his submission, which was well received, and Bagot managed to escape from Bristol into Cheshire, where he was captured but ultimately pardoned, though not for some years. It is worth adding that Adam of Usk joined Henry's train at Bristol, so that his chronicle is of peculiar value for the history of the next three months.

At this stage Henry seems to have deduced that Richard, wherever he landed, would make for north Wales and Cheshire, whither Salisbury had preceded him; he accordingly marched north again, this time up the valley of the Wye, in order to forestall him, and arrived at Chester upon the 9th of August, accompanied by archbishop Arundel.[4] The deduction was correct, for in any case Richard's main army had disappeared,

---

[1] *Ann. Ric.* pp. 243-4.   [2] *Ibid.* p. 244, and Tout, *Chapters*, iv, 58.
[3] M. V. Clarke, *Fourteenth Century Studies*, p. 101.   [4] Usk, pp. 25-6.

largely owing to the treachery of Albemarle, who now openly deserted him, and of Worcester, who had decided to join his relatives the Percies and formally broke his steward's wand of office. Apart from this Richard's forces had been demoralised by their fatal division into two detachments entirely out of touch with each other and both imagining that they had been betrayed; his only hope was clearly to rejoin Salisbury in north Wales.[1] The royal baggage, plate and chapel furniture were therefore abandoned at Haverfordwest[2] and travelling light Richard took the coast route at top speed for the rendezvous with his advance guard which had been arranged for Conway. In spite of Richard's greater rapidity of movement Henry, having the shorter inland road to follow, seems to have reached Chester about two days before Richard reached north Wales. On his arrival he at once sent Arundel and Northumberland as envoys to Conway castle, knowing that Richard would be there sooner or later; his excellent intelligence as to Richard's real and probable movements after landing may plausibly be attributed to information supplied by Albemarle, Worcester or other renegades.

Meanwhile Richard, passing through Carmarthen, Harlech, Carnarvon and Beaumaris, reached Conway, only to find that, as Creton, who was probably at Flint,[3] reports, the rank and file of his northern army, depressed by a rumour that he was dead and tired of waiting for confirmation, had simply melted away. This final disaster was probably due to incompetence rather than treachery; Creton, who knew him well, vouches for Salisbury's loyalty and good intentions. He had apparently advanced as far as Flint, where he may have left Creton on his subsequent retreat to Conway—this at least would account for the lack of probability in Creton's narrative of Richard's movements up to the point at which Richard was taken as a prisoner to Flint. It is in fact to this unfortunate passage in Creton, who did not even know when Richard left Ireland, and to the malicious gossip of the *Annales*,[4] that we owe the legend accepted

[1] *Ann. Ric.* pp. 248–9 makes Richard desert his army—it was *vice versa*.
[2] Galbraith and Clarke, *op. cit.* p. 72.   [3] *Ibid.* p. 69.   [4] p. 249.

even by Tout as well as all previous historians, of Richard's "aimless wanderings" in north Wales with their alleged evidence of "crazy panic". Actually, as Galbraith and Clarke have shown, events moved with logic and rapidity; the synchronised dating which they have reconstructed from the mutually hostile accounts of Usk and the Dieulacres chronicle, coupled with the record evidence, has entirely demolished the older view, which in any case depends either on making Richard leave Ireland too early or, more commonly, on putting his surrender to Henry too late, and sometimes on a confusion of both.

Even in Conway castle, however, left only with Salisbury and a handful of loyal followers, Richard had not yet surrendered and there was no need for him to do so. There was friendly shipping in the harbour, which the castle commanded, and he could still have slipped away by sea, either back to Ireland or to Bordeaux, or even to the court of his father-in-law, who owed him something in return for the countenance he had—probably in ignorance—given to Henry's designs. The fact that he did none of these things can no longer be explained by the theory of a tame surrender, and we know that he was not taken in Conway by force; actually Richard still trusted surprisingly and rather pathetically in the regality and it was only by the basest of stratagems, which they afterwards did their best to conceal, that the Lancastrians finally got him into their hands. Their official version of events, which is to be found in the *Annales* and the rolls of parliament, is indeed naïve enough to make the king abdicate voluntarily at Conway, confirm his abdication *hilari vultu* in the Tower and express no wish to confront parliament or undergo any form of trial, but this version can no longer stand against the critical analysis of Galbraith and Clarke,[1] based upon the buttressing of Creton's much more plausible story with the entirely independent testimony of the Dieulacres chronicle.

The actual facts, as far as they can now be reconstructed, seem to be as follows. Henry, appreciating the strength of

[1] *Fourteenth Century Studies*, esp. pp. 76–8.

Richard's position and anxious to get him into his power, sent a small deputation to Conway led by the earl of Northumberland and archbishop Arundel.[1] This deputation offered Richard terms which in the circumstance he might well have accepted, namely, that he should restore the Lancastrian inheritance to its rightful lord and surrender five unnamed members of his council for trial in full parliament; there was no question of his being deposed. After some hesitation and admittedly with certain *arrières pensées*—he is said to have remarked "there are some of them whom I shall flay alive"—Richard agreed to these terms; an oath was sworn by all parties to them on the Host and it was under this safeguard that Richard voluntarily left the castle and the ships and his last chance of safety. The later Lancastrian story was concocted to veil the gross treachery which followed when Richard fell into an ambush, perhaps set by Northumberland himself, upon the road and was lodged as a prisoner at the next castle, Flint, the first stage of the long *via dolorosa* which was to end at Pontefract six months later. Northumberland afterwards denied complicity in any scheme to make Henry king, but there seems to be little doubt that he was at least deeply involved in the squalid plot which put Richard at the mercy of his enemies.[2]

From this point up to the famous interviews in the Tower Creton appears to have been an eyewitness and his account has not been seriously challenged. Richard was taken into Henry's presence for the first time at Chester, where on the 19th of August writs were issued in his name for a parliament to meet at Westminster on the 30th of September;[3] these were followed on the next day by a proclamation to the sheriffs, also in Richard's name, euphemistically explaining what had taken place and bidding them restore order. The king was then taken through Lichfield, Coventry and St Albans to the Tower of

[1] Usk, p. 28, and *Rot. Parl.* iii, 416, mention the archbishop, but Northumberland appears to have led the deputation.

[2] Hardyng's *Chronicle*, p. 352. I am not convinced by Dr Wilkinson's arguments in favour of his complete innocence in *E.H.R.* liv, 215–39.

[3] Tout, *Chapters*, iv, 61, says the 20th—an obvious misprint.

London, which he reached about the end of the month. The hostility of the Londoners towards him is illustrated by a story in Usk[1] of the arrest of Roger Walden, Slake[2] and another Ricardian while the citizens were searching for Richard on some false report at Westminster; when the people of London discovered his true whereabouts they are said to have sent a deputation to Henry on his march through the midlands asking for Richard's instant execution.[3] Against this animosity may be set the equally well-attested story of an attempted rescue of Richard somewhere between Lichfield and Coventry; the *Annales*[4] says Cheshire men were responsible, but Creton[5] attributes it to Welshmen. The *Annales* adds that all this time Richard was treated *reverenter et honeste* by Henry, but that is not the impression given by Creton, especially after the Lichfield episode.

On the arrival of the Lancastrian army in London the fiction of continuity was carefully maintained and all acts of state were still carried out in Richard's name; thus on the 3rd of September he was made to appoint to the treasurership, vacant through the death of Wiltshire, a wealthy esquire of Henry's called John Norbury, who had shared his exile and was to give useful financial support during the next reign.[6] On the 5th he was forced to supersede Stafford as chancellor by a senior clerk of chancery, John Scarle, who was an old adherent of Lancaster and had been chancellor of the duchy as far back as 1382;[7] Stafford, however, was not disgraced and actually recovered the great seal for a period after Henry had become king. Moreover, these were the only important administrative changes; thus Richard Clifford, the keeper of the privy seal, was declared loyal and continued in his office and, as Tout has shown,[8] one of the most striking features of the whole revolution from the administrative point of view in general is the complete absence of any further purge of the civil service.

As regards the magnates it was naturally a different story.

---

[1] p. 28. [2] Similarly arrested in 1388. [3] Creton, pp. 176–7.
[4] p. 251. [5] p. 177. [6] See A. Steel in *E.H.R.* li, 29–51.
[7] Tout, *Chapters*, iv, 61–2. [8] *Ibid.* pp. 64–8.

Exiles such as Warwick and Cobham, though not Norfolk, were of course recalled,[1] while of the Ricardians Wiltshire was dead and Salisbury imprisoned, though he was soon released. The others simply lost their new honours;[2] Albemarle, in spite of his treachery to Richard, Surrey, Exeter and Dorset, reverted to the rank of earl and the new earl of Gloucester to that of baron. They also, as was to be expected, lost their offices—Westmorland and Northumberland becoming marshal and constable respectively, while Thomas Percy was deprived of his stewardship, though with compensations due to his last-minute change of front or, more probably, to the importance of his relatives.[3] Of the courtier bishops Walden naturally had to surrender Canterbury to Arundel, but soon became bishop of London, while of the others only Thomas Merke of Carlisle was punished somewhat later in the usual way by translation to a Clementine see, and in his case there was special reason for the step in view of the gallant stand he made for Richard's rights before he was finally deposed.

The continuance of Clifford in office is the more remarkable in view of the fact that one of Henry's first steps on seizing power had been to send letters under the privy seal in Richard's name to all the leading monasteries ordering them to produce their chronicles for the whole period since the Norman conquest[4] in order that they might be examined by a special commission of "sages in the law", on which Adam of Usk himself sat, the object of which was in theory to advise on the best method of deposition, but in fact to discover if possible some shadow of an historical, that is, of an hereditary, claim on Henry's part to the crown. This commission spent the greater part of September in sifting the chronicles and had reached a positive conclusion by the time that parliament was due to

[1] *Ann. Ric.* p. 252.
[2] The *Traïson* (pp. 72, 223) says that "parliament" demanded the death of the three *duketti*.
[3] Tout, *Chapters*, iv, 63–4.
[4] *Ann. Ric. loc. cit.* No trace of these letters exists, but there is no doubt that they were issued.

meet; this was, briefly, that there was no shadow of support to be found for any hereditary claim but that Richard could be deposed by the authority of the clergy and people, whatever precisely that might mean. Their advice was certainly not what Henry had been hoping for and was brusquely rejected by him, as can be seen by the course of subsequent events, but the incident is none the less of great importance for the light it throws on the conditions under which the principal chroniclers would be required to write up their account of the revolution and for the help which it gives in the very difficult problem of reconstructing the play of forces inside the Lancastrian party during the critical month of September 1399.[1]

This reconstruction, though necessary, is bound to be strictly hypothetical, but this much at least is clear. We know from the terms in which Henry ultimately claimed the throne that he personally was determined to base that claim in any event first on descent and secondly on conquest; what then was his hereditary claim? The answer is supplied in his own words, "right descent from Henry III"—not, be it noted, from Edward III. In spite of Stubbs's arguments to the contrary[2] this can hardly mean anything else in the circumstances than an appeal to what is known as the Crouchback legend, namely the theory that Edmund, the supposed second son of Henry III, had really been the eldest son but in view of his deformity had been passed over for the succession to the throne in favour of his younger brother, Edward. If this story were true neither Richard nor any of the three Edwards should have reigned and the rightful king was none other than Henry Bolingbroke himself, direct heir of Edmund through his mother, Blanche of Lancaster; no Salic law had ever been recognised in England—

[1] The whole problem is the subject of a major controversy, which has not reached any generally accepted conclusion. See G. T. Lapsley, *E.H.R.* xlix, 423–49, 577–606; liii, 53–78; H. G. Richardson, *ibid.* lii, 39–47, and *Bull. Inst. Hist. Research*, xvi, 137–43; B. Wilkinson, *E.H.R.* liv, 215–39. I have in general followed Mr Lapsley, as far as I can understand his arguments.

[2] *Constitutional History*, ii, 506–7. I follow Mr Lapsley's counter-arguments, *loc. cit.*

the empress Matilda, for example, had transmitted her claim to
Henry II—and descent through a woman was therefore no bar
to the crown. Unfortunately the story was a transparent fiction,
popularly said to have been concocted by John of Gaunt himself, and it was dismissed as such after investigation by the
commission upon which Usk sat, but it is none the less clear
that Henry clung to it unblushingly in order to defeat all rival
claims. When the time came for the actual usurpation he
continued to assert it, not only in words, but in the care he took
with the traditional ceremonies for the coronation of a king by
hereditary right, particularly his unction with a new flask of
specially discovered sacred oil,[1] and in his insistence in face of
Richard's protests that the abdication carried with it not only
the loss of all the sacred and thaumaturgical aspects of the
kingship but also, by implication, their transference to himself
as rightful heir. As Wallon has said, "jamais on ne vit plus
saint homme d'usurpateur".

So far we are on fairly firm ground, but we are reduced to
little more than speculation when we turn to consider, as we
must, the effect produced by this patently absurd claim (rejected by his own experts) upon Henry's own supporters. It
will be seen in due course that chief justice Thirning objected
even to the second ground on which he claimed the throne,
namely right of conquest, and in fact induced Henry to insert
a saving clause in it, and it is legitimate to suppose that the
claim to hereditary right, which was placed by Henry in the
foreground, produced as strong, or even stronger, objections.
What then was the programme of these supporters?

It is not necessary in the first place to disbelieve the assertion
made by the Percies in later years when they were in revolt
against him that they personally had indeed helped Henry to
recover his Lancastrian inheritance but had never intended that
he should become king at all.[2] Others may or may not have

---

[1] Another legend in itself, see *Ann. Ric.* p. 300. H. G. Wright gives the
story in detail in "The Protestation of Richard II in the Tower in September
1399", *Bull. John Rylands Library*, vol. xxiii.

[2] Hardyng, *loc. cit.*

been of this opinion, but it is at least a probable guess that Henry did have to reckon with such an attitude among a section of his temporary friends. It is, however, even more probable that a larger party, led by archbishop Arundel, had from the beginning meant to make him king but, it is important to add, king only on their own terms.[1] The events of 1386–8 and 1396–9 had acted as a forcing-house of constitutional theory and it seems fairly certain, if only from a comparison of the two sermons preached by Arundel on the 30th of September and the 6th of October, as well as from the acts of Henry's parliaments, that something approaching a true understanding of parliamentary sovereignty was at last in the air. Some sort of judgment of Richard in parliament was clearly expected by contemporaries and this expectation was undoubtedly disappointed by what actually took place, for while something resembling a parliament was held and detailed articles of accusation were read aloud to it Richard was never allowed to appear in person and there was no form of trial. There was, in fact, a stiffening of opinion between the holding of this first assembly and that which met on the 6th of October; in the first Henry was merely warned by Arundel to do God's will and not his own or to beware the consequences, while in the second he was told that justice, respect for law and respect for property were essential to the kingship, and that the king must therefore not be arbitrary in his behaviour, but must act by the common advice and assent of wise and responsible men.[1]

So far, it may be argued, this is simply good Bracton; the king is under God and the law and as God's vicar can do nothing but what is conformable to the law. But Bracton had gone on to say that if none the less the king breaks the law God alone can punish him, and this is emphatically not the sentiment of 1399 though it had apparently still been the sentiment of 1388— since if there had ever been a direct attack on Richard at all in 1387–8, it had been confined to two or three extremist magnates, kept secret and hurriedly abandoned. Arundel had already said at Flint that when the king erred the great lords could judge the

[1] *Rot. Parl.* iii, 415.

king,[1] and article after article of the *gravamina* implies that the sole protector of the joint interests of the crown and the *respublica* is parliament. Parliament had already changed the law against the king's will in 1388 and though it had then to some extent vitiated its action and unconsciously abdicated the powers to which it was implicitly laying claim in trying to bind all future parliaments, the same mistake—and this is of supreme significance—was not made in the assembly which met upon the 6th of October 1399. It is difficult to deny the name of parliament to this assembly,[2] whatever may be thought of that of the 30th of September, and in reversing the acts of 1397–8 and reaffirming those of 1386 and 1388 it was not only affirming the power of parliament to make and unmake law, for on this occasion it carefully omitted the attempts made in 1388 and 1398 to bind all future parliaments and thus achieved for the first time a true *de facto* sovereignty of parliament. For if the king is under God and the law and parliament may make and unmake law against the king's will, as it is now recognised that it was qualified to do in 1388, then the king is under God and parliament, and that perhaps is the main achievement of the revolution of 1399.

It may of course be argued that the right to make and unmake law and to punish the king if he errs does not carry with it any right to depose a king and to determine the succession, or alternatively that if it carries such a right in logic the theory of parliamentary sovereignty was still so young in 1399 that this most drastic of all its implications had not yet been admitted. It is certainly true that the deposition of Edward II, whatever else it may have been, was not a parliamentary deposition any more than Richard's temporary removal from the throne, if it took place, at the end of 1387 was a parliamentary deposition, nor was Richard when he declared "compassing the deposition of the king" to be treason in 1398 necessarily or probably thinking of any parliamentary method. It is more arguable

[1] Lapsley, *loc. cit.*
[2] H. G. Richardson, in "The Elections to the October Parliament of 1399", *Bull. Inst. Hist. Res.* xvi, 137–43, seems to argue that the assemblies of 30th September and 6th October stand or fall, as parliaments, together, but I do not find his arguments convincing on this point. See below, pp. 279–80.

that the commission of September 1399 was thinking of something of the sort when it reported that the king might be deposed by "the clergy and people", though from the large number of canonists and civilians sitting on this commission it is quite as likely that they had such continental precedents in mind as the "deposition" of Frederick II by the council of Lyons. And yet it is surely probable that what Arundel and his friends had in mind was to let the parliament called for the 30th of September meet in due form and carry out the change with its sanction and approval, nominally in Richard's own name. This could have been done by inducing it to fix the succession on Henry, of course at Richard's nominal suggestion, as it may perhaps have done once already on the Mortimers, after which an abdication could have been extorted from Richard, which in turn would have automatically made Henry king. It would also, in Arundel's view, vacate the writs and cause parliament to be dissolved before the process of transfer was quite complete, but Henry would already be enough of a king to summon a new parliament in his own name in which the abdication could be formally accepted, and he would then be king by an undoubted parliamentary title which would powerfully reinforce the nascent theory of the sovereignty of parliament. It was precisely this state of affairs which Henry was determined to avoid.

We do not know how he avoided it; we only know that it was in fact avoided—but it is not difficult to reconstruct the arguments that Henry could have used. The time factor was powerfully in his favour, for Adam of Usk implies[1] that the commission on which he sat did not discuss Henry's claim by descent until after the 21st of September, and parliament was due upon the 30th. Henry may well have stampeded Arundel and his friends by insisting on the futility of the commission and stressing the fact that something must be done before parliament met to make sure that Richard would not still remain king, for a full parliament was an incalculable body—it had been difficult enough to control in 1388—and who could say

[1] p. 30.

whether the piteousness of Richard's present position and respect for the sacred nature of the kingship might not enable
friends or neutrals to revive the figment of bad advice and keep
him on the throne with new advisers? Or again, even supposing
that parliament agreed first to name Richard's successor and
then to accept Richard's abdication, what successor would they
name? There was the powerful interest of the Mortimers and
even Henry must have admitted that many people would consider the hereditary claim of the young earl of March through
his grandmother Philippa to be superior to his own. It is even
possible that parliament had consented to the Mortimer succession as long ago as 1385,[1] and if so there was a still more
powerful reason for reminding Arundel that the new earl was
a child of eight and for asking him whether he could seriously
maintain that it was in the interest of the realm to suffer another
long minority with all that that implied. We may even guess
that the Percies were already known to be discontented and
certain to oppose Henry's claim, if not to assert their own—
a suggestion which has in fact been made but is perhaps too
fantastic to be taken seriously. Archbishop Arundel at least
wanted to see Henry king; he might therefore be persuaded to
begin by extorting Richard's instant abdication before parliament
could do anything about it.

It is at this point that Arundel must have introduced the
new objection—for new it was—that the immediate abdication
of the king would automatically vacate the writs of parliament,
so that "parliament" when it met would not be a parliament at
all. It is true that in his sermon of the 6th of October after the
event[2] he maintained that it was not the abdication but the acceptance of the abdication by parliament which had that effect, but
at that date he was desperately trying to paper over the cracks
in the revolution and give it a parliamentary air, and the evidence
of contemporaries is against him. For example, since Adam of
Usk knew[3] that the cession of the crown would *ipso facto* and

---

[1] The point has already been mentioned, *supra*, p. 214.   [2] *Rot. Parl.* iii, 415.
[3] pp. 36, 39. He also three times describes the parliament of 1397-8,
not that of 1399, as Richard's last parliament.

immediately invalidate the writs, his statement that by the 30th of September Richard had already "deposed himself" suggests that to his mind the decisive act was the abdication on the 29th, not the acceptance of the abdication on the next day. When the doctrine originated we do not know—it certainly did not hold and was not known at the time of Edward II's deposition—but it appears to have been generally recognised in the last quarter of the fourteenth century. Indeed if it were not so it is difficult to see why Arundel should have opposed an immediate abdication, while as things were his objections merely provided Henry with another powerful argument in its favour. In the end Arundel gave way and an immediate abdication was decided on, though Henry must have agreed then or later to the taking of certain measures intended to disguise its full legal effects.

In the first place, of course, the abdication had to be "voluntary" and this accounts for the insistence in the Lancastrian record that it was done *hilari vultu*, cheerfully. According to the *Annales*[1] everything went like clockwork. On the morning of the 29th of September Richard was solemnly visited in the Tower by a committee representing the "estates of parliament" and sages of the law, whose object was to induce him to repeat or implement the promise to resign the crown which he is ingenuously said already to have made at Conway. The authority behind this committee was certain lords spiritual and temporal, justices and other persons assembled at Westminster *in loco consueto consilii*. There is, it will be noticed, a distinct suggestion that this authorising body was itself a parliament, which it could not have been on the 29th of September, as the writs were made out for the 30th;[2] this suggestion was perhaps the first of Arundel's attempts to regain the ground that Henry had made him surrender. Richard is said to have replied to it by asking for an interview with Henry and the archbishop and a copy of the terms of abdication. Later in the same day they came to him, with certain other lords, in whose presence Richard cheerfully (*hilari vultu*) read aloud

[1] pp. 252–4. [2] Lapsley, *loc. cit.*

and signed[1] a document asking that Henry should succeed him as king and that formal announcement should be made by proxies to the "estates of the kingdom" next day. He also gave Henry the signet in token of his wishes.

The objections to this scene lie not only in its intrinsic improbability—the misleading reference to Conway is alone ground for suspicion—but also in the fact that not only the *Traïson* and the Dieulacres chronicle but even the strongly Lancastrian Adam of Usk and Monk of Evesham make no mention of it; the Dieulacres chronicle indeed says that Richard resigned his crown to God though not to Henry, but the *Traïson* does not mention any form of renunciation and maintains that he demanded to the last that he should meet parliament.[2] It is of course impossible to say what Richard's condition really was at this time or by what means the signet, and perhaps the signature, were extorted from him, but the statement of that hostile witness, Adam of Usk, rings true when he says[3] that he himself had visited Richard on the 20th of September and found him "very melancholy". Perhaps it is true that he did make some sort of a fight for a public hearing, but it is just as likely that since the final collapse of his regality at Flint he had fallen into a waking coma from which he never wholly emerged. One of the last pictures we have of him during the second "tyranny", drawn by an unfriendly chronicler,[4] depicts him sitting on his throne in silence upon crown-wearing days from dinner until vespers: "if he looked at anyone the person had to bow the knee." It was the last stage of his illness; the regality had grown until it had swallowed the entire world and

[1] Richard is known to have signed minor documents of state during his reign, but this is the first time in English history that signature replaces sealing on a major document of state.

[2] There is evidence that what Richard resigned was the *regimen*, the governance of the kingdom, not the *regnum*, the kingdom itself. See H. G. Wright, "The Protestation of Richard II", *Bull. John Rylands Library*, vol. xxiii.   [3] p. 30.

[4] *Eulogium Historiarum*, iii, 378. The year is 1398, after the Shrewsbury parliament. It is perhaps one of these solemn crown-wearings which is illustrated in the frontispiece to this book.

as Richard looked around him he saw nothing but the mirror of his royal personality, inhabited by flickering shades whose movements could be governed by a glance. In August 1399 at Flint the magic mirror was broken and it is probable that the force of the reaction turned Richard into a mumbling neurotic, sinking rapidly into a state of acute melancholia, in which he could offer only the feeblest of resistance from the first, while before long it would be totally impossible to rouse him. Meanwhile the Lancastrian revolution proceeded on its carefully ordered way.

On the 30th of September not only the "estates of parliament" but also the "people of the kingdom"—probably the tumultuous London mob referred to by many of the authorities —met in the great hall at Westminster *propter factum parliamenti*, and to this assembly Richard's abdication was communicated by his two proxies, the bishop of Hereford and the archbishop of York. The question now arises whether this body was a parliament at all or whether the writs had not in fact been vacated by Richard's action in the Tower upon the previous afternoon. Although there is a constant suggestion in the Lancastrian "record and process" that it was none the less a parliament and remained one at least until Henry had become king, it is never described as such in so many words in that record and there are many other features of it which are highly suspicious and irregular. Mr Richardson has, it is true, pointed out[1] that it is specifically called a parliament in one place and one only, namely, in the coronation roll of Henry IV, but this may be due to an adoption, innocent or otherwise, by the clerk who compiled that roll of the view disingenuously put forward by Arundel in his sermon of the 6th of October that it was the acceptance of the abdication, and not the abdication itself, that had invalidated the writs. Subsequently Mr Richardson has argued[2] that if the meeting on the 30th of September was not a parliament neither was the meeting of the 6th of October, which has universally been agreed to be a true parliament, on the ground that while fresh writs were issued

[1] *E.H.R.* lii, 39–47.   [2] *Bull. Inst. Hist. Research*, xvi, 137–43.

by Henry they were simply *pro forma* and the same persons were automatically returned without any pretence of fresh election in the interval, for which indeed there would have been no time. He suggests that if these persons were not members of a parliament on the 30th they cannot therefore, without fresh election, have become members on the 6th; or rather that, since it is generally agreed that they were members on the 6th they must also have been members on the 30th. The difficulty is a real one, but if the logical point is pressed it seems better to conclude that neither meeting was technically a parliament, though the second observed all the forms of one apart from the election issue and has acquired the title by prescription, rather than to suppose that there was no revolution at all.

For, as Mr Lapsley has shown, the assembly of the 30th of September, unlike its successor and in spite of the insinuations of the record and the statement on the coronation roll, did not observe the true forms of a parliament. The throne remained vacant and the king unrepresented; there was no opening discourse, for archbishop Arundel's sermon came later in the day; the commons neither retired nor chose a speaker; no receivers and triers of petitions were appointed; there was no ordinary judicial work; and finally a mob of "people" (*populus*) was present as well as the estates[1]—all features highly unparliamentary in character. The presence of the London mob may very well have been a last-minute touch introduced by Henry himself with the idea of driving a last nail into the pretence of a parliamentary title, which Arundel was so reluctantly surrendering. It is not unlikely that it was based on the confused and difficult precedent of Edward II's deposition,[2] certain features of which, since whatever it was it was not parliamentary, Henry may perhaps have consented to follow as a sop to the "constitutionalists". The main stages in that de-

---

[1] I cannot accept Dr Wilkinson's argument in *E.H.R. loc. cit.* that on this one occasion in English history *populus* and *status*, as against *clerus*, were identical as they never were before or have been since.

[2] For the details of this deposition see M. V. Clarke, *Medieval Representation and Consent*, ch. ix.

position had been a "voluntary" resignation made under duress at Kenilworth, while parliament was sitting at Westminster, in favour of a legitimate heir such as Henry was now claiming to be, and the resignation had been formally accepted in the first instance not by parliament at all but by a separate body at Kenilworth representing the "estates of the realm"—a phrase which until the fifteenth century was by no means identical with the "estates of parliament".[1] Further, parliament, both in considering the whole position and in confirming the acceptance, had been bodily invaded and influenced by the Londoners, just as it was in 1399. The fact that in 1327 the writs were not held to be invalidated by the cession of the crown, so that the last parliament of Edward II had automatically become the first parliament of Edward III, would not perturb Henry in the least; it suited his book perfectly to adopt the new theory upon that point for obvious reasons. Least of all had there been any "statute" of deposition in 1327 and as Maitland has said "the precedent created was one for revolution rather than for legal action"—the very point which must have commended it to Henry, though he was far from wishing to follow it in every detail.

Meanwhile, upon the 30th of September 1399 "estates" and "people" severally accepted Richard's abdication but requested that his "insufficiency" should be made clearer by reading aloud certain articles of accusation (the *gravamina*). The reason for this request is probably to be found in the specific statement both of the *Traïson*[2] and the Dieulacres chronicle that Richard or his friends did in fact demand a public hearing; it is true that the *Traïson* places this demand upon the 1st of October, when no meeting took place, but that is a venial error and there is other evidence to suggest that it was made, and made upon the 30th,

[1] S. B. Chrimes, *English Constitutional Ideas in the Fifteenth Century*, p. 115.

[2] This is now a better authority than Creton, whom it copies for the history of the past few months. Creton had gone home at this stage and was getting the information for the last section of his narrative at second-hand from a French priest in Henry's service.

most probably when Richard's condemnation was invited without any defence being allowed and even without any specific charges having as yet been made against him. This evidence has been found by Professor Galbraith and Miss Clarke[1] in the unpublished part of what is called *Giles's Chronicle*, which is a composite work covering the period 1377–1455. The upshot of their long and ingenious argument is that the section of this chronicle covering the year 1399 may in part be derived from material collected by a Ricardian chancery clerk, William Feriby, who survived the revolution; this material was later worked up into a general variant of the Monk of Evesham by a master of St Leonard's hospital, York.

In dealing with the deposition this chronicle provides two descriptions of the same event, one of which is scored through, but neither of which is to be found elsewhere. Both of them assert that when Richard's resignation was read in "parliament" and his condemnation invited, voices were very definitely raised against it on the ground that the resignation had been forced on him and that he was being condemned unheard. We are not told in these passages whose these voices were, but we know from the *Eulogium* that Thomas Merke, bishop of Carlisle, was present and it is to him that the *Traïson* assigns a spirited protest both against the general competence of the lords to judge the king and their special iniquity in judging him in absence, "without hearing what he has to answer or even his being present". We do not know what other voices, if any, were raised besides Merke's, but the probability that Merke had the great courage and loyalty to make such a speech is enhanced by the fact that after this he alone among the courtier bishops was singled out for punishment, and in any case it is most likely that it was to silence such voices, whose words were carefully expunged from the official record, that the articles of accusation, or some of them, were now produced and read, *pro omni scrupulo*, as the *Annales* says,[2] *et sinistra suspicione tollendis*.

The thirty-three articles themselves have frequently been re-

[1] *Fourteenth Century Studies*, p. 84.   [2] p. 258.

produced and analysed[1] and a passing mention has been made of some of them already. They simply represent an unanswered speech for the prosecution, which takes the form of a naturally one-sided résumé of the events of the past twelve years; they are in fact *pièces justificatives* and little more. The most striking feature of them is the continued insistence throughout that Richard had broken his coronation oath and the steady emphasis in consequence on moral guilt and perjury. There is nothing new in them, little logic and less constitutional theory; except in so far as the theory that breach of the coronation oath disqualifies from kingship may be thought constitutional, they are all detail and special pleading.[2] Richard is charged no less than eight times with having violated his official promises to keep the peace towards clergy and people, to do justice in mercy and truth and to maintain the laws, together with the further offence of not having obtained and followed the good advice (no. 23) by which alone, being but human, he could have kept them.

Having heard these charges the estates and people pronounced that there was ample ground for deprivation and proceeded to set up a committee of deposition. This committee then declared Richard worthy to be deposed and did depose him; the estates accepted their report and appointed proctors to renounce their homage and allegiance to the king. But without waiting for this formality, which in fact did not take place until the next day, Henry now stood forward and claimed the throne, "since it was evident that the kingdom of England was vacant", by right of descent vindicated by conquest. There is little ground for the belief expressed by Ramsay[3] among others that in this short speech he "insinuates rather than asserts three claims", the third of which is "parliamentary election", though it is true that he submitted to some form of acclamation or admission of them, which was done by the lords spiritual and temporal

[1] E.g. by Stubbs, Ramsay and others. Text in *Rot. Parl.* iii, 417–22; *Ann. Ric.* pp. 259–77.
[2] Cf. J. E. A. Jolliffe, *The Constitutional History of Medieval England*, pp. 468–7.   [3] *Genesis*, ii, 366.

both severally and collectively *cum toto populo*. Henry, who was now called king, then showed the signet as evidence of Richard's wishes and the archbishops enthroned him, after which Arundel preached on the text *vir dominabitur populo*, issuing the mildest of general warnings to Henry to rule well and wisely and justifying what had been done on grounds of sheer expediency. Henry then returned thanks and denied any intention of expropriation as a result of conquest—this appears to have been due to the expostulations of chief justice Thirning. He proceeded to commission his chief officers and justices and actually apologised to the estates for his intention, which he now declared, of re-summoning them with fresh writs for a parliament on the 6th of October, assuring them that it was only to spare labour and expense that he intended the same persons, that is those actually present, to constitute his own first parliament.

On the next day, the 1st of October 1399, the proctors of the estates reported these proceedings to Richard in the Tower and renounced their homage and allegiance, Thirning carefully pointing out to Richard, in effect, that the body which had met the day before in order to receive his abdication was a convention of the estates and people, who were in Westminster because they had been summoned to a parliament. It was on this occasion that with a dying flare of interest in his fate "Richard maintained that the spiritual authority imparted to him by his hallowing was indelible, and could not be renounced by him, a doctrine emphatically rejected by the chief justice";[1] but even after this the *Annales* cynically maintains the fiction of his cheerful bearing.[2]

The revolution of 1399 was now complete, and it will be seen that the supposedly parliamentary nature formerly assigned to it can no longer be maintained. Following Dr Chrimes[3] we may say, after reviewing the two depositions of the fourteenth century, that whatever theory on the subject may have been evolved by 1399 was perhaps something like this. To depose a king it is first necessary to make him abdicate and to see that his abdication is accepted by his people, or at least by some of

[1] Ramsay, *Genesis*, ii, 368–9.   [2] p. 286.   [3] *Op. cit.* p. 345.

them. Even then there is enough regality left in him for some
form of deposition, based on definite charges, to be required
and an important element in this is still a formal renunciation
of homage and allegiance. The "estates of parliament" as such
need not enter into the process at all, though the "estates of the
realm", with which they are shortly to be identified, would
seem to do so. It is, however, becoming an academic question
whether parliament itself cannot in fact depose a king, with
or without abdication, always provided that he has offended
against justice and broken the moral law; parliament has not
yet tried to do so, but its sovereign nature is slowly being
realised and there are some men in 1399 who are of the opinion
that it ought to try, and who even endeavour after the event
to put up a pretence that it has tried and has been successful.
Acquiescence in this pretence was the main price paid by Henry
for the throne, and even when we throw in as a makeweight
his declaration safeguarding property rights, it must be admitted that it was a small price to pay. Its inadequacy is shown
by the rapid disillusionment of the country after 1399, by the
extraordinarily quick waning of Henry's temporary popularity
and by the risings of 1400, 1403 and 1405. In 1404 a man got
into trouble for saying that the king had not been "elected by
the magnates and state (sic) of England, but by the London
rabble",[1] and there are the famous words attributed to Henry
on his death-bed: "only God knows by what right I took the
crown."[2]

[1] Chrimes, op. cit. p. 118.   [2] Jolliffe, op. cit. p. 488.

EPILOGUE

RICHARD was taken from the Tower on the 28th of October 1399 to Gravesend and thence, disguised as a forester, to the castle of Leeds in Kent, and so to Pontefract castle. Here he is said by Adam of Usk[1] to have been starved to death by his jailor, Sir Thomas Swinford, in February 1400. The *Traïson* confirms Swinford's jailorship and the story seems probable, though the date given by Usk—the last day of February—is certainly too late, for Richard was already dead by the 17th of February, when the issue roll records a payment made for conveying his body to London. As regards the manner of his death the hostile St Albans chronicles assert that he deliberately starved himself, while the *Annales* in particular adds the picturesque touch[2] that he was persuaded to do so by his friends—the implication that his "friends" had access to him may be noted—and that he repented of his decision and tried to take some food, but that it was then too late.

All the other chronicles ring various changes on the story, becoming more detailed the later they are in date. The editor of the *Annales*, Riley, insists in his introduction on the way in which, according to this chronicle, the top of Richard's head and his throat were concealed, the face only being left visible that all might recognise it, when the body was brought to London. He asks whether it was Richard's body at all and, if so, whether it was thus wrapped up in order to conceal blows inflicted by Piers Exton, one of Henry's squires, who according to an anonymous French secondary authority, copied by the monk of St Denis and ultimately by Shakespeare, murdered him with violence at Henry's orders. However, in 1873 dean Stanley opened the tomb in Westminster Abbey and found that the skeleton showed no decisive signs of violence.[3] The Piers Exton story, which is of late and dubious origin, may therefore be rejected in favour of some form of starvation, whether self-

[1] p. 42.   [2] pp. 330–1.   [3] *Archaeologia*, vi, 315.

inflicted or not, assisted possibly by smothering, and there is no real doubt that it was in fact Richard's body which was brought to Westminster in February 1400 and given honourable burial.[1] But in spite of this posthumous tribute and the precautions taken over it the reaction which had already set in against the Lancastrians and was probably the direct cause of Richard's death was maintained for years to come.

The first outbreak took place in January 1400 with the rebellion of the *duketti*; the earls of Kent and Salisbury lost their lives at Cirencester as a result and Huntingdon was killed in Essex, Rutland once more playing traitor. It immediately became clear that Richard could not be allowed to live, and the council minute of about the 8th of February which recommends that Richard, "if alive", should be placed in safe keeping and, "if dead", should be shown to the people is justly characterised by Ramsay as a "murderous suggestion".[2] But even after this there was a widespread refusal to believe in Richard's death, and progressive disillusionment with Henry IV led to a considerable increase in Ricardian sentiment from 1402 onwards.[3] The Franciscans in particular took up his cause and some suffered death for it; the rebel Percies in 1403 proclaimed his existence in Cheshire, and the earl of Northumberland still affected to think it possible he was alive in 1406, though he had already accused Henry of his murder. Even as late as 1418 Sir John Oldcastle refused to acknowledge the authority of the parliament which was trying him "so long as his liege lord, king Richard II, was alive in Scotland",[4] and a modern editor of the *Traïson*[5] has tried to show that Richard really did survive for many years in that country, but was either too imbecile or too magnanimous—it hardly matters which—to try to recover

[1] Cf. H. Wallon, *Richard II*, ii, 367–8 ff., 521.
[2] *Genesis*, ii, 369–70.
[3] There is an interesting set of special commissions issued to local gentry in that year enjoining them to stop loose talk in taverns and other "congregations" against the new dynasty. See *C.P.R.* 1401–5, p. 126.
[4] *The St Albans Abbey Chronicle*, 1406–1420, ed. V. H. Galbraith, p. 117.
[5] B. Williams, *Traïson* (1846), preface, pp. l–lxxiii.

his throne. But these lingering echoes are the common after-
math of revolutions and the hard fact remains that medieval
divine right was dead by 1400—smothered, or starved, in
Pontefract castle—and that in spite of Henry and his sacred oil
all through the blood and turmoil of the fifteenth century the
battle would be to the strong and the race to the swift.

APPENDIX

The following notes on some of the principal chroniclers mentioned in the text may be of interest.

(1) *Walsingham*

Thomas (of) Walsingham was a monk of St Albans, who became precentor and *scriptorarius* under the great abbot Thomas de la Mare (1349–96). The traditional view that de la Mare singled him out and gave him his original literary inspiration is probably correct. The exact dates between which he lived are less certain, but the MS. *Liber Benefactorum* of St Albans,[1] which was written in 1380, contains the sentence, *T. de Walsingham, precentor, istum librum compilavit*, which suggests that he was already well established in his two offices by that year. Moreover, since the list of monks in which this statement occurs is given in order of seniority, and twenty-one names precede while thirty-two follow Walsingham's, it would seem that in 1380 he was already a fairly senior member of his house. Again, this MS. makes it clear that by 1380 the new scriptorium, with the building of which Thomas Walsingham, according to his own accepted account,[2] was closely associated, was in full production; the beginning of his literary career can therefore be ante-dated to the last years of Edward III's reign.

Thomas Walsingham remained precentor and *scriptorarius* of St Albans until 1394, when de la Mare sent him as prior to Wymondham in Norfolk. De la Mare, however, died in 1396 and the new abbot, John Moot, recalled Walsingham to St Albans some time in 1397.[3] The reason for this recall, as given by Walsingham himself, was the wish he expressed to the new abbot *claustrali quiete vacare*, but the real reason was probably his own administrative incompetence in the responsible office of prior. This is suggested by the fact that, although still a comparatively young man, he does not seem to have held any further office at St Albans, but to have spent

---

[1] British Museum, Cottonian MSS. Nero, D. vii.
[2] *Gesta Abbatum*, iii, 393.
[3] *Victoria County History of Norfolk*, ii, 342.

the rest of his life in continuing his literary work. The only other facts known about him are that he dedicated his *Ypodigma Neustrie* to Henry V in 1420 and probably died about 1422.

The details of Walsingham's literary life-work have only recently been determined.[1] It has long been agreed that he compiled the *Gesta Abbatum*, to which may be added the *Liber Benefactorum*, and also wrote the *Ypodigma Neustrie* and the chronicle which has been printed as the *Historia Anglicana*. The crucial question is whether or not he also wrote the *Chronicon Anglie* and the *Annales Ricardi II et Henrici IV*, both of which are of the first importance for the history of his time. Their editors, Sir E. Maunde Thompson and H. T. Riley, while admitting that both are St Albans chronicles, have denied the authorship of Walsingham, and have therefore been obliged to postulate a whole imaginary "school" of anonymous St Albans writers, in addition to Walsingham himself. Professor Galbraith, on the other hand, argues most convincingly that they were all written by Walsingham.

Setting aside the three generally admitted works, Professor Galbraith points out that we have Walsingham's own word for it that he wrote two other chronicles: one, a long history of his own times, to which he often refers as his *Chronica Majora*, and another shorter history, in which he condensed his own work. As now printed the first part of Walsingham's original long chronicle for the period up to 1382 can be found in Maunde Thompson's edition of the *Chronicon Anglie*; it is continued up to 1392 in Riley's edition of the *Historia Anglicana* and from 1392 to 1406 in the *Annales Ricardi II et Henrici IV*. Finally it is brought to 1420, where it stops, in a MS. printed by Professor Galbraith himself in 1937 under the title of *The St Albans Abbey Chronicle, 1406–1420*. The short chronicle, on the other hand, unlike the long, is not wholly in print. The first part of it, to 1382, exists only in two unprinted MSS. in the Bodleian Library; a second section, 1382–8, may be found in the latter part of the printed *Chronicon Anglie*; for a short third section, 1388–92, we must return to one of the two Bodleian MSS. (it is not in the other MS.); while from 1392 to 1420 it constitutes the *Historia Anglicana* for those years, as printed by Riley.

[1] By V. H. Galbraith, *E.H.R.* xlvii, 12–30, from whom these and the foregoing details are taken.

More pertinent perhaps than these bibliographical complexities, so skilfully unravelled by Professor Galbraith, is the subject of Thomas Walsingham's prejudices and weaknesses as a man and as an historian. He was, of course, a loyal member of the great house of St Albans and friendly to the allied abbey of Westminster. This colours his account of the Peasants' Revolt, in which St Albans suffered severely, and also of the years 1396–99, when both the prior of Westminster and the new abbot of St Albans, John Moot, were in opposition to Richard.[1] He was naturally orthodox in religion and therefore does Wyclif and the Lollards less than justice—a failing which is aggravated by the fact that he had no special means of knowing anything about them, and is therefore often inaccurate and confused. He is, however, valuable in so far as he inserts into his chronicles documents relating to Wyclif, though even then his text is apt to be shaky.

Walsingham was personally timid and, as we have seen, probably unpractical; like many of his kind, he is therefore all the more violent in his writings. On matters in which he has no obvious bias of his own he aims at effect, as many second-rate writers have done, by adopting what he takes to be the popular view of his day and then grossly exaggerating it. Since the popular view is an inconstant thing, this practice frequently led Walsingham into serious inconsistencies as an historian; for example, in his treatment of John of Gaunt, whom in early life he attacked with incredible bitterness. When, however, Gaunt's son seized the throne Walsingham changed his mind about the new king's father, omitted certain passages from his *Chronica Majora* and probably rewrote others. Even as he left it, however, Gaunt is evidently a villain up to 1389, when he suffers a miraculous change of heart which, it is suggested, is mysteriously due to the results of his Castilian expedition: anyhow, after 1389 nothing is too good for him. It may be noted that most contemporary opinion, as far as we can judge, passed through precisely the same unreasoning phases.

Walsingham may therefore in the last resort be treated as a fair example of the more orthodox, cautious and conventional public opinion of the upper classes of his day, and this is important in an age when a real public opinion was coming into existence in those

[1] *Traïson*, pp. 3–4.

classes and was beginning to play its part in public affairs. One last point worth noting is that he is consistently hostile to the royal court, and especially to Richard II.

(2) *The Anonimalle Chronicle of St Mary's, York*

This chronicle has special value through being an independent compilation entirely unaffected by Walsingham's prejudices against such men as Gaunt; moreover, it has often inside information of its own, not found in other chronicles. This is especially true of its account of the Good Parliament of 1376 and of the Peasants' Revolt.

As an historical composition, however, the *Anonimalle Chronicle* does not attain a high standard, for as its editor, Professor Galbraith, points out, St Mary's, unlike St Albans, was not an abbey where professional historians were encouraged. Its unofficial nature is further illustrated by the fact that it is written in colloquial Anglo-French, instead of the conventionally florid Latin of the regular monastic histories. The provenance of the chronicle is established by four internal references, and internal evidence again proves[1] that the long passage dealing with the Peasants' Revolt was inserted between 1396 and 1399.

The literary sources of this passage are not known, but by far the greater part of the account has probably been borrowed from another chronicle. Professor Galbraith has drawn attention to the double introduction of the revolt[2] and to the reappearance in a later passage[3] of the clerical half of the poll-tax, which has already been mentioned at the beginning of the story;[4] it is significant that these two mentions occur immediately before and after the long account of the revolt, which is therefore clearly an interpolation, somewhat clumsily made.[5]

The interpolation and its setting have, however, been worked over by a single hand—in fact the compilation of the entire chronicle from 1356 and 1381 is undoubtedly the work of one person.[6] Original composition seems to have been this compiler's last resort.

[1] See Professor Galbraith's Introduction to his edition, p. xxiii.
[2] pp. 133–4 of his edition.   [3] p. 151.   [4] p. 132.
[5] Cf. the double mention of the parliament of Northampton, pp. 132, 152.
[6] Introduction, pp. xxxiii–iv.

Long and short extracts from other chronicles, news-letters and official documents are ingeniously dove-tailed by him without acknowledgment into his text; hence the real value of the chronicle, as Professor Galbraith says, lies more in the fresh information it gives than in its comments on events or in the political attitude of the compiler. Indeed, apart from the usual monastic hatred of anyone who, however innocently, injures the interests of his abbey, the compiler has no views, no heroes, no consistency; he merely copies mechanically the conflicting judgments of his different sources concerning the same men. It is a practice which may irritate the reader but provides a useful mirror of contemporary opinion and a still more useful control of the prejudice to be found in other writers.

The interpolation itself has been discussed by G. Kriehn,[1] who on general grounds of "vividness" would put its original composition, as distinct from its insertion in the chronicle, not later than June 1382. Professor Galbraith thinks that it was originally written in English and inserted in a lost London chronicle, from which it was stolen by the compiler of St Mary's, but he agrees with Kriehn's view that it first saw the light in the form of notes made by an eyewitness of the revolt in the immediate following of the king. He goes on to suggest that this original author may have been the poet and civil servant, Thomas Hoccleve. Thus the writer shows a most exact and intimate knowledge of the posts held by the legal and financial crown officials mentioned in the narrative, and a still more remarkable acquaintance with the minutiae of chancery procedure and of procedure in the offices of the signet and the privy seal. Such knowledge would most probably be possessed by a clerk of the privy seal, the only office which was in touch with all these different departments, and Thomas Hoccleve was such a clerk. Moreover, the account is vivid and well written, showing considerable dramatic sense and literary ability; and Hoccleve was a poet.[2]

That Hoccleve's account of the rising, if it is his account, was incorporated in a lost London chronicle is suggested by the resemblance of the version in the Monk of Westminster[3]—a resemblance

---

[1] *American Historical Review*, vii, 266–8.

[2] For Hoccleve, or Occleve, and his career see *D.N.B. sub nom.* and Tout, *Chapters*, v, 106–10.

[3] Analysed by Galbraith, *Anonimalle Chronicle*, p. xliii, and by Tait in *D.N.B.* "Wat Tyler".

so close that it implies a common source. Since no such source is known it becomes necessary to assume one, and in the circumstances it is easiest to postulate a London chronicle of the type that became so common in the fifteenth century. Moreover, a Yorkshire monk, looking for an account of the revolt some fifteen years later, would naturally go first to a London chronicle rather than to any other kind of document. These, in brief, are Professor Galbraith's theories.

More recently Professor A. F. Pollard has put forward other views.[1] Professor Pollard suggests that, while Professor Galbraith is clearly right in assuming that the vivid descriptions of the Peasants' Revolt and of the Good Parliament, to which may be added the account of the Gloucester parliament of 1378, are all taken by the compiler from some outside source, that source might just as well be John Prophet[2] as Thomas Hoccleve. He himself, however, is inclined to press the claims of a third candidate, Master John Scardeburgh. Scardeburgh was a clerk in chancery from at least 1373, when he was, moreover, already receiving the 100s. *per annum* which was then associated with a chancery clerk who had been detailed for work in the "common house" of parliament. From 1387 he was definitely a commons clerk, so that he may safely be presumed to have had first-hand experience of life in London and Westminster and of the outstanding parliaments of this period. More than this, he had a Yorkshire connexion, which did not exist in the case of either Prophet or Hoccleve, for from 1380 Scardeburgh held a prebend in "the chapel of St Mary's and the Holy Angels, York (otherwise St Sepulchre's)". John Ball, one of the most famous leaders of the Peasants' Revolt, had been a priest on the same foundation, and even though Scardeburgh is hardly likely to have known Ball personally and may seldom have visited York, the string of coincidences is sufficiently remarkable to make it a plausible theory that he took a special interest in the revolt, as well as in his parliamentary duties, and delighted in retailing information on both subjects to his friends in York. This is, however, a crude interpretation of Professor Pollard's much more cautious

[1] In "The authorship and value of the 'Anonimalle Chronicle'", *E.H.R.* liii, 577–605.
[2] Secondary of the privy seal, who was acting as clerk of the council in the thirteen-nineties. See *supra*, pp. 194–5.

attitude towards the evidence which he has brought together; for the time being, at any rate, it must remain a theory and nothing more.

(3) *The Monk of Westminster*

Higden's *Polychronicon* ends in 1344, but the MS. at Corpus Christi College, Cambridge, after leaving a gap of two years, has a continuation by "a certain monk of Worcester, John Malvern", whose work runs from 1346 to 1381 with additional matter from 1381 to 1394. The portion from 1381 onwards has been edited by J. R. Lumby as vol. ix of the *Polychronicon* in the Rolls Series.

Dr J. Armitage Robinson, has however proved[1] that the second continuation of this MS. is not by John (of) Malvern at all, but by a third and different hand. Thus whereas the first continuation exhibits a noticeable ignorance of and lack of interest in the house of Westminster and its affairs, such as the ravages caused there by the Black Death and the notorious Hawley-Shakell case of sacrilege, which defiled the abbey church at the beginning of Richard II's reign, the second continuation displays a close and accurate knowledge of Westminster history. Under the years 1386 and 1387, for example, it gives a detailed account of the disputed abbatial election of William Colchester, and tells in detail how the king wanted to commend John Lakyngheth but eventually supported Colchester against a third party "provided" by the pope. Again, it contains a full and accurate account of Tresilian's case in 1388, when the question of sanctuary at Westminster was once more raised; it continually returns with interest to the general problem of sanctuary; and it frequently mentions the king's devotions in the abbey and the importance which he, like Henry III and, oddly enough, king John, attached to the Confessor's shrine. There is therefore every probability that this part of the chronicle was written by an actual monk of Westminster, and it remains to suggest possible candidates.

In dismissing two rather unlikely fifteenth-century names Dr Armitage Robinson pointed out that the work is certainly contemporary; it reads like that of an eyewitness of many of the events

[1] "An Unrecognized Westminster Chronicler", *Proc. British Academy,* 1907–8, pp. 61 ff.

described, and furthermore, it calls John Malvern, author of the first continuation (from 1346), "a monk" of Worcester, whereas he became prior in 1395—a fact of which (since Worcester was a cell of Westminster) no Westminster writer can possibly have been ignorant. The year 1394/5 is also the period at which the narrative breaks off abruptly, as if the writer had died or left the abbey; it is therefore improbable that he was a monk who was active at Westminster after that date.

This leaves only two likely candidates for the authorship. The first of these is Thomas Merke, one of Richard's best and most loyal friends, who became bishop of Carlisle in 1397 and stoutly defended Richard in 1399 even while he was in process of being deposed. However, although Merke at one time was certainly a Westminster monk he was so well known a figure that it seems incredible that he could have written a chronicle all attribution of which to him has perished. It is therefore more likely that the writer was that very John Lakyngheth whom the king wanted to commend as abbot. Lakyngheth was cellarer, and twice treasurer, of Westminster; he was clearly a royalist, which suits the general tone of the chronicle; and, above all, he died in 1396, within two years of its ending. But his authorship, though probable, has not been definitely established, and Tout has taught us to refer quotations merely to an anonymous monk of Westminster.

Whether Lakyngheth or another, this second continuator of Higden has considerable merit. His work is well written in comparatively simple, if not classical, Latin, and is free from anything but purely local prejudice; moreover, what prejudice there is seems to be on the king's side, and so supplies a much-needed corrective to the bias of Thomas Walsingham. He has, it is true, more than a tendency to recapitulate and ramble, and his power to digest material which he wishes to incorporate in his narrative is not great; but, if he was not a very clever man, he leaves us with the impression that he was educated, honest and well meaning. His judgment, for what it is worth, is an independent judgment; he does not seem to have come under any undue influence from either side; he is never turgid, and though pious, his piety never descends into pietism. In fact, among the rather second-rate historians of the day it is fair to assign the unknown monk of Westminster a worthy place.

(4) *Adam of Usk*

All the relevant facts may be found in the Introduction to E. Maunde Thompson's edition of this chronicle.[1] Born of poor parents at Usk about 1352, Adam, with the help of the third earl of March, proceeded to become an exhibitioner in laws at Oxford about 1368; this would involve taking holy orders. He was made a papal notary by cardinal Pileo di Prata in 1381 and became an "extraordinary", or supernumerary, lecturer, in canon law at Oxford in 1387. Five years later he was practising in the archbishop's court at Canterbury, where he remained until some time after 1399.

In spite of this legal career Adam from the first showed tendencies towards restlessness and violence; thus he is mentioned as the leader of serious riots at Oxford in 1388–9. His first appearance in politics was in September 1397, when he was present at the autumn parliament, probably as a protégé of archbishop Arundel, with whose temporary eclipse he seems to have been associated. Thus he reappeared two years later in the company of Arundel and Henry, duke of Lancaster, and accompanied them to Chester, sedulously begging favours all the way for himself, his native town of Usk and for his friends. On returning to London with the Lancastrian army and its captive king, Adam was appointed, in his capacity as a canon lawyer, to the special commission of "sages in the law", which was to advise on Henry's claim to the crown. He visited Richard in the Tower, was present at Henry's coronation and first parliament and continued to practise as a lawyer until 1402. In that year, however, he fell from grace even more seriously than he had done at Oxford and was exiled to Rome for horse-stealing.

In 1408, being still an exile and unpardoned, Adam formed the ingenious plan of first joining, then deserting and probably betraying, his rebel compatriot, Owen Glendower, in order to worm his way back into favour with Henry IV. This he seems to have achieved, not without considerable danger and hardship, but even then he was not pardoned until 1411. After that he appears to have resigned himself to the life of a parish priest in or near his birthplace; he died about 1430.

This is not an attractive career and it is not made more attractive

[1] See Bibliography.

by the rhetorical and conceited tone of Adam's *Chronicon*, in which he sets out to tell the story of his own times. The picture emerges of a pushing, vulgar attorney without principle or scruple, alternately bullying, patronising or betraying his associates and fawning unceasingly, but without much success, on Henry and Arundel. There was a rotten streak in Adam—the Glendower episode is particularly unpleasing—and for all his knowingness he is as long-winded and credulous in his writings as the most cloistered of the monks whom he, as a secular priest and man of the world, affects to despise.

None the less we cannot afford to ignore him as an historian— the extent to which so able a writer as Wallon went wrong in his account of Richard's last three years through being ignorant of Usk's work (which had not then been discovered) is sufficient evidence of that. For Adam after all witnessed, and even took some part in, stirring events, and if, as seems to be the case, he only wrote of them long afterwards from memory, his recollections still have first-hand value for the years 1397 and 1399. The bias is of course strongly Lancastrian, but allowance can be made for that and other defects; the main facts cannot be disputed or the general value of the narrative denied.

(5) *The French Chronicles of Richard's Deposition,*
(a) *Creton,* (b) *Traïson et Mort de Richard II*

It is now known that these two chronicles, though by different hands, are so closely related that they must be considered together. It is another unfortunate defect in Wallon's work, for example, that he treated both Creton and the *Traïson* individually as first-hand evidence at all times, whereas they frequently borrow from one another and on such occasions obviously represent only a single source. Moreover, neither of them as yet has found a modern editor; the 1819 edition of Creton was produced for antiquaries rather than historians, and although Benjamin Williams's edition of the *Traïson* in 1846 is prefaced by a long introduction, this contains a good deal of wild speculation, some inconsistencies and many errors of fact.

In spite of Benjamin Williams's theories very little is known for certain about the authorship of the *Traïson*, though it is evidently in large part an eyewitness account of the last three years of Richard II's reign. More, however, is known of Creton, a French squire who composed a metrical history on the same theme. He too was an eyewitness; he came to England about 1398 in company with another Frenchman of some distinction and armed with letters from Charles VI. By virtue of these letters Creton and his friend were able to accompany Richard II to Ireland in 1399; they also elected to remain with him when he returned to England, at any rate up to the early days of his captivity.

Creton's poem, in which he tells of his experiences, obviously has some relation to the prose account which is to be found in the *Traïson*, but a close comparison of the two narratives shows that they differ from and supplement each other to such an extent that they are clearly by different hands. Since, then, Creton may have used, but did not write, the *Traïson*, which in any case begins well before he reached England, it remains to find another Frenchman who may have written it. The most plausible suggestion is that it was written by a member of the household, possibly a clerk, of the young queen Isabella—one, perhaps, who came to England with her in 1396. This would explain the date at which the narrative begins, a year earlier than Creton's; the obviously eyewitness account in it of Richard's final leave-taking of the child queen, to whom he was much attached, in April 1399, in the deanery at Windsor; and finally its reliance on Creton for what happened to Richard in Ireland and elsewhere from that time on until his captivity.

Once Richard is a prisoner in Henry's hands, however, the value of the two French chronicles is reversed. Creton and his friend go home, and Creton's narrative professedly relies from this point on information sent him by a clerk whom Henry brought with him from Paris in 1399. The *Traïson*, on the other hand, once more becomes of first-class importance and remains so until the end of the reign.

The value of both these chronicles to the historian is considerable, once their general relationship has been understood. Of the two the *Traïson* is the more naïve and suggests a less able and interesting mind than Creton's; on the other hand, its author is more impartial, since Creton, though by no means blind to Richard's faults, is whole-heartedly and even violently devoted to his cause. (The

Traïson too is friendly, but perceptibly cooler.) Allowing for their curialist bias and French proclivities, the reader may therefore find in both narratives an admirable control on the highly prejudiced accounts of Walsingham,[1] Adam of Usk and the official Lancastrian records. Their general trustworthiness has, moreover, been reinforced of late, as Professor Galbraith and Miss Clarke have shown,[2] by the newly discovered Dieulacres chronicle, the product of a small Staffordshire house which had no particular axe to grind—for this chronicle more than once confirms detail hitherto found only in the Frenchmen and suggests that while they, no more than the Lancastrians, tell the whole truth, they represent upon the whole the more trustworthy of the two points of view.

[1] More especially in the *Annales Ricardi II.*
[2] *Fourteenth Century Studies*, pp. 53–98.

BIBLIOGRAPHY

This list includes only the main authorities, with special reference to recent work: the most useful items are marked with an asterisk. For a fuller bibliography see *Cambridge Medieval History*, vol. vii.

(1) DOCUMENTS

Calendar of the Close Rolls, 1272– . London, 1892– .

Calendar of the Fine Rolls, 1272– . London, 1911– .

Calendar of Letter-Books of the City of London. Letter-Book H, circa 1375–99, ed. R. R. Sharpe. London, 1907.

Calendar of the Patent Rolls, 1216– . London, 1893– .

Diplomatic Correspondence of Richard II, ed. E. Perroy. Camden, 3rd ser. xlviii. London, 1933.

Documents Relating to Cambridgeshire Villages, ed. W. M. Palmer and H. W. Saunders, vol. ii. Cambridge (no date).

*English Constitutional Documents, 1307–1485, ed. Eleanor C. Lodge and Gladys A. Thornton. Cambridge, 1935.

Fasciculi Zizaniorum, ed. W. W. Shirley. Rolls Series. London, 1858.

Foedera, ed. T. Rymer. 20 vols. London, 1704–35.

Illustrations of Chaucer's England, ed. Dorothy Hughes. London, 1919.

Issues of the Exchequer...from King Henry III to King Henry VI inclusive. Extracted and translated by F. Devon. London, 1837.

John of Gaunt's Register, 1379–83, ed. Eleanor C. Lodge and Robert Somerville. Camden, 3rd ser. vols. lvi–vii. London, 1937.

"Peasants' Rising and the Lollards (The)." A collection of unpublished documents forming an appendix to *England in the Age of Wycliffe*, ed. E. Powell and G. M. Trevelyan. London, 1899.

Proceedings and Ordinances of the Privy Council, ed. Sir Harris Nicolas. 7 vols. London, 1834–7.

Rotuli Parliamentorum (1278–1503), ed. J. Strachey. 6 vols and index. London, 1767–83.

Select Cases before the Council, ed. I. S. Leadam and J. F. Baldwin. Selden Society. London, 1918.

Select Cases in Chancery, ed. W. P. Baildon. Selden Society. London, 1896.

Select Documents of English Constitutional History, ed. G. B. Adams and H. M. Stephens. New York, 1921.

Select Pleas in Admiralty, ed. R. G. Marsden. Selden Society. London, 1892.

Statutes of the Realm. 9 vols. with 2 index vols. London, 1810–28.

Wykeham's Register, ed. T. F. Kirby. 2 vols. Hampshire Record Society. London, 1896.

(2) CHRONICLES, POEMS, ETC.

★*Annales Ricardi II et Henrici IV.* J. de Trokelowe, *Chronica et Annales,* ed. H. T. Riley. Rolls Series. London, 1866.

★*Anonimalle Chronicle (The),* 1333–81, ed. V. H. Galbraith. Manchester, 1927.

Chronicon Anglie, 1328–88, T. Walsingham, ed. E. Maunde Thompson. Rolls Series. London, 1874.

★CRETON. *French Metrical History of the Deposition of Richard II,* ed. J. Webb (with translation) for the Royal Society of Antiquaries. London, 1819.

Eulogium Historiarum, ed. F. S. Haydon. 3 vols. Rolls Series. London, 1858–63.

EVESHAM. *Historia vitae et regni Ricardi II...a monacho quodam de Evesham consignata...,* ed. T. Hearne. Oxford, 1729.

★FAVENT, T. *Historia Mirabilis Parliamenti,* ed. M. McKisack. *Camden Miscellany,* vol. xiv. London, 1926.

FROISSART, JEAN. *Chroniques,* ed. Kervyn de Lettenhove. Brussels, 1863.
—— *Œuvres,* t. 25, ed. Kervyn de Lettenhove. Brussels, 1870–77.

HARDYNG, JOHN. *Chronicle,* ed. Henry Ellis. London, 1812.

★*Historia Anglicana,* T. Walsingham, ed. H. T. Riley. 2 vols. Rolls Series. London, 1863–4.

HOLINSHED, RAPHAEL. *Chronicles.* 6 vols. London, 1807–8.

KNIGHTON, HENRY. *Chronicon,* ed. J. R. Lumby. 2 vols. Rolls Series. London, 1889.

★MONK OF WESTMINSTER. Higden's *Polychronicon,* vol. ix, ed. J. R. Lumby. Rolls Series. London, 1886.

Piers Plowman, ed. W. W. Skeat. 4 vols. Early English Text Society. London, 1867–85.

Political Poems...from...Edward III to...Richard III, ed. T. Wright. 2 vols. Rolls Series. London, 1859–61.

Select Early English Poems, ed. Sir Israel Gollancz, No. 3. *Winner and Waster.* London, 1924.

★*Traïson et Mort de Richard II,* ed. B. Williams. English Historical Society. London, 1846.

★USK, ADAM OF. *Chronicon,* ed. E. Maunde Thompson. London, 1904.

(3) MODERN WORKS

ARMITAGE-SMITH, Sir SYDNEY. *John of Gaunt.* London, 1904.

ASHLEY, Sir WILLIAM JAMES. *James and Philip van Artevelde.* London, 1883.

BALDWIN, J. F. *The King's Council.* Oxford, 1913.

BARRACLOUGH, G. *Papal Provisions.* Oxford, 1935.

Cambridge Medieval History, vol. vii. Cambridge, 1932.

CHRIMES, S. B. *English Constitutional Ideas in the Fifteenth Century*. Cambridge, 1936.

*CLARKE, M. V. *Fourteenth Century Studies*. Oxford, 1937.

* —— *Medieval Representation and Consent*. London, 1936.

COOPER, C. H. *Annals of Cambridge*. 4 vols. Cambridge, 1842–52.

COULTON, G. G. *Chaucer and his England*. London, 1908.

—— "The Peasants' Revolt", in *Great Events in History*, ed. G. R. Stirling-Taylor. London, 1934.

CURTIS, E. *History of Medieval Ireland*. 2nd ed. London, 1938.

—— *Richard II in Ireland, 1394–5*. Oxford, 1927.

Dictionary of National Biography, especially "Richard II".

GRAY, H. L. *The Influence of the Commons on Early Legislation*. Cambridge (Mass.), 1932.

Historical Essays in Commemoration of the Jubilee of Owens College, Manchester, ed. T. F. Tout and James Tait. Manchester, 1907.

Historical Essays in Honour of James Tait. Manchester, 1933.

HOLDSWORTH, Sir WILLIAM S. *History of English Law*. Vols. i–iii. 3rd ed. London, 1922–3.

Interim Report of the Committee on House of Commons Personnel and Politics, 1264–1832. Cmd. 4130. London, 1932.

*JOLLIFFE, J. E. A. *The Constitutional History of Medieval England*. London, 1937.

JUSSERAND, J. J. *English Wayfaring Life in the Middle Ages*, tr. Lucy Toulmin-Smith. London, 1892.

LECHLER, G. V. *John Wycliffe and his English Precursors*, tr. Lorimer. London, 1884.

LEVETT, A. E. *Studies in Manorial History*, ed. H. M. Cam, M. Coate and L. S. Sutherland. Oxford, 1938.

MOBERLY, G. H. *Life of William of Wykeham*. London, 1887.

OMAN, Sir CHARLES. *The Great Revolt of 1381*. Oxford, 1906.

—— *The Political History of England, 1377–1485*. London, 1910.

OTWAY-RUTHVEN, J. *The King's Secretary and the Signet Office in the Fifteenth Century*. Cambridge, 1939.

OWST, G. R. *Literature and Pulpit in Medieval England*. Cambridge, 1933.

*PERROY, E. *L'Angleterre et le grand schisme d'Occident*. Paris, 1933.

*PETIT-DUTAILLIS, C. *Studies Supplementary to Stubbs's Constitutional History*. 3 vols. (English edition.) Manchester, 1908–29.

PLUCKNETT, T. F. *Concise History of the Common Law*. 2nd ed. London, 1936.

POLLARD, A. F. *The Evolution of Parliament*. 2nd ed. London, 1926.

POWELL, E. *The Rising in East Anglia in 1381*. Cambridge, 1896.

RAMSAY, Sir JAMES. *The Genesis of Lancaster, 1307–99*. 2 vols. Oxford, 1913.

—— *The Revenues of the Kings of England*. 2 vols. Oxford, 1925.

RÉVILLE, A. *Le Soulèvement des travailleurs d'Angleterre en 1381*. Paris, 1898.

STUBBS, W. *The Constitutional History of England.* 3 vols. 2nd ed. London, 1875.

*TOUT, T. F. *Chapters in Mediaeval Administrative History.* 6 vols. Manchester, 1920–33.

* —— *Collected Papers.* 3 vols. Manchester, 1932.

*TREVELYAN, G. M. *England in the Age of Wycliffe.* 4th ed. London, 1909.

UNWIN, G. (ed.). *Finance and Trade under Edward III.* Manchester, 1918.

UNWIN, G. *Gilds and Companies of London.* 3rd ed. London, 1938.

VICKERS, K. H. *England in the Later Middle Ages.* 3rd ed. London, 1921.

*WALLON, H. *Richard II.* 2 vols. Paris, 1864.

WILKINSON, B. *Studies in the Constitutional History of the Thirteenth and Fourteenth Centuries.* Manchester, 1937.

WORKMAN, H. B. *John Wyclif.* 2 vols. Oxford, 1926.

(4) PERIODICALS

ARMITAGE ROBINSON, J. "An Unrecognized Westminster Chronicler." *Proceedings of the British Academy,* 1907–8, pp. 61 ff.

ATKINSON, R. L. "Richard II and the Death of the Duke of Gloucester." *English Historical Review,* xxxviii, 563–4.

BETTS, R. R. "English and Čech Influences in the Husite Movement." *Transactions of the Royal Historical Society,* series iv, vol. xxi, 71–102.

COULTON, G. G. "The Chronicler of European Chivalry." *The Studio,* special winter no. 1930.

CRUMP, C. G. and JOHNSON, C. "The Powers of Justices of the Peace." *English Historical Review,* xxvii, 226–38.

CURTIS, E. "Unpublished Letters from Richard II in Ireland, 1394–5." *Proceedings of the Royal Irish Academy,* vol. xxxvii, section C, 276–303.

*EDWARDS, J. G. "The Parliamentary Committee of 1398." *English Historical Review,* xl, 321–33.

GALBRAITH, V. H. "The Articles laid before the Parliament of 1371." *English Historical Review,* xxxiv, 579–82.

—— "Thomas Walsingham and the Saint Albans Chronicle, 1272–1422." *English Historical Review,* xlvii, 12–30.

HOLDSWORTH, Sir WILLIAM S. "The Influence of the Legal Profession on the Growth of the English Constitution." *Proceedings of the British Academy,* 1924.

KRIEHN, G. "Studies in the Sources of the Social Revolt in 1381." *American Historical Review,* vii, 254–85, 458–84.

*LAPSLEY, G. "The Parliamentary Title of Henry IV." *English Historical Review,* xlix, 423–49, 577–606.

* —— "Richard II's Last Parliament." *English Historical Review,* liii, 53–78.

LEWIS, N. B. "Article VII of the Impeachment of Michael de la Pole in 1386." *English Historical Review,* xlii, 402–7.

Lewis, N. B. "Re-Election to Parliament in the Reign of Richard II." *English Historical Review*, xlviii, 364–94.

—— "Simon Burley and Baldwin of Raddington." *English Historical Review*, lii, 662–9.

—— "The 'Continual Council' in the early years of Richard II, 1377–80." *English Historical Review*, xli, 246–51.

*Myres, J. N. L. "The campaign of Radcot Bridge in December, 1387." *English Historical Review*, xlii, 20–33.

Pollard, A. F. "The authorship and value of the 'Anonimalle Chronicle'." *English Historical Review*, liii, 577–605.

Richardson, H. G. "Heresy and the Lay Power under Richard II." *English Historical Review*, li, 1–28.

—— "Richard II's Last Parliament." *English Historical Review*, lii, 39–47.

—— "The Elections to the October Parliament of 1399." *Bulletin of the Institute of Historical Research*, xvi, 137–43.

* —— "The Parliamentary Representation of Lancashire." *Bulletin of the John Rylands Library*, xxii.

Shaw, P. "The Black Prince." *History*, xxiv, 1–15.

Stamp, A. E. "Richard II and the Death of the Duke of Gloucester." *English Historical Review*, xxxviii, 249–51.

*Steel, A. "English Government Finance, 1377–1413." *English Historical Review*, li, 29–51.

—— "Practice of Assignment in the Later Fourteenth Century." *English Historical Review*, xliii, 172–80.

* —— "Sheriffs of Cambridgeshire and Huntingdonshire in the reign of Richard II." *Proceedings of the Cambridge Antiquarian Society*, xxxvi, 1–34.

—— "Some Aspects of English Finance in the Fourteenth Century." *History*, xii, 298–309.

Waugh, W. T. "The Great Statute of Praemunire." *English Historical Review*, xxxviii, 173–205.

—— "The Great Statute of Praemunire." *History*, viii, 289–92.

Wedgwood, Josiah. "John of Gaunt and the Packing of Parliament." *English Historical Review*, xlv, 623–5.

Wilkinson, B. "The Deposition of Richard II and the Accession of Henry IV." *English Historical Review*, liv, 215–39.

Wood-Legh, K. "Sheriffs, Lawyers and Belted Knights in the Parliaments of Edward III." *English Historical Review*, xlvi, 372–88.

Wright, H. G. "Richard II and the Death of the Duke of Gloucester." *English Historical Review*, xlvii, 276–80.

—— "The Protestation of Richard II in the Tower in September 1399." *Bulletin of the John Rylands Library*, xxiii.

INDEX

Authorities mentioned in Appendix and Bibliography are not given here